D0531908

High Road to Promontory

HIGH ROAD TO PROMONTORY

Building the Central Pacific
(now the Southern Pacific)
across the High Sierra

BY GEORGE KRAUS

AMERICAN WEST PUBLISHING COMPANY

PALO ALTO / CALIFORNIA

Library of Congress Catalog Card Number 70-77826

DEDICATION

—to Robert Hancocks, who in his late thirties became interested in the history of Southern Pacific and its forerunner, Central Pacific. His years of study, upon which this book is based, were never completed, for he died without warning at the age of forty-five.

—to Bob's wife Esme and his son Richard, and to the many friends who aided him in this initial research, but whose names were not recorded. I offer thanks for all contributions, great or small, that may be reflected in this book, and regret that they must be offered anonymously. I can only hope that inclusion in this book constitutes a sufficient reward.

—to my mother, Elsie, Anne, Karl, and the rest of my family.

FOREWORD

THE PACIFIC RAILROAD SURVEY, completed in 1855 after two years of grueling effort in western America's almost trackless mountains and plains, pointed to the fact that California was an isolated and defenseless land. In war, her forts might be demolished and her territory occupied before troops or munitions could be sent by way of Panama, the only possible route for moving large numbers of men and the hardware of war. In a month, California might easily be lost before any aid could arrive.

Most important, however, was the need for faster and more reliable communications between this isolated outpost and the settled and industrialized East.

Despite many reports to the contrary, California and Californians were of one mind concerning the need for a Pacific Railroad. They were almost universal, too, in their opinion that such a project was too formidable for anyone less than the federal government or a corporation with the government's financial backing.

As early as May 1, 1852, two years after California became a state, a legislative act* proclaimed that "the interests of this state, as well as those of the whole Union, require the immediate action of the Government of the United States for the construction of a national thoroughfare connecting the navigable waters of the Atlantic and Pacific oceans for the purpose of national safety, in the event of war, and to promote the highest commercial interests of the Republic, and granting the right-of-way through the states of the United States for the purpose of constructing the road."

This, then, is the story of the conception and construction of the Cen-

---

*State of California, 1852, p. 50.

tral Pacific, the most difficult section by far of the nation's first transcontinental railroad. It is an epic tale, for the builders of the Central Pacific had no convenient pass such as the Rockies afforded the Union Pacific for its leg of the transcontinental line. Instead, they were confronted by the Sierra Nevada's seemingly impassable granite spires. It is the story of a battle fought by a small group of men who earned victory by thorough planning, persistent effort, and willingness to carry on against desperate and largely unknown odds.

Rich as is the country opened up by their efforts today, it was then a wilderness, remote, unpopulated, and with little future promise. Everything known of the country a railroad must traverse to link East and West would discourage the venture.

It was known, for instance, that any transcontinental railroad must cross two mountain chains popularly regarded as impassable barriers. Still fresh in the memory of emigrants who crawled westward were mountain trails so steep that wagons had to be lowered by rope. Cutting through rocky and precipitous passes, they knew, would be literally done by hand. Moreover, little was known of the principles of traction. Only a few years earlier, even engineers generally believed that gravity would defy any attempt to drive a locomotive uphill.

While Californians agreed on the need for transportation facilities more convenient to the East, none was willing to risk fortune or reputation on so unlikely a task as constructing a transcontinental railroad.

Shortly before his death, Collis P. Huntington, the financial wizard of the Big Four, told a San Francisco gathering of Southern Pacific officers on May 16, 1900: "I remember well, when we were organizing the Central Pacific Railroad movement, how some of your wisest men here laughed at us, and shrunk away when we asked them to share the risks with us, and the gain, if there should be any."

But the Big Four did risk their fortunes and reputations, and they succeeded in an almost impossible endeavor. Much "general" information—and misinformation—is available about the first transcontinental railroad, the Big Four, Theodore Judah and Central Pacific's financial and political problems. Historians have clouded in generalities the events leading up to the fateful meeting between Judah and the Big Four, and the details of construction of the Central Pacific. That is indeed unfortunate, for the details are a fascinating story.

The story of the struggle as told by the men involved, by their wives, contemporary company records and newspaper accounts combine to give an accurate and moving chronicle of the construction challenge of the nineteenth century.

Although this book deals mainly with construction of the western end of that transcontinental railroad, the appendix will include biographies of the Big Four, Theodore Judah, and other principals; a necessarily skeletonized account of what transpired in later construction in other states and areas of California; and a brief survey of what the railroad meant to California and the West.

We are fortunate in that a permanent record of Central Pacific's construction was made by photographer Alfred A. Hart, of Sacramento, who was hired by Central Pacific President Leland Stanford in 1864 to follow the construction crews along the line to chronicle its progress. Whenever an inspection train left Sacramento, Hart, with his wet-plate outfit, stereo camera, and assistants, was on that train. He was the only photographer to have such privileges on the C.P., and they were continued until some time after the last spike was driven at Promontory, Utah, May 10, 1869.

Robert Hancocks, who studied Hart and his work extensively, once said that he was "greatly disturbed to see Hart's fine work credited to other contemporaries" including C. E. Watkins and Edward J. Muybridge, both of San Francisco. "His work has been circulated around the country as their photos or without credit at all," he charged, demanding that "it is high time that Hart's name be identified with his camera."

Hart's stereos and captions are a significant contribution to this book, as are the detailed descriptions of many of Hart's photographs provided by Central Pacific chief engineer Samuel S. Montague and his assistant, J. M. Graham. Perhaps this book will restore much-deserved credit to Hart.

For their help, guidance, and encouragement, I should like to thank historian David Myrick of San Francisco, and the Sacramento Pioneers, especially Dr. V. Aubrey Neasham, Dr. Robert McGowan, and Walter Frome. My thanks go also to the Southern Pacific Company for opening its files to me, to the Bancroft Library of the University of California at Berkeley, to the Stanford University Library at Palo Alto, and to the Huntington Library at San Marino, California.

GEORGE KRAUS
San Francisco, California
November 15, 1968

TABLE OF CONTENTS

ONE

AN ISOLATED LAND

PEOPLE FAMILIAR WITH CALIFORNIA, focal point of the greatest human migration in history and one of the most energetic manufacturing and industrial areas in the world, may find it difficult to realize that in 1845, a little more than a century ago, Daniel Webster addressed the United States Senate opposing development of the West.

"What do we want," he asked, "with . . . this region of savages and wild beasts, of deserts of shifting sands and whirlwinds of dust, of cactus and prairie dogs? To what use could we ever put those endless mountain ranges, impenetrable and covered to their bases with eternal snow? What could we de with the western coast line three thousand miles away, rock-bound, cheerless and uninviting?"

In 1845, when Webster's eloquence pictured the bleakness of the remote western lands for his colleagues, fewer than four hundred Americans lived in California. After the cry of "Gold!" echoed eastward in 1848, followed by the fevered rush for hoped-for wealth, California's population multiplied 250-fold to some one hundred thousand Americans, most of them men. They came by covered wagon across the dry plains that rolled endlessly westward from the Missouri River; they clawed their way over the fastnesses of the mighty Sierra Nevada; they sailed from East Coast ports around Cape Horn or crossed the forbidding Isthmus of Panama. Whatever the route or the means of transport, the journey to California offered incomparable hardships and consumed many months. Of those who set out with high hopes, many did not arrive.

Hubert Howe Bancroft, in his *History of California,* VII, described the situation: "The sunburned immigrant, walking with his wife and little ones beside his gaunt and weary oxen in mid-continent, the sea-sick traveler, the homesick bride whose wedding trip had included a passage of the Isthmus, the merchant whose stock needed replenishing; everyone prayed for a Pacific Railroad."

Four of these immigrants had survived the hardships of the journey, and had, by 1855, become successful merchants in Sacramento. Now all were experiencing the difficulties of living and conducting business in California's "golden land." Collis P. Huntington and Mark Hopkins, already well-known merchants in Sacramento, became partners in a hardware business at 54 "K" Street.*

In that same year, 1855, Leland Stanford moved the Stanford Brothers' dealership in oils and groceries from Michigan Bluff, in the Sierra, to 56-58 K Street, next door to Huntington and Hopkins. The following year, when Stanford's new and larger quarters were completed nearby on Front Street at the corner of L, the Huntington-Hopkins store was enlarged to include the quarters Stanford had vacated. In the interim, Charles Crocker had established his highly successful dry goods store at 246 J Street, just two blocks away. Long before their association with Central Pacific, these prominent Californians, who became known as the "Big Four," were associated in other joint enterprises.

October, 1856, according to the Sacramento *Union,* Leland Stanford, Charles Crocker, Mark Hopkins and future Central Pacific Secretary E. H. Miller organized a state convention in Sacramento to form the California Republican Party. E. B. Crocker, Charles's brother and later a director of the railroad, was president of the Republican Club and chaired the convention. Stanford was the party's nominee for state treasurer in the election of 1857 and its nominee for governor in 1859 and again in 1861, when he was elected.

Long before the formation of the Central Pacific, Stanford and Huntington showed an interest in transportation. An item on the incorporation of the California and New York Steamship Company appeared in the Sacramento *Union* of May 13, 1857. Stanford was listed as a stockholder and director of the million-dollar company, which would establish "a people's line of first-class steamships between San Francisco, New York and New Orleans."

Both Stanford and Huntington were involved in another early venture —the Wagon Road Company. The *Union* reported on June 12 of that year that the Wagon Road board of directors had met in Placerville. There, enough money was subscribed to start improving the road to Slippery Ford. The improved road, it was said, would afford a shorter route for freight

---

*Complete biographies of Leland Stanford, Charles Crocker, Collis P. Huntington, and Mark Hopkins, as well as railroad engineer Theodore Judah, are presented in the appendix.

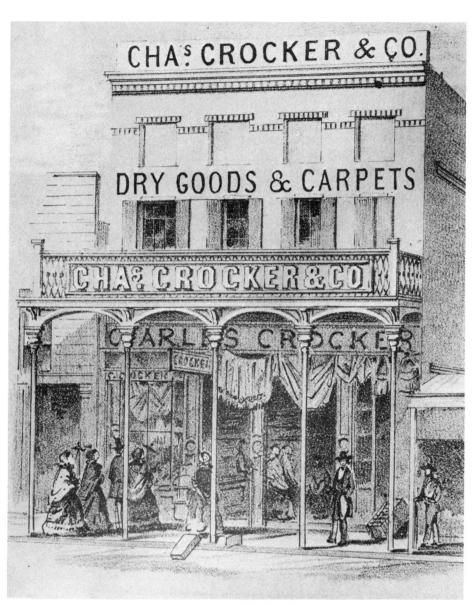

*The Crocker store on J Street, Sacramento
(taken from an 1857 lithograph).*

and passengers from Sacramento and Folsom to Carson City, Nevada, via Placerville. It would connect with the newly-opened Sacramento Valley Railroad, California's first, then operating between Folsom and Sacramento. A *Union* reporter accompanied Stanford, Huntington, and eight other Wagon Road Company directors over the new route by stage. The trip took some thirteen hours less than was required by the former route via Oroville, the newspaper reported four days later. Also, "after the road is improved, the trip can be made over the Sierra and back in less than five days and is a triumph for Johnson's Route [via Johnson Pass over Echo Summit]." How long Stanford and Huntington were involved in the Placerville enterprise is not known.

By January 1, 1856, the Sacramento Valley Railroad—also with dreams of a transcontinental connection—started operations to Adler Creek and became the first railroad in California. It took only a few more weeks (Feb. 22) to open the line to Folsom. However, the monetary crisis of 1855 all but ended this pioneer operation, and further immediate construction was out of the question.

Theodore Dehone Judah—who had been chief engineer of the S.V.R.R.—left to devote his time to a project that had been an obsession with him since his arrival in California: the "Pacific Railroad." Judah made the first of four trips East in 1856 to solicit aid for his dream project, but had little success. Again, in 1857, Judah visited Washington, after carefully reviewing the railroad surveys that had been made ten years before by the U.S. Army Engineers. These had been published as *The Pacific Railroad Surveys of 1853-55,* a twelve-volume work detailing the flora, fauna, native Indian tribes, and other information not related to a railroad route. But Judah recognized that the reports neglected the more practical information that would be required if the great project was to obtain support more tangible than Congressional oratory.

Consequently, Judah set forth what he considered to be the practical considerations in a pamphlet, which he had published at Washington, D.C., in 1857 and distributed to members of Congress during the session of that year.* Judah characterized construction of the Pacific Railroad as the "most magnificent project ever conceived" and stated that at that time the project had been "in agitation for over fifteen years." He pointed out that private money could not be obtained, since no survey had yet been made upon which financiers could base practical and accurate costs; for "when a Boston capitalist is invited to invest in a railroad project, it is not considered sufficient to tell him that someone had rode [*sic*] over the

---

*T. D. Judah, *A Practical Plan for Building the Pacific Railroad* (Washington, D.C.: Henry Polkinborn 1857), Library of Congress.

ground on horseback and pronounced it practicable. He does not care to be informed that there are 999 different varieties and species of plants and herbs, or that grass is abundant at this point; or buffalo scarce at that. His inquiries are somewhat more to the point. He wishes to know the length of your road. He says, let me see your map and profile, that I may judge of its alignment and grades. How many cubic yards of the various kinds of excavation and embankment have you and upon what sections?

"Have you any tunnels and what are their circumstances?

"How much masonry and where are your stone?

"How many bridges, river crossings, culverts, and what kind of foundations; how about timber and fuel?

"Where is the estimate of the cost of your road, and let me see its detail?

"What will be its effect on travel and trade; its business and revenue?"

Judah called for a preliminary survey by carefully planned and adequately financed parties to prepare definite estimates considering profiles, curves, necessary construction materials, and other data. He believed that stock in such a railroad would find ready sale.

Sensible as these proposals were, nothing came of them. They elicited much talk, but Congress was not yet ready to act, hamstrung as it was by the slavery question. Southern legislators could not support a northern road lest northerners fan out and absorb public lands along its route. The North feared that such a road would provide the South with a link to bind to the slave-holding states the territory recently acquired from Mexico, including California.

The Sacramento *Union* assessed the situation on January 29, 1859: "A Californian, Judah, in Washington City, who is well informed as to the prospects of California interests in Congress, writes, 'that there is no chance this session of Congress to do anything toward developing the Central Route. The President [James Buchanan] is in favor of the extreme Southern Route for the Pacific Railroad, and, it is understood, will veto any bill for a road over any other to the Pacific.' "

The only practical solution to the many disputes over routing, the *Union* declared, would be "for Congress to pass a bill authorizing the building of two roads, making the same appropriation of land or bonds to each, and then let their friends, North, South, East and West go forward and build them if they can."

Throughout the 1850's, Californians were repeatedly disappointed by the failure of Congress to pass legislation to establish a Pacific Railroad. At each congressional session, sectional jealousies and the rivalries of ambitious politicians continued to defeat every such proposal. By the spring of 1859, it seemed clear that if anything was to be accomplished, the West must move of its own accord.

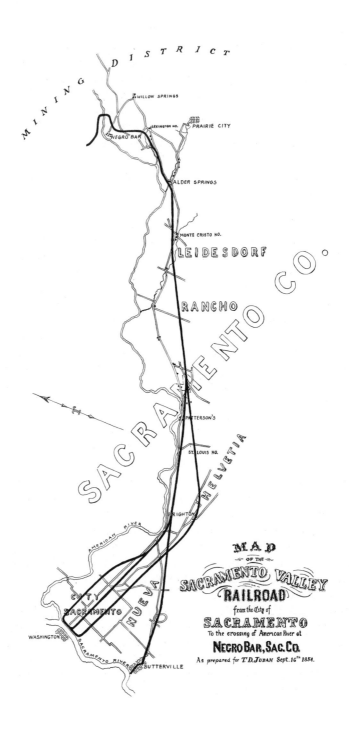

MAP
OF THE
SACRAMENTO VALLEY
RAILROAD
from the City of
SACRAMENTO
To the crossing of American River at
NEGRO BAR, SAC. CO.
As prepared for T. D. JUDAH Sept. 16th 1854.

MINING DISTRICT

WILLOW SPRINGS
LEXINGTON HO.
PRAIRIE CITY
NEGRO BAR
ALDER SPRINGS
MONTE CRISTO HO.
LEIDESDORF
RANCHO
PATTERSON'S
ST. LOUIS HO.
HELVETIA
BRIGHTON
AMERICAN RIVER
CITY SACRAMENTO
NUEVA
WASHINGTON
SACRAMENTO RIVER
SUTTERVILLE

SACRAMENTO CO.

The Sacramento Valley Railroad, the first in California, had transcontinental dreams itself. Her chief engineer, T. D. Judah (at right and below, on the locomotive's tender) went over to the Central Pacific to pioneer the "most magnificent project ever conceived"—the construction of the Pacific Railroad.

On April 5, the California Legislature voted for a Pacific Railroad Convention, to be held on September 20 at Assembly Hall on the corner of Kearny and Post streets, San Francisco. It was to be composed of delegates not only from various sections of California, but from the state of Oregon and from Washington and Arizona territories.

Judah returned from the national capital in time to participate in the convention as a delegate from Sacramento. Experienced in dealing with Congress, Judah was convinced that the only way to obtain passage of enabling legislation was to eliminate the question of routing from congressional debate by providing that the private company undertaking the project should select its own.

Even at this early stage, there was friction between San Francisco and Sacramento interests over the route of the railroad; but Judah, regarding such action as premature and unwise, remained convinced that nothing could be expected from financing sources until careful and proper surveys had been made and costs approximated: "There were only two measures worthy of important consideration . . . and if the convention would unite harmoniously in recommending them as the proper measures to be adopted, they would have accomplished the main objects for which they were called together," he later wrote in a letter to the editor of the *Union*.

"The first was with regard to a proper survey of the line or lines so as to enable us to speak understandingly of the relative merits, length and cost of various routes and upon this information to determine upon and adopt the proper route or line.

"The second was to decide upon the manner in which the Federal Government could properly extend her aid in the construction of the road, calling upon her emphatically to respect the views of the convention on this subject as an expression of the views and opinion of the people of the whole Pacific Coast, not only of the state of California." He went on to say that in his opinion, the convention had accomplished this unanimously with "no political, local or sectional considerations."

Any private company would "be forced to settle down upon the central line as the one for the road," the *Union* concluded in a reply published the following day. "If Judah's plan as recommended by the convention should be favorably acted upon by Congress, no legislation as to the route would be required; the line would be left solely to the selection of those who furnished the money to lay down the rails. They would, of course, consult their own interests, as well as those of the country, and the result would not be in the least doubtful."

The Pacific Railroad Convention formally requested Congress to lend its aid by granting lands to California, by guaranteeing interest on the bonds through the territories, and by remitting the duties on railroad iron for the entire distance.* It asked that in California the road run from San Francisco around the South Bay, through Stockton, and eastward over whatever route the legislature might select. In addition, the delegates recommended state and county aid, relief of stockholders from personal and individual liability, and an actual survey of various passes through the mountains. They also appointed Judah as their accredited agent to Washington. Less than a month after the convention adjourned, Judah sailed for Panama on the steamer *Sonora.*

On his arrival in the East, Judah immediately prepared a bill embodying the convention's chief recommendations, sending copies back to California for endorsement and formal approval at a second session of the convention in Sacramento.

That the Big Four were well aware of the projected Pacific Railroad became apparent in 1859, when Horace Greeley made his famous trip west on behalf of the project. Among the Sacramentans who greeted him and escorted him on his speaking trip through that section of the state were Huntington, Hopkins, and Crocker. Stanford was busy conducting an unsuccessful campaign for governor.

Greeley was wholly behind the project. "Let us resolve to have a railroad to the Pacific—to have it soon," he wrote, on his return to the East, in *Overland Journey to California.* "It will add more to the strength and wealth of our country than would the acquisition of a dozen Cubas. My long, fatiguing journey was undertaken in the hope that I might do something toward the early construction of the Pacific Rail road; and I trust that it has not been made wholly in vain."

Meanwhile, in Washington, Judah sought out members of Congress and on December 6, 1859, succeeded in gaining an interview with the President, who, when presented with a copy of the Pacific Railroad Convention memorial, expressed himself generally in favor of the Pacific railroad. Newly-elected California Congressman J. C. Burch, who journeyed east with Judah on the *Sonora,* agreed to sponsor legislation in the House.** However, sectional controversies over the route soon arose again, and the House bill, though twice reported onto the floor in different forms, was at last put over for consideration until the next session, which would begin in December, 1860. The Senate, meanwhile, was so harassed by the larger question of slavery and secession that Senator Gwin of California, sponsor of the railroad bill in that chamber, could not even get his

---

*It should be noted, however, that the Central Pacific received no land grant aid from California.

**This agreement was included in Judah's report to the Convention Committee and reprinted in full in the Sacramento *Union* of July 25, 1860.

*Hank Monk and Horace Greeley on the
Overland Stage at Placerville, 1859.*

compromise bill called up for consideration.

While Congress was thus occupied, Judah busied himself studying the operation of locomotives on heavy grades. His observations later became highly important in solving the question of crossing the Sierra Nevada, for Judah was able to state with authority that grades as steep as 350 feet per mile could be overcome with perfect safety.

Although the work of the Pacific Railroad Convention in 1859 and Judah's subsequent trip to Washington resulted in no further direct or formal action, they affected public opinion significantly. The proposed Railroad Bill of 1859, on which various interests had almost compromised, became in many respects the forerunner of the Pacific Railroad Act that Congress finally passed in 1862.

Far from discouraged by Congress' failure to act, Judah, with characteristic enthusiasm, began mapping out a railroad over the Sierra Nevada. He had become increasingly aware that plans submitted earlier had proven unsuccessful before Congress because, while admirably suited to senatorial eloquence, they were uniformly based upon hope and hypothesis, not upon demonstrated fact. He was convinced, therefore, that nothing definite could be accomplished in Washington until more concrete action was taken in California. He determined, therefore, that he would not again ask Congress to offer some hypothetical company the right to build the railroad, and later select its own route. The company should be organized and itself present Congress with accurate and definite surveys of a chosen route. That company must stand ready, he felt, to accept any reasonable proposal and to start actual construction immediately.

"In Washington, he labored largely at his own expense, as from time to time he went on there," Mrs. Judah later wrote of her husband's efforts, "till he made up his mind that he would never go to Washington again until he had been over the Sierra Nevada Mountains, made a survey and would go back with maps, profiles, estimates, etc., for a railroad across them.

"How we used to talk it all over and over on the steamer enroute to California in July, 1860. Three weeks from the time we arrived in California, he was in the mountains, accompanied mostly by Dr. D. [Daniel] Strong, whose friendship was assured, and who was truly a mountaineer."

Dr. Strong had spent considerable time attempting to re-establish wagon travel through Dutch Flat—a traffic that was eliminated, ironically enough, by the Johnson Pass Wagon Road Company in 1856, which Stanford and Huntington had organized. Now he lent his energies to locating a pass through the mountains for a railroad.

Apparently, Judah was still employed by the Sacramento Valley Railroad. L. L. Robinson, trustee and superintendent of that railroad, told the first Nevada Legislature, "after all other employment failed him, I hired

23

Judah to explore the Sierra Nevada Mountains for routes for wagon roads north of the South Fork of the American River, and at the same time to act as agent for the Sacramento Valley Railroad and solicit freight."

This testimony was borne out by the October 6, 1860, issue of the Sacramento *Union,* which quoted the Nevada (City) *Journal:* "Mr. Judah is on his way over the mountain to inform himself relative to the practicability of the passes to the east of us for railroad purposes, preparatory to a visit to Washington. Mr. Judah is acting agent of the Sacramento Valley Railroad, and is offering liberal inducements for teamsters to load their wagons at Folsom rather than at Sacramento."

Meanwhile, Doctor Strong had discovered what he considered a practical route for a railroad across the Sierra, a passage used for many years by westbound wagon trains through Dutch Flat and the Donner Pass. He wrote to Judah, who had been searching for a pass north of the thirty-second parallel, and suggested that he come to Dutch Flat to check what Strong believed was a gateway through the rocky wall. Judah promptly responded and, with Strong's aid, raised enough money in Dutch Flat to finance an investigation.

"Dr. Strong used to tell a thrilling story of their last night in the mountains," Mrs. Judah later wrote. "They came near being snowed in, obliged to get up in the middle of the night from their camp and start out in darkness to find the trail, and none too soon were they.

"Judah could not rest or sleep after they were in town and in the store [until] he had stretched his paper on the counter and made his figures thereon. Then turning to Dr. Strong, he said for the first time, 'Doctor, I shall make my survey over the Donner Pass, the Dutch Flat Route, above any other.' "

The morning after their return, according to Strong, "Judah came into my place and said to me, 'give me some writing materials' — I produced same and he sat down and drew up what he called 'Articles for Association' and he shoved them across the table to me and said 'sign for what you want.' "

Convinced they had found a feasible route over the mountains, Judah and Strong drew up a stock subscription agreement for a railroad across the Sierra, to be known as the "Central Pacific Railroad," the first record of that name. As yet, of course, the Big Four were in no way connected with the enterprise.

Judah's "moonlighting" apparently aroused the ire of his employer — the Sacramento Valley Railroad. Superintendent Robinson later reported that "during Judah's exploring service for [the S.V.R.R.] . . . he projected what became known as the 'Dutch Flat Route' and his report to the press was made without the consent or knowledge of the railroad, they feeling

Dr. Strong's drug store
at Dutch Flat, on the
route of the westbound
wagon trains.

An overview of Dutch
Flat, where the Central
Pacific planned a
wagon road as a "cash
register" for railroad
empire.

such a report should have been made to them." As a result, Robinson said, he was forced to discharge Judah.

California law at this time provided that a railroad corporation must have bonafide capital stock subscriptions of one thousand dollars for each mile of projected road, with 10 percent to be paid before incorporation. Therefore, Strong and the now unemployed Judah immediately began canvassing likely prospects for the stock subscription. Strong was widely acquainted in the business community and met with fair success.

Judah, meanwhile, prepared and published a report, detailing results of their investigation and drawing attention to "some newly discovered facts with reference to the route of the Pacific Railroad through the State of California." Published in San Francisco November 1, 1860, the eighteen-page pamphlet read in part: "Confident of the existence of a practicable line across the Sierra Nevada Mountains, nearer and more direct than the proposed line via Madelin Pass and headwaters of the Sacramento *(Pacific Railroad Survey of 1853-55),* I have devoted the past few months to an exploration of several routes and passes through Central California, resulting in the discovery of a practicable route from the city of Sacramento; upon the divide between the Bear River and the North Fork of the American, via Illinoistown [Colfax], Dutch Flat and Summit Valley to the Truckee River which gives nearly a direct line to Washoe with maximum grades of 100 feet per mile—the elevation of the pass is 6,690 feet."

This route saved 150 miles over Lieutenant Beckwith's proposed route through Feather River Canyon, later used by the Western Pacific. But of greatest importance was its direct line to Nevada's Washoe country, which, all agreed, probably would be one of the chief sources of business for such a railroad. Settlements already existing along the line could also be expected to supply local business.

The Pacific Railroad Bill was scheduled to come before Congress in December. The measure provided for generous assistance from the federal government and required that construction within California be effected by a California corporation.

Judah proposed that such a corporation be formed at once "for the purpose of constructing a road through the state upon this route, in anticipation of the passage of this bill."

Largely through Dr. Strong's efforts, subscriptions in the amount of $46,500 were procured in Dutch Flat, Illinoistown [Colfax], Grass Valley, and Nevada City. Since the length of the proposed road within the state was estimated to be 115 miles, about $70,000 more was needed to conform to the California law governing stock subscriptions. The promoters hoped to obtain the necessary balance in San Francisco and Sacramento.

Armed with his pamphlet and much other data, Judah proceeded to

San Francisco. Exhilarated by initial successes, he wrote to Strong on November 14, 1860, "I have struck a lucky streak and shall fill up the list without further trouble. I have got one of the richest concerns in California into it."

His optimism was unwarranted. San Franciscans had largely financed the disastrous Sacramento Valley Railroad and they well remembered their losses. San Francisco's rich listened to Judah, smiled at his enthusiasm, and closed their wallets, regarding him as an enthusiastic lunatic—"Crazy Judah."

His wife later described her husband's reaction: "Mr. Judah left me at the Russ House [San Francisco] where we were stopping, firm in the faith that the gentlemen he was to meet that evening would give him the aid he required to make his survey the following spring, and would be his backers and form the Pacific Railroad Company. He left me in high hopes. His high hopes were doomed to disappointment; and why? Not because they did not believe in Judah, but they all had large interests in various ways. If Congress did not pass a Pacific Railroad Bill, no road could be built, and even then it was generally thought it would take from twelve to twenty years to build it, in spite of Mr. Judah's honest assertion 'seven years would build it, under the provisions of such a bill,' as he believed could and would be passed. They did not give the encouragement he asked. Weary and disappointed that night on his return from the meeting, his words were these: 'Anna, if you want to see your friends in the morning you must pack your bag and trot around to see them, for I am going up to Sacramento on the boat tomorrow afternoon. Remember what I say to you tonight, so you can tell me sometime, not two years will go over the heads of these gentlemen I have left tonight, but they would give all they hope to have from their present enterprises to have what they put away tonight."

So Judah returned to Sacramento and on the very next day called together a few local businessmen for a meeting at the St. Charles Hotel— about thirty of them, according to Dr. Strong.

Leland Stanford later offered an account of this first meeting with Judah: "At first, I had no personal acquaintance with him [Judah]. The first time that my attention was called to the question of the construction of the railroad was by a gentleman by the name of James Bailey [a Sacramento jeweler], who was afterwards the secretary of the Central Pacific. Mr. Bailey came down to see me and told me that Judah had discovered in the mountains a pass over which a railroad could be built, and desired that I should see Mr. Judah. I told him I would be glad to see Mr. Judah, but did not know that we would care to do anything in this matter. I told him, however, that I would talk with Mr. Huntington and others about it. We fell into conversation upon the subject, and the result was that we agreed

An early stage coach on the wagon road over the Sierra. The trip took four to five days, carrying passengers, baggage, and mail.

to have a meeting the same evening at my house. We then fully considered the subject and discussed the matter one way and another. We afterwards met again, when Mr. Hopkins joined us, and the result was that we concluded that we would make the acquaintance of Mr. Judah. Neither of us was acquainted with him, and we invited him to meet us and make our acquaintance. He came down with Mr. Bailey and we had a conversation."

Among those present were Stanford, Huntington, Hopkins, Crocker, Dr. Strong, Lucius A. Booth, James Bailey, Cornelius Cole (a Sacramento lawyer and later congressman and senator from California), B. F. Leete (one of Judah's surveyors), and several others—possibly including the Robinson brothers of the Sacramento Valley Railroad.

In his explorations, Judah told the group, he had crossed the crest of the Sierra on no less than twenty-three separate occasions. From his "barometric reconnaissance," he had become convinced of the feasibility of the "Dutch Flat Route," but financial backing was necessary so that an exact instrumental survey of the proposed line could be made.

Mrs. Judah outlined her husband's arguments before this merchant group: " 'You are tradesmen of Sacramento city', Judah told the men. 'Your property, your business is here; help me to make this survey; I will make you the company; and with the bill passed you will have control of business interests that will make your fortune in trade, if nothing more. Why, you can have a wagon road if not a railroad'. "

Huntington was a skeptic, who felt that a railroad project such as Judah described "was so big there was not much use starting our expecting to do much toward building it." Nevertheless, he persuaded six others to join him in a pledge to pay the costs of the survey. Hopkins, although much in doubt about the gigantic difficulties posed by construction in the mountains, followed his partner's lead. Huntington then talked with Leland Stanford, who agreed to pay one-seventh of the cost. Charles Crocker, Lucius A. Booth, and Charles Marsh (all friends of Huntington), James Bailey, and Judah completed the group of seven backers.

Meanwhile, during the 1860/61 session of Congress, the House of Representatives passed a bill providing for two railroads. The Senate amended the bill to call for three. The House retaliated by refusing to take any action on the Senate bill. Despite this impasse, however, the stage was set for further action.

In the meantime, on December 20, 1860, South Carolina seceded from the Union. Other Southern states quickly followed. Three months later, on April 12, 1861, Fort Sumter was attacked, and the Civil War began. The war, of course, eliminated southern influence from the selection of a Pacific Railroad route and restricted the choice of any route to northern territory. It forcefully brought home to Congress the fact that rail communications with the Pacific slope were not merely desirable for commercial and other related reasons, but were essential to military security. At the same time Congress was aware of particularly strong southern sentiment in California, which, it was feared, might either sway the new state toward the Confederacy or even bring about its return to Mexico.

When members of Congress attempted to persuade Lincoln that the federal government should build the Pacific Railroad, he is said to have replied, "The national government has its hands full carrying on the war. Private enterprise must build the Pacific Railroad. All the government can do is aid, even admitting its construction is a political as well as a military necessity." The proponents of the Pacific Railroad sent word to California that passage of a Pacific Railroad bill at the next session of Congress was a certainty.

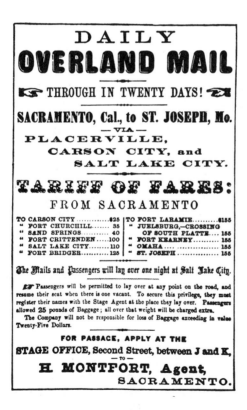

TWO

JUDAH SURVEYS THE SIERRA AND THE
CENTRAL PACIFIC IS ORGANIZED: *1861*

I F YOU WANT TO SEE the first work done on the Pacific Railroad, look out of your bedroom window. I am going to work there this afternoon," Judah told his wife in March, 1861. They were stopping at the Vernon House in Sacramento, where Judah, after waiting for improved weather, was forming a crew for the instrumental survey.

"We organized a corps of engineers in the spring," Charles Crocker later said, "and sent them with Mr. Judah at the head to run a line along the mountains to the Big Bend of the Truckee River [at the present site of Wadsworth, Nevada]. It was merely a trial line; what we called a base line —but from that we found that the grades which Judah had said could be obtained were actually practicable, and were obtained."

On April 30, 1861, Mark Hopkins, treasurer of the newly formed company, called an organizational meeting of stockholders of the proposed Central Pacific Rail Road of California. The Big Four apparently decided to organize without waiting for the results of Judah's survey which would require six months to complete. They drew up articles of association, to which thirty-one stockholders, subscribing to a total of 1,250 shares, affixed their signatures.

The California legislature passed a new act covering incorporation of railroads in the state on May 20, 1861, a bill that Crocker doubtless helped to formulate, as he was then serving a two-year legislative term.

The Central Pacific Rail Road of California was incorporated formally under the new law on June 28, 1861, with these officers: Stanford, president; Huntington, vice-president; Hopkins, treasurer; James Bailey, secretary; Judah, chief engineer. The directors were Stanford, Crocker, Bailey, Judah, L. A. Booth, Huntington, Hopkins, Dr. Daniel W. Strong, and Charles Marsh. Capital stock was set at $8,500,000, divided into 85,000 shares at $100 each. Huntington stated later that the combined wealth of the five principals—that is, the Big Four and Judah—at this time amounted to $159,000.

The historian Bancroft commented upon the organization of the Central Pacific and called attention to the group's inadequate financial base: "Indeed, when it is remembered that neither Congress, individual states, nor syndicates of capitalists had yet been found willing to lay hold of so stupendous and hazardous an enterprise as that of constructing a Pacific Railway at that time, the audacity of the Sacramento corporation in attempting the most difficult portion of it appears an act of madness or of inspiration. Few were found to give material encouragement to the project, and many said that those Sacramento merchants who had ventured upon it would sink their personal fortunes in the canyons of the Sierra."

The summer and fall of 1861 were busy. In June, 1861, only nine days before the filing of the Central Pacific articles of incorporation, Stanford had been nominated as the Republican candidate for Governor of California. Judah wrote to Strong, "Election and politics so monopolize everything here now that our people have very little time to talk railroad matters, but promise as soon as election is over to get together. A good deal depends upon the election of Stanford, for the prestige of electing a Republican ticket will go a great way towards getting us what we want—I am trying to put my little road upon its legs, and it looks rather favorable, but like everything else, can do nothing with it until after election."

Judah completed his survey early in August. The Sacramento *Union* of August 7, 1861, reported with satisfaction that "when the Pacific Railroad next comes up in Congress, Californians will be able to say to members: We are now prepared to lay before you a perfectly reliable report of a competent engineer. The problem as to crossing the Sierra Nevada has been solved."

Huntington, Crocker, and Stanford joined Judah in the Sierra at various times for a personal look at the projected route. A practical man, Huntington also wanted to inspect other possible routes.

The Sacramento *Union* of November 11, 1861, devoted considerable space to a survey Huntington and Judah made of the Feather River route:

"The only thorough reconnaissance of that route that has ever been made so far as we are advised was made last August by T. D. Judah, engineer of the Central Pacific Railroad Company, accompanied by C. P. Huntington, one of the directors; A. A. Sargent, California delegate to Congress; and Charles Marsh, as far as Long Valley, down the Middle Fork of the Feather River to the neighborhood of Nelson's Creek.

"At that point the canyon of the river commences. Huntington and Judah determined to explore that canyon, a feat, they were informed by those living along the river, that had never been performed by mortal man. They employed a Chinaman to aid in conveying blankets and provisions. They were seven days working their way through the canyon from Nelson's Creek to Bidwell's Bar, a distance of 70 miles.

"The entire distance was through rock granite, slate and marble, the walls rising from two to three thousand feet, cut through on an extremely crooked line with angles of every variety. Between 30 and 40 tunnels in solid rock would be required to turn points and the bed for a railroad [would have to be] blasted in the wall of rock for nearly the whole distance.

"No trail practicable for mules had ever been found across the canyon of the Middle Feather between Nelson's Creek and Bidwell's Bar; so Huntington and Judah were told by miners who lived up on the benches and descended into the canyon by steps [and] in some cases by ropes. The miners also assured them that the water in the river rose the past winter fully 75 feet. This examination of the canyon demonstrated its utter impracticability for railroad purposes."

That same summer, Stanford, Huntington, and Crocker covered the proposed Donner Pass route with Judah. Stanford later recalled:

"I remember that while we were making our explorations, we came to the summit, and at Donner Pass we looked down on Donner Lake, 1200 feet below us, and then looked up at the drifts above us, 2000 feet, and I must confess that it looked very formidable. We there and then discussed the question of the paying qualities of the enterprise and we came to this conclusion: That if there was a way by which a vessel could start from San Francisco or from New York and sail around Cape Horn in behind those mountains, we could not afford to compete. If this could not be done, however, and if we had only the ox and mule teams to compete with, we saw that we could obtain such a rate for carrying freight and passengers that we could afford to build the road with the prospect of further developments in Nevada. At that time the business of Nevada was very promising and we had an idea, like everybody else on this side, that most of the mountains in Nevada were filled with mineral wealth."

A comparison of the various routes revealed that the one through Dutch Flat and the Donner Pass was the most practical, with advantages over the others on at least thirty counts. However, Huntington found that Judah's estimates provided for too much earthwork, and not enough work in rock; he made such changes in the figures of the estimates as his judgment dictated.

Through the summer the Big Four devoted their energies to Stanford's

Donner Lake, from the summit.

Leland Stanford.

campaign for the governorship, which he won on September 4, 1861, with 55,935 votes against 32,872 for McConnell and 30,944 for Conness. On October 1 Judah placed before the partners a written report on the results of his months of careful work since the preliminary report was published a year earlier.

His initial survey extended eighty-one miles from base to summit of the Sierra Nevada, with a rise of seven thousand feet. However, he had discovered a ridge or spur of remarkable surface regularity; hence, the line would rise a maximum of only 105 feet per mile. This unbroken route along the ridge also eliminated the necessity of crossing any of the major canyons and only one important stream, the Little Bear River, which would require a bridge only fifty feet high.

As to the problem of attacking a double summit, the survey was particularly fortunate, for Judah had discovered what was apparently the only way to avoid entirely the second mountain range. A northern route surveyed by Lieutenant Beckwith over what was then known as Madelin Pass had shown two distinct summits thirty-five miles apart. The main wagon road from Placerville to the Washoe country crossed over Johnson's Pass through Lake Tahoe Valley, and then over Daggett's Pass through the second summit ridge. Judah's plan avoided this second ridge by taking advantage of the Truckee River Canyon, which first leads north from Lake Tahoe, then east by an easy grade through the ridge and down to the Nevada plains at the Big Bend of the Truckee.

Generally, this later report differed somewhat from Judah's findings of 1860. He recommended that the route be moved slightly to the west, through Lincoln rather than through Folsom. Other changes came later, the most important being a shift to the American River side of the ridge, which was considered better suited for a railroad than the Bear River side. The line ran up the divide between the rivers "from gap to gap"—"gaps" being the low points along the ridge—in order to secure the best possible gradients. Judah also showed the actual grades that would be encountered and compared them with grades on selected eastern railroads. The plan called for eighteen tunnels, which he described in detail, with the longest 1,370 feet in length. He estimated total construction costs to the state line at an average of $88,428 per mile. Beyond the Big Bend of the Truckee, the cost would drop to an average of $83,600 per mile. The line proposed in the survey of 1861 would save, according to Judah, 184 miles between Council Bluffs and the Pacific, when compared with the Beckwith route, and not less than $13,500,000 in total expenditure. From the Big Bend of the Truckee, the Central Pacific could extend eastward along the Humboldt River—a route Judah considered preferable to the more southerly one explored by Captain Simpson during the Pacific Railroad Survey of

Freighting over the Placerville Road.

An 1854 lithograph of Virginia City.

1853-55—and then to the Great Salt Lake.

Judah also pointed out that his route ran through extensive forests of pitch and sugar pine, fir, and especially abundant quantities of cedar and tamarack, which would furnish excellent crossties. Passenger transit would be reduced to eight and one-half hours between Sacramento and what is now Reno. He considered the Donner route more favorable because it offered an easy connection to Oregon and Washington. It would be accessible to newly-discovered silver deposits near Lassen's Meadows on the Humboldt River and, because of lower freight rates, would permit shipment of low-grade silver ores from Nevada to Europe for refining. Nevada citizens would save as much as a million dollars annually on freight costs. In addition, the superior character of the soil along the proposed line argued in its favor.*

That same summer (1861), considerable traffic had sprung up between Nevada and Sacramento over the Placerville Turnpike. Hopkins had taken pains to count the number of teams and passengers traveling over the road in order to ascertain the amount and value of this commerce, which would, of course, be handled by the Central Pacific as soon as significant portions were completed.

Now the Big Four determined to take full advantage of the trade by opening their own wagon road. On November 27, 1861, articles of association for the Dutch Flat and Donner Lake Wagon Road Company were drawn up between Stanford, Crocker, Huntington, Hopkins, Bradley, and Strong. The road was to run from Illinoistown [Colfax] in Placer County, California, to Virginia City and the Washoe Valley in Nevada Territory. The agreement was to continue for ten years, unless dissolved earlier by unanimous vote of the stockholders, or for such further time as they might mutually agree upon. Four hundred shares of stock at a thousand dollars each were issued; Crocker was named president, and Hopkins, secretary and treasurer.

Primarily, the wagon road was designed to aid the Central Pacific in crossing the mountains and help avoid construction delays; to transport freight from Nevada points to the end of the railroad at Dutch Flat, and then to succeeding points along the line as the completed railroad gradually moved eastward; to haul supplies in ox- and mule-drawn wagons to construction forces working in advance of the railhead as far away as the eastern slope of the Sierra; and, as a toll road, to control freight shipments

---

*William Hood, for many years chief engineer of the Central Pacific, declared in 1925 that, in his opinion, Judah's reasons were "as valid today as when Judah wrote his 1861 report. Were there now no railroad over the Sierra," Hood stated, "the Donner Lake Route would still be selected over all others as the best possible route over the range."

over portions of the road as it was completed. Three toll gates, at Dutch Flat, Polley's Station, and Donner Lake, were established along the sixty-seven-mile-long road between Dutch Flat and the top of Dog Mountain.

In November, 1861, the Central Pacific group organized and incorporated the Nevada Railroad Company, which was authorized to construct a railway and telegraph line through Nevada Territory for a distance of 275 miles. Early in November, the Nevada Legislature passed "An Act granting certain persons the right to construct a railroad from the Western to the Eastern boundary of Nevada," which was approved and signed by the governor on the twenty-fifth. A subsequent act of the Nevada Legislature that same year extended the time for making the survey and filing maps, as required by the first act.

Everything was now ready for the campaign to secure approval and aid from Congress for the transcontinental railroad.

THREE

THE PACIFIC RAILROAD BILL: *1862*

Armed with his completed survey, maps, and detailed figures, Judah was confident that he could sway Congress. In a letter to Strong dated September 2, 1861, Judah wrote, "I think the next Congress will be a favorable one to procure lands from the government, and perhaps it may be money; but of the latter, I do not feel by any means so certain; but the lands do not create any debt, and the feeling towards California ought to be a good one."

He had devoted August and September to mapping the surveys, making profiles, and gathering information for use in the campaign to win congressional approval. His letter to Strong continued, "Our office is getting along rather slowly. I hope to get everything finished so as to be able to go on by 1st October, if they still desire me to go." He added that the election of Stanford as governor, for which all his Sacramento associates were then laboring, would be of great assistance.

On October 9, 1861, the Central Pacific's directors, pleased with the preparatory work, resolved "that Mr. T. D. Judah . . . proceed to Washington on the steamer of the 11th Oct. . . . as the accredited agent of the Central Pacific Company of California, for the purpose of procuring appropriations of land and U. S. Bonds from government, to aid in the construction of this road."

On his arrival in the East, Judah sent the company this account of his journey: "I collected together all the maps, profiles and field notes, etc., of our recent survey and sailed for the Atlantic states on October 11, 1861.

"Our Congressional representative, Mr. Aaron A. Sargent, being a fellow passenger, a good opportunity was afforded for explaining many features of our project not easily understood, without more than a cursory examination, which explanations were of great service to us in future operations.

"The trip also afforded an opportunity to write a portion of the report of our recent survey, which being subsequently completed in the city of New York, I procured 1,000 copies to be printed, distributing a portion of the same among railroad men, where like to do us most good, sending copies to President Lincoln, the heads of departments and to our Senators and Representatives in Congress. It was also published in the railroad journals and thereby obtained considerable circulation before the meeting of Congress.

"Meeting in New York our Senator, Hon. Jas. A. McDougall, chairman of Senate Pacific Railroad Committee, after a long and exceedingly satisfactory interview, I left fully satisfied that in him the Pacific Railroad had a firm friend not likely to be discouraged by the threatening aspect of our affairs, but ready and anxious to adopt the plan best calculated to make the Pacific Railroad a success in the present session of Congress, and to urge the same to speedy termination.

"Mr. McDougall requested me to arrive at Washington at least a week before the meeting of Congress, to assist him in preparing a bill, so as to have it ready to introduce at an early day."

The Civil War was now raging, a factor that greatly enhanced the chances of support. Not only had the obstructionist southern senators and representatives left Congress, but the war had already demonstrated the necessity for better liaison between the various sections of the country under control of the federal government. Also, Judah was, by this time, well known in Washington. He had been present during three previous congressional sessions and had actively lobbied for passage of a bill to grant lands to the state of California for purposes of railroad aid and had labored for adoption of some practicable Pacific Railroad scheme. The chief difficulty, as he clearly recognized, had been the nebulous character of these previous proposals. Now, however, he brought with him detailed engineering plans and supporting data, together with the fact of an existing corporation, ready to start building from the western end of the route.

Judah arrived in Washington before the session started, as Senator McDougall had requested, to assist in drafting a bill following the general outline of that submitted during the preceding session. As it now appeared advisable to take up the matter first in the House rather than in the Senate, Congressman Sargent took active charge of the campaign. Sargent had not been assigned to any of the standing committees, but only to the Special Committee on Pacific Railroads, so he was free to devote his energies to that one subject.

Congressional attention was naturally riveted upon the war between the states, and it was most difficult to distract it long enough to consider the railroad project. But on January 31, 1862, Sargent boldly obtained the floor in midst of debate on another matter and spoke at length about the Pacific Railroad as a military necessity to the nation. While the House appeared somewhat astonished at the newcomer's daring, his move proved wise, for it drew the attention of the members to the subject.

Sargent dwelt at length upon Judah's accomplishments and estimates, calling attention to the fact that, for the first time, Congress had before it a complete survey of the proposed route. He compared Judah's work with the former barometric reconnaissances of Beckwith and others, pointing out the savings that would be afforded by using the newly discovered route over Donner Pass.

The immediate result of Sargent's action was the appointment of a special subcommittee of the House of Representatives to draw up a proposed bill. Meanwhile, Judah had obtained an appointment as secretary of the Senate Pacific Railroad Committee, the chairman of which was Senator McDougall. Upon Sargent's motion, he was also named clerk of the new House subcommittee and later became clerk of the main House committee, appointments which had an important bearing upon the fate of the Pacific Railroad movement. Without these appointments, which gave Judah a semi-official standing, it is possible that the bill could not have been guided through Congress to enactment as law. Judah, now in the key position, had charge of all committee papers and documents and the privilege of the floor of both Senate and House. Although these appointments have been characterized as of "doubtful propriety," there is no evidence that Judah ever misused the trust by asking special consideration either for himself or for those he represented. On the contrary, he sought only what he considered to be truly in the public interest: aid to the railroad.

The bill that finally became law was introduced into the House of Representatives by Sargent on March 4, 1862, and was referred to the Pacific Railroad Committee, reported upon ten days later, and made a special order for March 25. On April 8, it was sent to the House, sitting as a committee of the whole.

The legislators seemed assured that the railroad bill would do more for the country than for the builders of the Pacific Railroad. On March 18, Pennsylvania's cautious Representative Campbell, chairman of the House Committee on the Pacific Railroad, said, "The road is a necessity to the government. It is the government that is asking individual capitalists to build the road. Gentlemen are under the impression that it is a very great benefit to these stockholders to aid them to an extent of about half the capital required. I beg leave to call the attention of gentlemen to the fact

Workshops at the Sacramento yard.

that it is the government which is under the necessity to construct the road. If the capitalists of the country are willing to come forward and advance half the amount necessary for this great enterprise, the government is doing little in aiding the company to the extent of the other half by way of a loan."

Later, Congressman White added, "It is not supposed that in the first instance the company will reimburse the interest to the government; it will reimburse it in transportation. I undertake to say that not a cent of these advances will ever be repaid, nor do I think it desirable that they should be, as this road is to be the highway of the nation."

Senator Henry Wilson of Massachusetts agreed: "I give no grudging vote in giving away either money or land. I would sink $100,000,000 in opening a railroad and do it most cheerfully and think I had done a great thing for my country. What are $75,000,000 or $100,000,000 in opening a railroad across the central regions of this continent, that shall connect the people of the Atlantic and Pacific, and bind us together? Nothing. As to the lands, I don't grudge them."

Spirited debates arose on such matters as the percentage of payments which should be required on subscribed capital stock, and ways to insure completion of the middle of the line by the companies that undertook construction at both ends. Congress feared, of course, that building might begin at either end and later be discontinued, and the nation be left with two unconnected railroads, one in California's Sierra Nevada, and the other in the Rocky Mountains. In the House, Mr. Kellogg offered an amendment requiring forty miles of the central division to be completed first.

This, of course, would have been ridiculously impractical, if not impossible, for rails and ties and all other construction materials, water, and food supplies would have had to be hauled by wagon and team for many hundreds of miles into the deserts and mountains of the West. Thaddeus Stevens aptly, if inaccurately, compared the proposition to the subterranean efforts of an over-acute squirrel who would begin at the bottom of its hole and burrow upwards to the surface.

Vigilance and effective parliamentary management brought the long debates to an end on April 9 and 10, when the Committee of the Whole set a week's postponement to "give time to consider." This was later extended to April 28, when the matter was again taken up during three more days of heated discussion, ending on the motion of Mr. Campbell to limit speeches to five minutes. This rule helped to silence objections raised by friends of adverse projects and skeptics who believed money appropriated on an overland railroad would be buried in the "Great American Desert." The bill finally passed the House on May 6 by a vote of 79 to 49.

Action then shifted to the Senate, where Judah called a Pacific Railroad Committee meeting for May 8. At a later session, some minor amendments and one major one relating to the Iowa branch were added to the bill, causing considerable confusion. During a breathing spell in which the Senate considered other legislation, however, Judah succeeded in effecting several compromises that effectively ended opposition.

Judah wrote the editors of the Sacramento *Union* on May 23, 1862, that "the Pacific Railroad is a fixed fact and you can govern yourselves accordingly." He added that the bill would come up "in about 10 days when, should our armies have met with no serious reverses, we may reasonably expect the passage of the Pacific Railroad Bill through the Senate." True to his prediction, on June 20, after four days of debate, the bill passed the Senate by a vote of 35 to 5. The House concurred in the Senate amendments a few days later, and the bill was signed into law by President Lincoln on July 1, 1862.

It provided for the appointment of five commissioners by the Secretary of the Interior and the creation of a corporation called the Union Pacific Railroad Company for the construction of the eastern link, and assigned the western portion of the road to the Central Pacific Railroad Company. The Union Pacific was to be constructed westward from a point on the 100th meridian of west longitude between the south margin of the valley of the Republican River and the north margin of the valley of the Platte River in the Territory of Nebraska to the western boundary of Nevada Territory. Capital stock of the Union Pacific was to be 100,000 shares at $1,000 each, or $100,000,000. The bill granted a right of way over public lands, giving alternate sections as designated by odd numbers to the amount of ten sections, or 6,400 acres, a mile; it also allocated financial aid in the form of government (6 percent currency) bonds at $16,000 per mile, which were to be a first mortgage on the road. The bonds were to be doubled and trebled for certain difficult and mountainous portions of the route. The bill further stipulated that the road was to be completed within twelve years and nothing but American iron was to be used in its construction. Its gauge was to be fixed by the President.

The Central Pacific was to construct "a railroad and telegraph line from the Pacific Coast at or near San Francisco or the navigable waters of the Sacramento River to the eastern boundary of California." The act also permitted the company to extend the road from Sacramento to San Francisco "with all rights, grants, donations, etc. given to that portion of the line west of the western base of the Sierra Nevada mountains."

The federal government gave the Central Pacific a right-of-way two hundred feet wide on each side of the railroad across all government lands, as well as the grounds necessary for stations, machine shops, and other necessary structures. It also was given the privilege of taking earth, stone,

Map of the designated Route" of the Central Pacific R. of California

Showing its General Location from the City of Sacram to Eastern boundary of Cal^a and to Big Bend of Trucke

The map filed by Judah
with the Secretary of the
Interior, June 30, 1862.
The line was later
modified to run through
Auburn, instead of
cutting north.

timber, and all other available material for construction from government lands adjacent to the road. The Central Pacific, like the Union Pacific, received every alternate section of public land, designated by odd numbers. Mineral lands were excepted, but it was provided that where mineral lands contained timber, that timber should go to the railroad.

The donated lands were to become the property of the Central Pacific as the road progressed, but no lands were to come into its possession until forty miles had been finished and approved. Only then could patents be issued for the lands on each side of the completed sections. The government further agreed that with each additional forty miles of railroad constructed, the government would issue Central Pacific $1,000 in United States bonds—to be repaid at the end of thirty years with interest at 6 percent—at the rate of $16,000 per mile.*

In view of the tremendous effort and expense involved in mountain construction, it was agreed that the government should advance money at the rate of $48,000 a mile for constructing the line through the Sierra Nevada. In consideration of the great distance of the Central Pacific from its base of supplies on the East Coast, the advance for the section east of the 150-mile limit between the Sierra Nevada and the Rocky Mountains was fixed at $32,000 per mile. As provided in the Pacific Railroad Act of 1862, the government bonds were to constitute a first mortgage on the company's entire property. The issuance of these bonds was thus a loan, not an outright subsidy.

The Central Pacific was required to complete fifty miles within two years of filing assent to the provisions of the act and fifty miles each following year, except in the mountainous regions, where twenty miles was fixed as the annual minimum. The act stipulated that the entire Pacific Railroad was to be completed by July 1, 1876, under pain of forfeiture.

It further provided that all compensation for services rendered the government should be applied to payment of bonds and interest until the entire amount was fully paid. After the road was completed and until the bonds and interest were paid, at least 5 percent of the net earnings were to be applied annually to payment of the debt.

Charles Crocker later said of the Pacific Railroad Bill of 1862: "The bill was not satisfactory. We built 18 miles under it and then applied for a change, finding that as the government held the first mortgage, we could not sell any other bonds, and the government did not give us any aid until we had built 40 miles of road which would take us to Colfax and we could not do that with the money we had.

---

*These government bonds and the accrued interest were paid in full by the railroad, although it was forced to sell the bulk of them to the investing public at substantial discounts rather than at the full face value.

"We could not borrow a dollar on the faith of the company. Mr. Stanford, Mr. Huntington, Mr. Hopkins and myself had to give our personal obligations for the money necessary to carry us from month to month. There was not a bank that would loan the company a cent. They had no faith in it. We bought the first 50 miles of iron on our own personal obligations. We procured from D. O. Mills, who was personally known to all of us, a paper testifying to our responsibility and our honor as men and merchants, and that whatever we agreed to do, he believed we would faithfully adhere to. Mr. Huntington bought the iron and gave our personal obligations for it, and put up the bonds of the company besides as security; and we entered into an agreement that we would be personally responsible as individuals for 10 years for the payment of the interest on those bonds. Those were the responsibilities we took, and if we had not done so there would have been no railroad.

"I would have been glad, when we had 30 miles of road built, to have got a clean shirt and absolution from my debts. I owed everybody that would trust me, and would have been glad to have them forgive my debts and taken everything I had, even the furniture of my family, and to have gone into the world and started anew."

Charles Crocker.

FOUR

HARNESSING THE ELEPHANT: *1862*

Huntington joined Judah in Washington for the final debate on the Pacific Railroad Bill, and shortly after its approval by President Lincoln, flashed the first word to his Sacramento colleagues by the newly established telegraph. "We have drawn the elephant," he said. "Now let us see if we can harness him."

In Sacramento the word spread quickly, causing great excitement. The *Union* reported on July 12, 1862: "The firemen's parade last evening in honor of the passage of the Pacific Railroad Bill was the most brilliant affair of its kind that has ever taken place in this city. The procession was a mile long and the route was one blaze of torches and fireworks from the time of starting to dismissal, and there were over 100 mottoes carried in the line, all of them appropriate and pithy."

Before Judah left Washington, the Pacific Railroad committees of both the Senate and House joined in a testimonial thanking him for his "valuable assistance in aiding the passage of the Pacific Railroad Bill through Congress." The testimonial, signed by forty-six congressmen and seventeen senators, continued: "Your explorations and surveys in the Sierra Nevada Mountains have settled the question of practicability of the line, and enabled many members to vote confidently on the great measure, while your indefatigable exertions and intelligent explanations of the practical features of the enterprise have gone very far to aid in its inauguration."

Judah reported to the Central Pacific on his activities in the Atlantic states after passage of the bill:

"I left Washington, Friday, June 27 [1862], for New York, for the purpose of making necessary inquiries and securing provisional contracts, if possible, for the iron equipment, etc., for the first 50 miles of our road. My desire being to make such contracts, if possible, for government bonds —and so that, if necessary the first 50 miles could be completed by the fall of 1863.

"Finding that iron was rapidly advancing in price, and mills beginning to refuse to take orders, most of them being filled up with orders for many months ahead, I placed matters in the hands of G. T. M. Davis, Esq., with instructions to immediately close some kind of arrangement with iron, locomotive and car men, upon the best terms he could get, before further advances took place. Any contract or arrangement not to be binding on us until ratified by the Central Pacific Railroad Company.

"Mr. Davis succeeded in making a contract with Norris & Co. of Philadelphia, for eight locomotives, deliverable in January, to be paid for entirely in government bonds, when issued. Also, obtained a proposition from the Lackawanna or Scranton Iron Company for 5,000 tons of rail, deliverable in time for the completion of our first 50 miles as proposed. Also obtained a proposition from Wason & Co. of Springfield, for eight passenger, four baggage and sixty freight cars, deliverable as above.

"All of these contracts and propositions to be subject to the approval of our Board of Directors, which was requested to be given within thirty days from July 21, 1862, they otherwise to be void. Unless these contracts are accepted by our company, I doubt if it will be possible to otherwise arrange to procure this material so that the first 50 miles can be finished by the fall of 1863, which I regard as quite essential to be done, in order to complete the entire line through California as contemplated in the bill."

Judah left the matter in the hands of Davis in New York and sailed for California July 21, 1862. On his return to Sacramento, he tendered a further report, which in part explained some behind-the-scenes maneuvering that led to passage of the Pacific Railroad Bill:

"It is not to be thought that all of these matters were being accomplished without opposition; they were done in the face of decided opposition and determined hostility from various parties, whose interests were antagonistic to our own, and who fought the bill with energy to the end.

"You will observe that much had not been accomplished, notwithstanding the fact that all other bills, at all other sessions, were framed upon the principle of recognizing but one company to build the entire road, which principle seemed to have been settled on by general consent, as evidenced by the discussions and vote upon the Curtis bill in the two previous sessions of Congress.

"Yet this was a bill recognizing the employment of companies already existing at either end, and making the appropriations direct to them for the construction of the road through their respective states, one of them being our own company.

"The Maine, or Perham Company, who have had bills before Congress at every session for the last six years, and who had their bill before both branches of Congress at this session . . . were entirely ignored, though appropriations increased throughout the whole bill and *double* the amounts contemplated in the Curtis bill, given to us, through the State of California to the Big Bend of Truckee.

"The right given us to build the *entire line* in California, either from the Sacramento river or from San Francisco; the Nevada company recognized, and $32,000 per mile with 6,400 acres of land per mile for that portion of the road; the lengths of sections across the Sierra Nevadas reduced from 40 to 20 miles; two years given us in which to build the first 50 miles, and only 50 miles per year required thereafter.

"And this bill approved and reported by both House and Senate committees at the same time — this was the first time that both Pacific Railroad Committees of Congress ever reported in unison the same bill, and at the time this was done, the Chairman of the two committees had not met or had any consultation on the subject. . . .

"The principles which produced this result were control and *harmony. . . .*"

Judah had already, on June 30, filed with the Secretary of the Interior a map of the route projected by his company. The act provided that, upon such filing, the lands for fifteen miles on either side of the projected route would be withdrawn from preemption. This was a first step at clinching the bargain between the Central Pacific and the federal government, since this simple device prevented speculation by outside individuals before the company had time to locate its lines with complete accuracy. Such lands, thus, could not be preempted or purchased until after the final location of the railroad and until federal authorities had made a final survey of these lands.

Judah outlined these provisions of the Pacific Railroad Bill in detail in his report of October 1, 1862, which also contained a statement of the advantages which, in his opinion, would accrue to the company through the new statute. He urged action to take advantage of the aid offered by the government and pointed out that the Central Pacific was given the privilege of constructing its line eastward from the California border until it should meet with Union Pacific's line building westward. This provision was of great importance, and Judah urged the company to make an immediate survey as far as Salt Lake City in order to determine the probable cost of such an extension "and to ascertain if sufficient inducement exists for your company to construct said road." He added that "I am

C. P. Huntington.

Mark Hopkins.

positive in the opinion that it will be found advisable to undertake the construction of about 300 miles next easterly from the state line of California."* Judah also pointed out that the Central Pacific was in a particularly advantageous position to take over the large and lucrative silver and passenger business in the Washoe region of Nevada, in addition to probable local business in those California communities through which the line would run. (Computations of travel on the main Washoe route through Strawberry Valley were included, and estimates were made of annual receipts of the road in California.) The new railroad could also expect transcontinental business from its connection with Union Pacific.

O<small>N AUGUST</small> 2, 1862, the Secretary of the Interior notified the Central Pacific that the government had withdrawn from preemption, private entry, or sale the lands shown on Judah's map filed on June 30. Before the company started actual construction along the route of Judah's survey, however, it made one last appeal for anyone with knowledge of a better route to come forward, to ensure that the best possible route was not overlooked. The Sacramento *Union* published the following notice:

THE CENTRAL PACIFIC RAILROAD COMPANY OF CALIFORNIA, DESIROUS OF OBTAINING FULL INFORMATION WITH REGARD TO ROUTES ACROSS AND PASSES THROUGH THE SIERRA NEVADA MOUNTAINS, WILL RECEIVE INFORMATION AND GIVE DUE CONSIDERATION TO THE MERITS OF ROUTES OTHER THAN THAT SURVEYED BY THEM, PROVIDED THAT PROPER SURVEYS AND RECONNAISSANCE ARE MADE OF SUCH ROUTES BY COMPETENT ENGINEERS AND FURNISHED TO THEM BEFORE THE FIRST DAY OF OCTOBER, 1862.

No route changes apparently were suggested, and the *Union* of October 15 reported that "the books of the Central Pacific . . . will be open to receive subscriptions to its capital stock, to the amount of eight million dollars, in Sacramento on the 22nd day of October and in San Francisco on the 28th day of October."

Marcus D. Boruck, who had been engaged to sell Central Pacific shares in San Francisco, later testified before the Pacific Railway Commission that during the latter part of 1862, he had opened a San Francisco office at the corner of Bush and Montgomery streets. Although it was kept open for twenty-two days, he managed to sell only three subscriptions of

---

*The language of the 1862 act was vague on the matter of the meeting of the two lines. This point was clarified in the acts of 1864 and 1866.

fifteen shares. "In the first place," he said in assessing the difficulty in promoting the sale of Central Pacific stock, "there was but a single newspaper in the city of San Francisco which favored the Central Pacific, and, I think, one or two outside of San Francisco. It was a very difficult matter for them to raise money from the monied men and they had to go along very slowly and do the best they could."

Meanwhile, in Sacramento, Judah got on with laying out the route. On November 6, 1862, the *Union* reported that "T. D. Judah, with a corps of ten or a dozen men, commenced yesterday the survey of the route for the Pacific Railroad. The route surveyed starts at Front and K Streets, runs up Front to I, across the slough east of the station house to Sixth and E Streets, and out the new levee. From this point it diverges to the north and crosses the American River about 100 yards below the site of Norris' bridge. The company camped last night on the north bank of the American River."

Huntington, who spent most of his time in the East after passage of the Pacific Railroad Bill, visited Sacramento shortly after Judah surveyed the route out of the city. He spoke later of the consequence of this visit, which hinted at differences of opinion concerning construction methods, which would continue between Judah and the Big Four. "It has been understood that the Central Pacific Railroad was to run up I Street in Sacramento and I had given orders that it was to go up that Street to Fifth and thence to B Street and out to the levee. Work had commenced, however, in running it by a point on the American River, where water overflowed every year, and would require more of the expensive rip-rap to be brought down from Folsom to protect the embankment. Work had been going on for several days when I walked out to see how affairs were progressing.

"Mr. Judah came up and said that the board of directors had given orders to have the work done that way but, I replied, it will cost $200,000 more at least to put the road here; it must go up I Street. I then sent for Mr. Cody and ordered him to move the road to I Street."

On this occasion, however, Judah prevailed; the line was built along the American River.

Unable by the sale of bonds to secure the funds necessary to start construction, the Big Four personally contributed $34,500 each for a total of $138,000, which they considered sufficient to build the first section —to reach at least to Newcastle, a distance of thirty-one miles. The railroad announced on December 4 that Timothy Dane and others had been assigned the right to construct all that portion of the railroad and telegraph line lying between the cities of Sacramento and San Francisco, which Central Pacific was authorized to build under Section 9 of the railroad bill.

This assignment included all Central Pacific's rights, grants, and donations. Huntington stated before the Pacific Railway Commission in 1887: "When we [he and Judah] were in Washington trying to get through the bill to give us aid, a certain party said that we must cut off our part at Sacramento and they must have the part between Sacramento and San Francisco, or else we must begin at San Francisco—we consented.

"We commenced at Sacramento, and assigned that part of the road, as agreed to, to Charles McLaughlin, and a man by the name of Houston, as I remember, and Judge Dane, and a number of others, and they located the road. We had nothing to do with them at the time. . . . They finally got embarrassed and did not see their way clear to complete the road to San Francisco; and said if we would take it and finish it to San Francisco, we could have it, and they would keep the land grant. They had built from San Jose toward Sacramento to a distance of about twenty miles."*

On December 22, the Sacramento *Union* shed more light on this matter: "A company has been organized to which the Central Pacific has assigned the rights to build, under the Pacific Railroad Bill, a railroad from San Francisco by way of San Jose and Stockton, to Sacramento, there to connect with the Central Pacific. This new organization is called the Western Pacific Railroad Company. From recent numbers of the San Francisco newspapers, it appears that the railroad jealousies which have been exhibited in that city have been removed by an action of the Board of Directors of the Central Pacific . . . in assigning the right to build under the Pacific Railroad Bill [to the Western Pacific]."

That the Central Pacific had been committed to yield this part of the line was confirmed by Judah on his return to Sacramento in 1862. "I would also state," he added, "that in pursuance of an agreement with Hon. J. A. McDougall and Hon. T. G. Phelps, made in Washington, I assigned to certain parties representing the interests of the San Francisco and San Jose road, the rights, grants and franchises given us for that portion of the road between Sacramento and San Francisco."

Toward the end of the year, the stage was finally set for construction

---

*The Western Pacific Railroad Company (not the Western Pacific of today) was incorporated December 13, 1862, to construct a railroad from San Jose through Santa Clara, Alameda and San Joaquin counties to Sacramento—a distance of 137.5 miles. It was capitalized at $5,400,000. The right to extend the road from Sacramento to San Francisco was given to the company with all rights, grants, donations, etc., by the Central Pacific, subject to the same conditions. Officers were Timothy Dane, president; E. S. Holden, vice president; E. T. Pease, secretary; R. Chenery, treasurer; and W. J. Lewis, chief engineer. The first twenty miles were to be built one year from July 1, 1865, and the entire road within four years thereafter. Congress later extended this by two years. The aid in government bonds amounted to $1,975,560. San Francisco contributed $200,000 in cash; Santa Clara county, $150,000; San Joaquin county, $250,000 in stock.

56

over the Sierra actually to begin. Since all of the money and supplies for the railroad would have to be procured in the Atlantic states, Huntington left Sacramento in December to take up residence in New York; it would prove to be his permanent home. He journeyed west only when business required; Mark Hopkins, who held Huntington's power of attorney, voted his interest in all matters.

On December 27, 1862, the Central Pacific announced that Charles Crocker & Company had been awarded a contract to build that portion of the road between the foot of K Street in Sacramento and the California Central line at a point later called Junction (now Roseville) comprising Sections 1 to 18, inclusive.

As the year 1863 dawned, the Central Pacific laid plans for the actual breaking of ground. The railroad was nearing reality, and its annual report for 1862, filed with the Secretary of State of California in February, 1863, told only of "the promise of things yet to come."

FIVE

THE MUSCLE, THE GOLD, AND THE IRON: *1863*

O<small>N</small> S<small>ATURDAY</small>, J<small>ANUARY</small> 3, 1863, the board of directors of the Central Pacific resolved "that the commencement of the work on the railroad of this company be inaugurated with proper ceremonies on the 8th instant at eleven o'clock A.M., at the foot of K Street. The public, societies and citizens generally are hereby invited to participate therein." They followed the resolution with a similar invitation to the state Senate, the Assembly, and the Sacramento Pioneer Association.

The Sacramento *Union* of January 9 best described the ground-breaking event:

"The skies smiled yesterday upon a ceremony of vast significance in Sacramento, California and the Union. With rites appropriate to the occasion, and in presence of the dignitaries of the State, representatives of every portion of the commonwealth, and a great gathering of citizens, ground was formally broken at noon for the commencement of the Central Pacific Railroad—the California link of the continental chain that is to unite American communities now divided by thousands of miles of track-less wilderness. Among the assemblage were pioneers who had assisted in laying the foundations of the Golden State, who had dreamed, toiled and schemed for years in behalf of this grand enterprise, and cling with steady faith, through many depressing defeats, to the belief that they would live to witness the consummation of their hopes; men who had more recently determined to devote their energies and their means to the execution of the project; representatives of the various sections of the State who appreciated the importance of the work to the whole Pacific Coast, no matter where the line should be located; high officials whose presence and earnest approval enhanced the dignity of the occasion; divines to invoke blessings on the work; and last, but not least, directors and contractors, who gave substantial assurance that the brain, the muscle, the gold and the iron were ready to make the railroad a reality. . . .

"The choice of scene for the ceremony was not favorable to the presence of the gentler sex, but the balconies opposite—on Front Street, above K—were adorned with a fair delegation. The great preponderance of pantaloons was a disagreeable necessity of the 'situation'. A stand was erected near the levee, a short distance above K Street, and the ends were adorned with the national flag. A general distribution of bundles of hay gave a comparatively dry footing to the crowd in the immediate vicinity. The Sacramento *Union's* Brass Band was stationed on the balcony of the American Exchange Hotel, and between the addresses enlivened the proceedings by playing the national airs and peculiarly 'Wait for the Wagon'. Two wagons adorned with flags, drawn by horses that were also decorated with the national colors, were stationed near the rostrum, with earth ready to be shoveled out for the railroad embankment. On one of these wagons was a large banner bearing a representation of hands clasped across the continent from the Atlantic to the Pacific, with the prayer of every loyal heart, 'May the Bond Be Eternal'.

"Shortly after twelve o'clock M., Governor Stanford appeared upon the stand, and the ceremonies of the occasion were commenced. C. Crocker introduced to the assemblage Leland Stanford, Governor of the state of California. In his speech, Governor Stanford said in part: 'I congratulate you upon the commencement of the great work which, in its results to the state of California and the Pacific Coast, and to the Nation itself, is to be what the Erie Canal was to New York and the Eastern States. This work will go on from this side to completion as rapidly as possible. There will be no delay, no backing, no uncertainty in the continued progress. We may now look forward with confidence to the day, not far distant, when the Pacific Coast will be bound to the Atlantic Coast by iron bonds that shall consolidate and strengthen the ties of nationality, and advance with giant strides the prosperity of the State and the Country. . . .'

"After a brief prayer by the Reverend J. A. Benton, Stanford was allowed to turn the first spadeful of earth for the project:

"The two wagons loaded with earth were driven up in front of the rostrum, and Governor Stanford, with a zeal and athletic vigor that showed his heart was in the work and his muscle in the right place, seized the shovel, and amid cheering of the crowd deposited the first earth for the embankment. The enthusiastic Charles Crocker promptly called for 'nine cheers' and the crowd, sharing his enthusiasm, cheeringly responded. The sun smiled brightly, and everybody felt happy because, after so many years of dreaming, scheming, talking and toiling, they saw with their own eyes the actual commencement of a Pacific Railroad. . . ."

With the beginning of construction that month, Charles Crocker retired from the board of directors, taking the title of general superintendent. His brother, Sacramento attorney E. B. Crocker, took his place on the board.

After the winter's high water had receded so that crews could get into the field, actual grading started in February under contract to Crocker, who subcontracted the project in sections to other firms. Besides grading, the only other work actually under way was construction of the American River Bridge, begun the previous December.

In March Charles Crocker and Professor J. D. Whitney, California State Geologist, surveyed the proposed rail line to locate the "base" of the Sierra, which the company was later accused of moving closer to Sacramento. In 1887 Crocker explained: "I took Professor . . . Whitney . . . on a little ride and I had a profile of the road from Sacramento City to Truckee Meadows with me. I showed it to him. I had a copy of the law and I read that to him. 'Now,' said I, 'Professor, we want to have you decide, or give your opinion of where this spot should be located.' The profile showed a perceptible rise from Arcade Creek up. It was getting up faster and faster as we went along. I did not ask him to do anything except that I wished him to decide where true justice would place the western base of the Sierra Nevadas. 'Well,' he says, 'the true base is the Sacramento River, but,' said he, 'for the purpose of this bill, Arcade Creek [seven miles from Sacramento] is as fair a place as any.' "

During that same month, March, 1863, Whitney addressed a letter to Stanford, in which he discussed the location of the western base of the Sierra Nevada, and cited geological authority. He wrote, "I would suggest, therefore, that the point where the line of the Central Pacific Railroad crosses Arcade Creek may with propriety be taken as the base of the Sierra, as from there commences a regular and continuous ascent, and in a distance of 150 miles from that point, the most difficult and mountainous portion of the route will have been traversed." This question was later settled by President Lincoln, who based his decision on Whitney's report.

That same spring the New York Central, Michigan Central, Baltimore & Ohio, Chicago & Northwestern, and Rock Island railroads told Congress that they had adopted four feet, eight and one-half inches as the standard gauge for their rails and urged that the new Pacific Railroad be established at the same gauge. President Lincoln had earlier fixed the official gauge for the transcontinental railroad at five feet, the gauge also required by the Central Pacific's state charter. Congress resolved a change in gauge to that of the eastern roads—the gauge in use by American railroads today.

Sacramento boomed in the sixties, as seen in the above
photograph of K Street, compared to the line drawing
of the Front Street area between I and K, circa 1849.

This decision imposed serious problems on the Central Pacific, since the specifications of all materials, locomotives, and other rolling stock ordered up to that time had been based on the five-foot gauge.

In view of Central Pacific's financial problems, and to further encourage construction of the railroad, California and several of its counties initiated legislative action to give financial help, culminating in a grant by the California Legislature of a cash subsidy of $300,000 to be paid on a mileage basis.*

In spite of the fact that the project seemed to be off to a good start, Judah wrote to Dr. Strong on May 13, indicating that all was not well between him and the Big Four. He had long opposed the policy by which a member of the company, Charles Crocker, could act as a contractor, bidding on construction work. His letter also indicated that he no longer was included in meetings scheduled from time to time by other officers.

"I had a blow-out about two weeks ago and freed my mind, so much so that I looked for instant decapitation. I called things by their right name and invited war; but counsels of peace prevailed and my head is still on; my hands are tied however. We have no meetings of the board nowadays, except the regular monthly meeting, which, however, was not had this month; but there have been any quantity of private conferences to which I have not been invited. I try to think it is all for the best, and devote myself with additional energy to my legitimate portion of the enterprise.

"On the 1st of April I presented my accounts to the board and insisted upon a settlement, but after backing and filling, the board adjourned, and to this day I do not know if they are considered as allowed, and there has been no regular meeting of the board since. . . .

"Much to my surprise, Mr. Hopkins has got me charged with 10 percent on my 150 original shares as cash advanced by him, and he says he knows of no agreement or understanding that it was to be allowed me as compensation for services rendered previous to the final organization.**

"All are elated at the vote in Placer County. Governor Stanford is in

---

*This act was repealed the following year. The state instead assumed payment of 7 percent interest on 1500 of the company's $1,000 bonds for a period of twenty years. In return for this aid, the Central Pacific agreed to furnish certain free transportation and render other service to the state government. First benefits of the act were not received by Central Pacific until January, 1865, after the California Supreme Court had ratified the legislature's action.

**Central Pacific Voucher No. 470 of July 1, 1863, shows that Judah was credited with $1,500 for his services in the reconnaissance survey in the Sierra. While Judah's letter suggests that he was not paid for this work, the voucher gives evidence that he was remunerated through the 10 percent stock subscription.

San Francisco, and if the vote carries in our favor there, the office of treasurer will be an important one.*

"I hope to put parties on the location of the second 50 miles this summer, so look out to see me up there before long."

Although the split between Judah and the Big Four had been widening for some time, their differences apparently erupted in July. Large sums of money for construction was needed immediately, and businessmen and bankers were not eager to invest in such a risky enterprise, especially in view of the war that was raging. In New York that spring, Huntington had had no success in disposing of the company's bonds. In the interim, Hopkins carefully husbanded dwindling resources at home. Judah had been schooled by eastern railroad engineers and desired to build "too well"—more expensively than his financial backers either desired or could afford. The Big Four, quite naturally, wanted to put up as little actual cash as possible, while Judah urged the necessity of an early survey through Nevada Territory in order to hold the Nevada charter. He also pointed out that actual contracts for second- and third-division construction must be let at once in order to insure completion within the time fixed by Congress.

Those unfriendly to the transcontinental railroad project were already saying that it was nothing but a huge swindle. As the Big Four were now largely concentrating on the wagon-road project over the mountains by way of Dutch Flat, the comment was that the new railroad's owners did not intend to lay any rails beyond Dutch Flat, that they were instead merely concocting a scheme to trap unwary investors. Whatever the facts regarding the wagon-road or the cause of delay, Judah was plainly impatient for work on the railroad to proceed. Moreover, he was not happy with Charles Crocker's role in the contracting arrangements.

Crocker, who had resigned his directorship in 1862, received the contract for construction as far as Newcastle; but records show that the directors at about this time, influenced by the "hue and cry" that Crocker was a favored contractor, informed him that he could build only two miles of this first division.** The "hue and cry" was Judah's. He also differed as to where the "base of the mountains" was located, refusing to sign the affidavit that had been prepared stating that the base was at Arcade Creek. According to Dr. Strong, Judah said, "We cannot sign it because the foothills do not begin here according to our surveys."

---

*In May, 1863, Placer County voters authorized the county to subscribe to $150,000 in bonds. San Francisco voted a $600,000 subscription. Court action by opponents of the C.P. held up delivery of these bonds until 1865.

**The twelve miles between Junction and Newcastle included sections 19 to 31. Crocker chose Sections 30 and 31, just below Newcastle.

The January, 1908, *Atlantic Monthly* outlined this critical period:

"During the summer of 1863, the affairs of the company assumed a critical aspect. Huntington had earlier gone East to arrange for rails and equipment. While there he had availed himself of the power of attorney he held from Stanford, Hopkins, Crocker and Judah to borrow $1,250,000 on their personal credit.

"This had been exhausted and the need of more funds was becoming more and more pressing. A division of opinion arose among the directors as to how these should be obtained. Three of them, including Judah and Bailey, were in favor of using the road and equipment as collateral for a new loan, while Huntington, Stanford, Hopkins and Crocker opposed it, on the grounds that a second encumbrance would so lower their credit as to prevent future loans except at ruinous rates.

"They wanted to have the directors put up personally to keep the work going until they reached Newcastle, when their Government subsidy* would commence to be available, and also because they would have a part of the road in operation to give them some standing as borrowers.

"The differences came to a showdown. Huntington and his supporters gave the others their option of four courses: buy us out, sell out to us, pay your proportion of what is necessary to keep the work going, or quit. In fact, for a few days work was suspended. Eventually Judah and his friends sold out their interests to the other side."

The withdrawal of Judah and other partners from the Central Pacific enterprise did not disturb Huntington, who regarded it as an opportunity to rid the company of those who seemed too weak to serve its interests well. He himself had no doubts, for he knew that the land and loans granted by Congress offered a prize more splendid than any gold or silver bonanza, a prize that probably would never have fallen to a small group of Sacramento storekeepers had not the Civil War prevented other men with greater influence and larger capital from competing for it. Huntington realized that the Central Pacific Railroad would be their reward and that only the strong could build it.

There is no doubt that Huntington took advantage of the conflict among the directors to cull what he considered the dead timber from his organization. He obviously considered carefully and decided that in the Big Four lay the strength needed for the enterprise. Stanford, although a storekeeper, had been a leader in California politics, and was currently Governor of California. Charles Crocker also was politically influential, as was his brother E. B. Crocker. And Huntington needed someone he could trust

---

*Loans to be repaid at 6 percent interest.

completely to protect his Sacramento interests; Hopkins, his old friend and partner, filled that need.

The rest could go.

Judah confirmed this split in a letter to his friend and ally, Dr. Strong, who was also a fellow stockholder and director:

"My Dear Doctor:

"You will excuse the long delay in answering your letter, but I have been waiting from day to day to have something definite to write about. Huntington has returned, and seems to possess more that usual influence. Stanford, who I told you was all right, is as much under their influence as ever.

"The wagon road seems to be a tie which unites them, and its influence seems to be paramount to everything else. I have had a big row and fight on the contract question, and although I had to fight alone, carried my point and prevented a certain gentleman [Crocker] from becoming a further contractor on the Central Pacific Railroad at present. . . .

"I believe I told you that the governor told me he would sell to Rohn his wagonroad interest. There is a good deal of negotiation going on, and from all indications all their differences are reconciled, all is smooth. They are a band of brothers again, and are going to let Rohn and Parish in with them. Rohn is with them a good deal, and told me today that he and Parish were going up Thursday next over the road, and that they offered him $30,000 interest, but he wants a controlling interest. Crocker and Huntington are going up Thursday and going over the new route across to Washoe City. They have been consulting and looking over the way every day, and do not hesitate to talk boldly, openly before me, but not to me, about it. They talk as though there was nobody in the world but themselves who could build a wagon road. They are going to take up this route. Crocker wrote to a Mr. Brown to meet them. He is going to take Rohn and Parish over it. He wants Huntington's judgment on it, and before they return they intend to take it up. . . .

"About coming down, do as you think best; it is not absolutely necessary; everything will go one way, and you are on the list; Marsh also. I would be very glad to see you and have you come down; but if you should not, write me, and send me yours and such other proxies as you have got. What do you think of going up immediately and taking up that route? Cannot a new company be organized for that purpose of persons whom you can control? But of course if they should know of it before the election they would decapitate you. Perhaps it is best to rest easy and come down at any rate when we will consult together.

"JUDAH"

65

Judah's report to the directors, when they met a few days later explained in detail why the Central Pacific could not utilize the old Sacramento Valley Railroad and its Auburn extension as part of the new line. The Central Pacific and its officers had been heavily criticized for not using that already existing line, a criticism that probably stemmed from the fact that the owners of the older line were anxious to rid themselves of it and were disappointed in not being able to do so. The S.V.R.R. was useless to the new road, for several reasons, Judah pointed out. First, the older line was eight miles longer than the projected route between the foot of K Street in Sacramento and Auburn. Second, the Pacific Railroad Bill appropriations did not apply to any line already constructed and thus no federal aid toward the purchase of the Sacramento Valley line could be expected. Third, because the act required the use of American iron, the English rails used in the original Sacramento Valley line to Folsom would have to be replaced. Besides, the extension to Auburn was constructed with rails that, although of American iron, were altogether too light. Fourth, the federal aid bonds were to constitute a first lien on the road; the older line was already heavily mortgaged. Fifth, in addition to relaying the S.V.R.R. with American iron, the new line would have to do a great deal of rehabilitation work. And finally, only the proposed Central Pacific location could secure the Marysville trade and prevent competition for this large business by some other line.

Judah pointed out that on the selected route via Dutch Flat, no less than five trial surveys had been run between Sacramento and Clipper Gap before the route via Antelope Ravine was finally adopted. Cost of the first division of fifty miles was estimated by him at $3,221,496. He declared that assistant engineer Samuel S. Montague was at that time—July, 1863—in the field with a survey party to find the location for the second fifty-mile division, which would bring the road to a point but six miles short of the summit of the Sierra Nevada.

At this meeting, the directors also approved the decision to build to Newcastle, thirty-one miles from Sacramento. Contracts to construct this second subdivision for the first division, comprising Sections 19 to 31 (Junction to Newcastle), were approved and awarded thus:

Sections 19–20   Cyrus Collins & Company
Sections 21–24   Messrs. Turton, Knox & Ryan
Sections 25–27   Charles D. Bates & Company
Sections 28–29   S. D. Smith
Sections 30–31   Charles Crocker

Of this thirteen-mile segment, Crocker's two miles were the heaviest. Moreover, he was later obliged to finish much of the work let to other contractors, because they began bidding against each other for labor, which

The Central Pacific's
first ticket office
on Front Street,
Sacramento, 1864.

The Broadway Wharf
at San Francisco,
where the steamers
departed to Sacramento.

The "Gov. Stanford," first locomotive on the C.P. roster.

*Freight was shifted from sailing craft to railroad cars
on the Front Street docks, Sacramento.*

was very scarce, and ran costs so high that they were unable to finish the job.

At the same meeting, Judah also reported that 6,000 tons of rail—sufficient to build sixty miles of track—had been purchased in the East and would be delivered at the rate of 500 tons monthly; the necessary spikes and iron also had been bought and were on their way. Six locomotives had been procured for use on the first fifty miles of railroad. Three of these, the *Atlantic, Pacific,* and *John Conness,* were bought from William Mason & Company, of Taunton, Massachusetts; one, the *Governor Stanford,* was ordered from Norris & Company, of Philadelphia; and two tank locomotives, the *T. D. Judah* and the *Collis P. Huntington,* from Danforth Cooke & Company, of Paterson, New Jersey. Purchase of two first-class passenger cars, two baggage cars, twenty-five platform freight cars, fifteen boxcars, and the necessary frogs, switches, turntables, and other supplies necessary for the first fifty miles was also announced.

The "elephant" that Huntington had referred to with apprehension was growing beyond all recognition. It is quite probable that during this period some of the organizers wished they had never heard of the Pacific Railroad, or at least wanted out of the gamble. At any rate, by the end of September, 1863, matters had deteriorated to the point that Judah left Sacramento for the East Coast with the expressed intention of obtaining other backing for the project. On October 9, he wrote his last, and perhaps most illuminating, letter to Dr. Strong, while aboard the steamer *St. Louis.* In it he declared:

"I have a feeling of relief in being away from the scenes of contention and strife which it has been my lot to experience for the past year, and to know that the responsibilities of events, so far as regards Pacific Railroad, do not rest on my shoulders.*

"If the parties who now manage hold to the same opinion three months hence that they do now, there will be a radical change in the management of the Pacific Railroad, and it will pass into the hands of men of experience and capital. If they do not, they may hold the reins for awhile, but they will rue the day that they ever embarked in the Pacific Railroad.

"If they treat me well they may expect similar treatment at my hands. If not, I am able to play my hand.

"If I succeed in inducing the parties I expect to see to return with me to California, I shall likely return the latter part of December."

Strained relations had obviously developed between Judah, Strong,

---

*While information is vague on this point, it appears that the Big Four had bought Judah's shares for about $100,000, while giving him an option to buy each of them out for the same amount.

Marsh, and other original backers on one hand and the Big Four on the other. Quite possibly Judah feared that there was truth in the allegation that the Dutch Flat wagon road promotion constituted a swindle, although it is probable that the wagon road actually was a secondary project to facilitate construction of the railroad by providing the means of getting workers and supplies to forward camps in the mountains.

Whatever Judah hoped to accomplish in the East—which very likely included backing by the Vanderbilt interests—soon became academic. He contracted yellow fever on the Isthmus of Panama and, by November 2, 1863, was dead.

Judah's chief aim was to complete the transcontinental road as quickly as possible. Had he lived, the history of western railroading might have altered its course, for it was not until Judah's sudden death that full control of the Central Pacific was obtained by the Sacramento merchants.

"When Judah sailed in 1863," his nephew asserted years later, "his plans were fully matured, his co-adjustors selected and the meeting arranged." He revealed that Judah had planned to attract capital in the East to buy from his former associates the company's charter and subsidies. He planned to place these, along with the management, in the hands of an entirely new group of men, of "known public spirit," who would "prosecute diligently the main work of completing the railroad." The November 5, 1863, issue of the San Francisco *Bulletin* seemed to echo this view: "At the time of his departure, the interior press stated that he went on business connected with the Central Pacific Railroad Company, but from a reliable source we are informed that his connection with the company had then ceased."

Leland Stanford, however, in a letter to the Nevada Legislature in February, 1865, stated that Judah had remained chief engineer until his death. Of all the Big Four, Stanford was the most friendly toward Judah throughout this trying period, and there is no actual evidence that Judah had completely severed his ties with the company before leaving for the East.

In a letter written after his death, Mrs. Judah outlined her understanding of her husband's increasing disillusionment:

"Judah used to say, when he came home from the Directors' meetings, 'I cannot make these men appreciate the 'elephant' they have on their shoulders; they will not do what I want and must do; we shall just as sure have trouble in Congress as the sun rises in the East, if they go on this way; they will not see it. Something must be done. I will not be stultified before Congress and the business world.' They did not ratify the contracts made in the East for iron and equipment before he went out and had three months in which to have them ratified. He had brought them a franchise and laid it at their door; rightly used, giving them unlimited credit throughout the world, and they would beggar it. He felt they were ungrateful to their trust and to him. Governor Stanford was a 'Judah man', and so long as he lived he was loyal to him, I believe. Charles Marsh and Dr. Strong were his fast friends. Mr. Judah saw he must place himself differently, and he went to work to accomplish it. It is best shown by his words to me on the steamer, enroute to New York in October, 1863. He had secured the right and had the power to buy out the men opposed to him and the true interests of the Pacific railroad at the time. Everything was arranged for a meeting in New York City on his arrival. Gentlemen from New York and Boston were ready to take their places. . . . Theodore said to me one day, lying in his berth, 'What can I not do in New York? I have always had to set my brains and will against other men's money. Now, with money—equal—what can I not do?' He knew what he could do; it was all laid out, but God willed it otherwise and called him home."

It is ironic that while Judah prepared for his trip to New York, the first supplies were arriving from the East. On October 6—four days before he sailed—the Sacramento *Union* reported: "FIRST LOCOMOTIVE FOR RAILROAD ARRIVES BY BOAT. Between 1 and 2 o'clock yesterday [October 5] afternoon, the schooner, *Artful Dodger,* arrived from San Francisco and took a berth opposite the foot of I Street. She had on board the locomotive, *Gov. Stanford,* a quantity of spikes and other material for the Central Pacific Railroad.

"This morning, the new discharging track of the company was extended to the schooner dock and the removal of the heavy machinery commenced about 10 o'clock.

"This is the first locomotive of the Central Pacific which has reached this point and numbers of people have been on the levee, looking at the engine which bears the name of the governor of the state.

"For the present, the engine will be placed on the levee near the intersection of I and Front Streets, there to await the completion of the engine house, which is to be of brick, of semicircular form, with its concavity opening towards First or Jibboom Street."

Other reports indicate that the railroad had started to erect dock and tracks along Front Street, but their big cranes were not yet in place. In fact, the railroad had no shops, few tools, and only a short stretch of track ready to receive the first motive power. The company's biggest building was a small tool house on the levee, which had been nailed together in one day at a cost of $150 for materials. This shed was designed by the frugal Huntington, who had rejected plans for a more elaborate building, and insisted on using this tool shed as the first ticket office when the line was opened to Newcastle the following spring. (The little building stood there on the levee near the foot of I Street until 1908, when it was demolished.)

Now that the heavy machinery was beginning to arrive from the East, assistant chief engineer Samuel S. Montague reported that during October, 1863, piles were driven along the edge of the river on Front Street, and several hand-operated pillar cranes were erected to lift the material off river schooners arriving from San Francisco. His report also indicated that the bridge across the American River was finished and awaiting the start of rail as were other trestling and bridges necessary to complete the road to Junction (now Roseville): "The trestling at Arcade Creek ["base" of the Sierra seven miles from Sacramento] is completed. It is 200 feet in length, and similar in plan to that at the American River.

"The bridge at Dry Creek [17 miles from Sacramento] is completed and consists of four 54½-foot Burr's truss resting on stone piers, and connected with the embankment at each end by shore bends of trestling.

"The Antelope Creek bridge [near Junction] consisting of one span of Burr's truss, resting upon substantial granite piers, is completed."

Central Pacific selected October 26, 1863, as the day the first rail was to be laid and planned a suitable celebration similar to the ground-breaking ceremony staged the previous January. Word was sent to Huntington, who had returned to the East after the July directors' meeting; but Huntington, knowing the condition of the company at that time and the purpose of Judah's mission to the East, opposed a celebration. "If you want to jubilate in driving the first spike go ahead and do it," he wrote. "I don't. These mountains look too ugly and I see too much work ahead. We may fail and I want to have as few people know it as we can and if we get up a jubilation any little nobody can drive the first spike, but there are many months of hard labor and unrest between the first and the last spike."

Huntington had his way, as he usually did—a fact indicated by the October 27, 1863, issue of the *Union:* "Yesterday morning the contractor to build a section of eighteen miles laid the first rail on the western end of the Pacific Railroad, as described in the bill passed by Congress. Quite a number of persons were present to witness the work, though no notice that it was to be done had been published. Those engaged in the enterprise did not choose to have any ceremony over the affair; they made a regular business matter of an event which in the eye of the public is the first certain step taken in building the great Pacific Railroad.

"Grading has been done, bridges built; but nothing looks to the public so much like making a railroad as the work of laying down the iron of the road bed. On the Atlantic side the contract for building the section through Kansas has been let two or three times, but up to this date we have seen no report of the rails being laid, though not long since we saw it stated that a shipment of iron had been made from New York for the Kansas section. . . .

The Dry Creek Bridge
was completed in 1863.

The credit, therefore, of having put the first rail on the line must be awarded to the California Central Pacific Company.

"A few weeks since it was reported that all the stock of the Union Pacific Railroad had been subscribed, the 10 percent paid in, and the company organized. This company is to build the road from the western line of Kansas to the eastern boundary of California. The law, however, provides that the California Central Pacific Railroad Company may continue to build east through Nevada and Utah Territories in the event of their building their road to the east of California before the Union Pacific Company reaches that point from the East with a railroad.

"The prospects now are that the California company will complete their road to the east line of the state before the Union Company finish theirs through Nebraska. In fact, the road must be built from the two ends; upon the center section little can be done until it can be reached by rail each way. Hence, the vast importance of pushing the work at the east and west ends of the Road as rapidly as possible.

"On this point, we maintain that the California Central Pacific Railroad Company has accomplished more than could have been expected under the circumstances. It is but little over a year since the Pacific Railroad Bill was received in California. It was signed by the President on the 1st of July, 1862, and reached California in August following. Within the intervening time the company has obtained subscriptions to the stock for nearly a million of dollars; sent an agent to the East, who purchased the iron and rolling stock for seventy miles of the road, six hundred tons of which have arrived, while four thousand tons are known to be afloat; seventy-five miles of the road have been carefully surveyed and located, and thirty miles put under contract, eighteen of which is now ready for the iron; and, as before stated, a commencement to lay it down was made yesterday. . . .

"When the cars are running fifty miles the company will, besides the earnings of the road, receive the $48,000 per mile loan donated by Congress, as well as the $10,000 per mile granted by the State to aid the enterprise. Therefore the completion of the first fifty miles solves the financial problem connected with building a railroad over the Sierra Nevada. That fifty miles the company will have in running condition before the first of December 1864, which is the date named in the bill for the completion of that section. Factious opposition to the issuing of bonds in San Francisco may cause delay but it will be only temporary. The road will continue to advance. The work of laying the rails has begun and it will continue until California and Washoe are united by iron bands and until the iron rails are stretched across the continent. It is hardly twelve months since work was actually commenced, and yet within that short space of time the greatest obstacles in the way of building a Pacific Railroad have been met and surmounted. With fifty miles of road in operation, the company will become an institution which will be recognized in the financial markets of the world. It will possess character and credit equal to millions, and will be enabled to proceed with full confidence in its resources and in the future."

However, after Judah's departure for the East, his friends left the company one by one. Apparently, they were given the same option as Judah: either to buy out the Big Four or be bought out themselves. The Dutch Flat and Donner Lake Wagon Road Company, of which Dr. Strong had been in charge since the spring of 1863, was removed from his direction on October 30 of that year and placed under the direction of R. H. Pratt, the Big Four's man. At that time, Dr. Strong disposed of thirty-six of his forty shares in the wagon road company and also withdrew his holdings in the Central Pacific.

Judah's estate was probated in 1863 in Greenfield, Massachusetts. The inventory listed fifty Central Pacific Railroad Company bonds of $1,000 each and an interesting agreement, signed by Charles Crocker, which would give Judah fifty additional $1,000 railroad bonds. These were never delivered, and after futile efforts to collect on this unrestricted contract, the administrator dropped his efforts and asked the court to declare Crocker's agreement valueless.

Although certain minor changes were made in Judah's survey on the ridge between the Bear and American rivers, the Central Pacific line, as actually built over the Sierra Nevada, was essentially that plotted by Judah. His was pathfinder's work, and without his enthusiasm, vigor, and perseverance, it is doubtful whether the Pacific Railroad dream would so soon have become reality. A railroad spanning the continent was, of course, inevitable; but that fact cannot detract from this young engineer's great contribution. He was an idealist and a dreamer, but he was also a practical man; and the accomplishments of his brief career attest to his astounding energy and imagination.

"Central Pacific Railroad has started to erect a substantial frame building 20 feet by 150 feet on the banks of Lake Sutter near Sixth and I Street," the Sacramento *Union* announced on November 6, 1863. This item heralded the start of the first building of what was to become that city's large railroad shops. This was the first of several wooden buildings built by the Central Pacific late in 1863. (This small group of buildings comprised the shops of Central Pacific until 1867, when plans were drawn and work started on the larger shops.) Benjamin Welch, a friend of Collis P. Huntington, was hired as superintendent of the shops, where twenty to thirty men were employed. Welch's official title was "car master"; but, in addition to supervising the building and maintenance of cars, he was also general superintendent of construction.

The same edition of the *Union* also carried an item indicating that enemies of the Central Pacific were still at work:

"Strange as it may seem, there is undoubtedly a very active opposition in San Francisco to building the Pacific Railroad and, to some extent, in other parts of the state. This opposition in certain sections arises from the selection of Sacramento City as a terminus of that route, and is attributable to local jealousy. Another opposition comes from the Sacramento Valley Railroad which is largely controlled by Pioche, Bayerque & Company of San Francisco. They oppose the enterprise on the ground that construction of a railroad from Sacramento to Dutch Flat and thence toward Washoe would damage the business of the Valley road, which runs from Sacramento to Folsom, as it would divert the Washoe [stagecoach] travel from that route. Another opposition is the Market Street Railroad [in San Francisco] owned by Pioche, Bayerque & Company.

"All these oppositions may be natural enough on the part of the interests affected, but with the public at large no such hostility should be felt. It looks as though the San Francisco Board of Supervisors were too much influenced by the managers and agents of the Valley and Market Street railroads when they refused to issue bonds voted by the people to the Pacific Railroad."

Huntington, in a letter written in May, 1874, to Philetus Sawyer in Washington, chairman of the House committee on the Pacific Railroad, commented on hostility experienced late in 1863: "This crusade against the railroad company had its origin far back in the history of the company, almost at its very commencement. It first originated with the owners of a railroad [Sacramento Valley Rail Road] running a short distance easterly from Sacramento who wanted to be bought, but careful surveys were made of that and various other routes, and it was determined that it was not on the proper location for a route over the mountains, and for that reason was rejected, and the company encountered the opposition of the owners. The opposition was not large or very formidable but it was persistent and malicious. It showed itself on the first and subsequent applications to Congress, but, as it was not then popular, it was secret and malicious. It showed itself, still secretly, in each application made by the company to the State of California for legislative aid—it showed itself more openly by endeavoring in common councils and Boards of Supervisors, and also before the courts, to prevent the company from realizing the benefit of the subsidies that had been authorized by legislative enactment and by popular vote. The effect of this opposition was to cause delay in realizing aid when most needed, and the expense in finally obtaining it. This opposition has not always been confined to the original opposers, but in most cases, it can be traced back to them, or to their successors."

*Stacks of 55-60 pound
iron rail awaiting the next
work train at the
Sacramento yards.*

On November 7, the *Union* again commented upon the difficulties encountered by the company in collecting $600,000 in Central Pacific bonds that San Francisco had agreed to buy. The article outlined the work that had been done, and concluded: "All this has been accomplished without failing in any instance to meet every obligation incurred to contractors and without creating any indebtedness. This simple statement is an ample vindication of the management of the directors as they can desire. No railroad on the Pacific side has ever been managed so successfully."

A brief announcement in the same issue promised that bigger things and better days were soon to come: "Yesterday afternoon steam was gotten up in the locomotive *Governor Stanford* at the foot of I Street. The engine could not be set in motion as it had not yet been placed upon the track. On Monday morning it is expected it will go to work hauling iron for the purpose of laying track."

Three days later, the *Union* triumphantly reported, "The first locomotive was started on the Central Pacific yesterday. A salute was fired in honor of the event. The kids got in on the first ride and had all the riding. When they were ready to take the 'State officers, bankers, editors, etc.', a salute was fired of thirty-five guns from a new twelve-pounder bought by W. Siddons. By eight o'clock that night the locomotive was in full working order and made a number of trips as far as 16th Street crowded with cheering passengers."

The embankment and tracks of the railroad had by then been built on the levee along Front Street to a point just north of First and Broad streets, in the American Fork addition; from there they curved eastward to Sixth and D streets, then northeast on the city levee to the crossing of the American River at Elvas. At a point a few feet north of First and Broad streets, piles were driven, upon which the first turntable—a fifty-footer of wood and iron bars operated by hand power—was erected.

Judah's death left the company without a chief engineer. His place was taken by Samuel Skerry Montague, a man who had worked under him on the surveys and who had acted in Judah's capacity after his departure for the East. The board of directors in their November, 1863, meeting named Montague acting chief engineer, and in March, 1868, promoted him to chief engineer, a position he filled until his death in 1883.

"The track of the Pacific Railroad is finished, it is stated, to the west side of the American River, and the engine now crosses," the *Union* announced on December 4, 1863, quoting a Leavenworth, Kansas, paper to the effect that forty miles of the eastern division of the Pacific Railroad (Union Pacific) had been graded and that the road "is going towards the Pacific at the rate of a mile a day." The *Union,* in defense of the Central Pacific, added: "In California something handsome has been done in getting the Pacific Railroad under way but we do not pretend to be pushing it ahead as they profess to be doing in Kansas. Within a dozen miles or so the railroad company here is compelled to begin the ascent of the dreaded Sierra Nevada. The heavy and costly work here is encounterd at the very start. Here we have to transport iron and rolling stock some 20,000 miles, but in the face of these difficulties the Central Pacific Company has within eleven months purchased the iron and rolling stock for seventy miles. The grade is finished for eighteen miles; a splendid bridge is built over the American River; the iron is laid for a mile beyond the bridge and by the first of January 1864 unless the iron on shipboard is detained beyond all calculations the road will be in running condition for eighteen miles."

The annual report of the railroad for the year ending December 31, 1863, showed still no revenue received and the bills beginning to grow. It read as follows:

The amount of Capital Stock subscribed $1,364,000.00

The amount of Capital Stock actually paid in 863,140.00

The amount paid for purchase of lands is 100.00

The amount expended on Construction 947,058.91

The amount expended for Buildings 1,578.19

The amount expended for Engines 67,995.59

The amount expended for Cars 50,073.12

The Indebtedness of the Company is

    In First Mortgage Bonds Issued. . . . .$ 785,000.00

    In Bills Payable (in U. S. Notes). 210,000.00

    In Unadjusted accounts about 5,000.00

The Amount due the Company is

    From Stockholders on Subscriptions. . . . .$ 500,060.00

    Balance on deposit in New York. 87,400.21

The amount received from transportation

    of Passengers, Property, etc. 000.00

SIX

ABRAHAM'S FAITH: *1864*

E̲ᴀʀʟʏ ɪɴ 1864, President Lincoln made a decision of great importance to the financially shaky Central Pacific. By the terms of the Pacific Railroad Act, the company was to receive a loan in bonds to the amount of $16,000 per mile for its line west of the base of the Sierra, and, because of the extremely high cost of construction in the mountains, $48,000 per mile for 150 miles east of that point. The Department of the Interior suggested that the end of the first fifty-mile segment be designated as the base of the Sierra and the beginning of the $48,000-a-mile construction. The California Supreme Court, however, had decided that the foothills of the Sierra began thirty-one miles from Sacramento, at Newcastle. It devolved upon President Lincoln to make the final decision as to where the increased payment would begin. He decided that, based upon Professor J. D. Whitney's earlier report, the point should be 7.18 miles east of Sacramento—a determination which meant a difference of more than $1,000,000 in the amount advanced to the company by the federal government.

In making the announcement, Lincoln expressed his belief in the importance of the Pacific railroad as a national undertaking and declared that he welcomed this opportunity to give the enterprise every benefit the law would permit. "Here is a case," he said, "in which Abraham's Faith has moved mountains."

Later in 1864, those opposed to the Central Pacific were still effective enough to cause a major financial crisis within the company, as Judah had predicted the previous fall. The Sacramento *Union* on January 28, 1864, described the company's opponents:

"It has been generally supposed for the last twelve years that every man in California was earnestly in favor of the Pacific Railroad but since the bill was passed by Congress, which insures the final completion of the great work, men are found in the state who are so intensely selfish as to oppose the Pacific Railroad unless they can have the building of it or dictate who shall do the work, or how it shall be done. Strange as it may sound this opposition has been developed to a greater extent in San Francisco, the commercial metropolis of the Pacific, and which by the railroad will be made one of the greatest commercial cities on the globe, than in any other portion of the state."

In spite of the continuing opposition, however, building progressed. Shortly after the beginning of 1864, C.P. locomotive No. 2, the *Pacific*, arrived in Sacramento and joined the *Gov. Stanford* in moving construction trains to the rail head. Charles Crocker & Company reported on February 29, 1864, that, following steady progress in construction, the road was "ready for business from Sacramento to the Junction [now Roseville] with the California Central Railroad—a distance of 18 miles." In a report to the directors, chief engineer Montague detailed progress: "On Sections 1 to 18 [first eighteen miles], 36 culverts are built in a thorough and substantial manner, of hard-burned brick, laid in hydraulic cement, with parapet walls, topped with granite six inches in thickness, securely fastened to the walls with iron anchors.

"The ties, furnished by the contractors, are of the best quality of Coast or Black redwood, and there are now delivered, in addition to those already used (sections 1 to 18), a sufficient number to lay 22 miles of track. [Cross ties 6 x 8 x 10 inches and 8 feet long are used.]

"The track has been laid in a thorough and workmanlike manner, and is ballasted with such material as could be obtained in the vicinity of the Road.

"Buildings. A 'Y' track has been constructed at the Junction [Roseville]. Suitable watering places have also been provided at Sacramento and Junction. A Fairbank's track scale of the capacity of sixty tons has been landed from the ship, and will soon be erected at the Junction."

The Central Pacific was now ready for business—as soon as it could obtain additional locomotives and passenger cars, equipment that was not long in arriving. "The first passenger car of the Pacific Railroad Company was completed last week and placed on the track on I Street," the *Union* announced in March 15. "Another finished car remains in the works of the Company on 6th Street and will be brought out in a day or two." Materials and equipment continued to arrive during the month, as the San Francisco *Daily Evening Bulletin* reported on March 22, 1864: "The ship *Success* from New York, which arrived on the 19th instant, brought a large amount of iron and rolling stock for the Central Pacific Railroad. Among the rolling stock is a first class locomotive engine named the *C. P. Hunting-*

ton. Some idea of the quantity of material, etc., brought by this vessel may be inferred from the amount of freight money due on the Bills of Lading, which is $12,781.44. By the ship *Mary Robinson,* which arrived last week, this company received two other first class locomotive engines, one of which is named the *T. D. Judah.* [The other was the *Atlantic.*] With these additions the Central Pacific Railroad Company has now on hand five engines to run the road."

A week later, the new locomotives were unloaded from the ships and assembled in a yard at the foot of I Street, adjacent to the old Goss & Lambart machine shops. The *Gov. Stanford* had the honor of moving the first revenue freight and also the first train carrying paying passengers. According to the *Union* of March 26, the locomotive "arrived at dusk last evening from the foothills with three carloads of granite, about thirty tons, all taken from the Brigham quarries on the line of the Pacific Railroad. This is the first freight which has passed over the Road."

"One year and four months after the groundbreaking ceremony . . . in Sacramento," Montague reported to the directors, "the first paying passengers . . . were hauled from Sacramento to Junction, [Roseville] a distance of 18½ miles. Trains are now running daily over the road to that point." Little freight, however, passed over the road until June 10, when it was opened to Newcastle, thirty-one miles from Sacramento. E. H. Miller, Jr., secretary of the road, reported for April 26–30, that 298 passengers brought in total revenues of $354.25. In May 8,900 passengers were carried for a total revenue of $4,291.25.

As the Central Pacific had no Sacramento passenger station, it converted the little tool house which stood on the levee on Front Street into a ticket office. The tool house served until the following year, 1865, when C.P. acquired the Sacramento Valley Railroad and with it the passenger station located on Front Street near K.

Meanwhile, the diminutive locomotive *C. P. Huntington* became operational on April 9 and, with engineer John E. Lonergan at the controls, the following day hauled three "platform" cars loaded with rails to the forward-moving railhead. As the little engine pulled its load across the American River Bridge, Alfred A. Hart, photographer for the Central Pacific, made several memorable photographs.

Despite Central Pacific's steady progress, attacks against the firm continued. The San Francisco *Alta California,* a leader in the campaign against the railroad and the "Great Dutch Flat Swindle," insisted that the railroad would be built only to Dutch Flat as a feeder to the wagon road that started at that point. Accordingly, the newspaper blasted the company on April 25, 1864: "The Sacramentans are determined to have no railroad but Dutch Flat. They have gone over to Stanford's moonshine project, and

Central Pacific Locomotive No. 4—"T. D. Judah."

Central Pacific locomotive No. 3, the "C. P. Huntington."

everything else must of course give way. . . . Though the Capital has aided in the raid upon this county for $600,000, upon Placer for $250,000, and upon the State for millions for the benefit of that scheme, it will yet prove its ruin. There will never be a railroad running from Sacramento, by way of Dutch Flat to Nevada Territory. There are obstacles in the way which cannot be overcome. The Pacific Railroad will follow another route, and that route will not be through the city of Sacramento nor anywhere in the vicinity."

The route to which the *Alta* probably referred was that of the San Francisco & San Jose Railroad, which in April, 1864, was operating fully between these two points, and was expected to be the first portion of a transcontinental route running south to the Colorado River and then across Arizona. This route was later used by the Southern Pacific Railroad, which was organized in 1865, and took over the San Francisco and San Jose.

The newspaper did not give up easily and on May 14 predicted that "the first fifty miles will exhaust all their resources soon. If all the counties subscribe, together with the state and government aid . . . it does not require much foresight to predict that the present company will stop at the end, or nearly so, of the first fifty miles. . . . The toll wagon road may run down to meet the railroad but it is doubtful whether the railroad will go further than the fifty miles to meet the wagon road."

The only opposition the *Alta* could offer, however, was verbal; and the railroad continued east, reaching Newcastle, thirty-one miles from Sacramento, by June 6, 1864.

"The road has been constructed in the most permanent and durable manner," Montague wrote in a report, "and the general character of the work will compare favorably with first-class railroad work in the eastern states. . . .

"Commodious freight and passenger deposits have been erected at Sacramento and Newcastle, and at the former place, an engine house, with stalls for five engines has also been built. Turntables have been built at both named places. Suitable watering places have also been provided at Sacramento, Junction and Pino.

"A telegraph line has also been constructed along the line of your Road, from Sacramento to Newcastle, and offices established at both named places.

"It may not be improper to state in this connection that the Commissioners appointed by the President of the United States in accordance with the provisions of Section 4 of the Pacific Railroad Act, have made a careful and thorough examination of your Road and the Telegraph Line connected therewith, and their favorable report has already been transmitted to the proper authorities at Washington."

Montague also informed the directors that he had filed a map with the Secretary of the Interior outlining the general route of the Central Pacific from Sacramento to the Big Bend of the Truckee River. That map, recorded by the Interior Department July 6, 1864, reflected a change in the original route.

"Coincidentally," only eight days after the Central Pacific announced opening of its line to Newcastle, the Dutch Flat and Donner Lake Wagon Road Company announced through its president, Charles Crocker, that it too was open for travel. The following advertisement appeared in the Sacramento *Union* on June 14, 1864: "The Dutch Flat Road is now open for travel, and teamsters can save three days in the round trip to Virginia City, and carry fully one quarter more freight on account of light grades. Plenty of freight can always be procured at Newcastle, the terminus of the Central Pacific Railroad. Until further notice all teams going west without load can pass free of toll. All those taking loads at Newcastle can pass free up to July 1, 1864.

"Teamsters, try it and see for yourselves."

R. H. Pratt, successor to Dr. Strong as head of the toll road, made it into an excellent highway at a cost of about $350,000, an expense borne by the associates as individuals and not charged to the railroad company. Pratt then took over all of the company's teamster operations. Later that year, the secretary of Central Pacific, E. H. Miller, described the wagon road:

"The present facilities afforded by your Road, and the connecting Stage Lines for the accommodation of travel across the mountains, are unequaled upon any other route.

"Persons traveling via the Central Pacific Railroad, and the Dutch Flat and Donner Lake Wagon Road, reach Virginia City in from four to six hours less time than by any other line. Since the California Stage Company placed their coaches upon this line in July last, the average time for the trips from Sacramento to Virginia has been but seventeen hours.

"This road, which was commenced in 1863, and completed in June, last, is by far the best road yet constructed across the mountains. It accomplishes the ascent of the Western slope of the Sierras with a much lighter maximum grade than has heretofore been deemed possible to attain within the limits of expense which such an enterprise would justify.

"The maximum ascending grade, [eastward] is but 10 inches to the rod, or less than one-half the maximum grade on the other most important roads crossing the mountains.

"It is constructed in the best possible manner, and is everywhere wide enough for teams to pass each other without difficulty.

After crossing the
American River Bridge,
four miles from
Sacramento, the line
stretched east on the
"12-mile Tangent."

"Commodious hotels have been erected along the route, and preparations are being made to keep the road open during the Winter.

"No difficulty is apprehended in doing this, as the snow-fall is believed to be much lighter upon this, than upon the other routes, via the Henness and Johnson passes.

"This comparative immunity from heavy snows, which frequently form a serious obstruction to travel across the mountains during the winter months, is chiefly due to the difference in altitude between this and the other routes named, there being several hundred feet in favor of this route."

Thirty-one miles from Sacramento, at Newcastle, the railroad would come to an absolute halt. Iron for another nineteen miles lay useless because there was not enough money for the necessary grading; in the eighteen months since the jubilant groundbreaking ceremonies, the Central Pacific had exhausted its financial resources. Huntington labored in New York and Washington with desperate energy but little result.

Painfully discouraged, Stanford returned to San Francisco and offered controlling interest in the road to any group of capitalists who could raise sufficient money to carry it across the Sierra, but his offer, too, met with no response. During testimony before the Pacific Railroad Commission in 1887 Stanford described the situation in which they found themselves: "We were forced to use our own individual credit to the fullest extent in the purchase of supplies, at one time to the extent of $600,000. We went on, however, and built the first thirty-one miles of road entirely from our own means. We had not then obtained any county or state aid. We built thirty-one miles of road but we were not able until we got this county aid to go further."

The situation was desperate enough to force Huntington's return to Sacramento, where he found the treasury practically empty, labor forces reduced to the minimum, and both Crocker and Stanford in despair. In no way could they hasten release of promised state and county help from the tangle of litigation in which the hostile interests had involved it. The Big Four agreed that in order to survive, they must finance the work a little longer. All means for doing so seemed exhausted, but the financial genius Huntington persuaded the others that each could do a little more. "Huntington and Hopkins," he said, "can, out of their own means, pay five hundred men for a year. How many can each of you keep on the line?" The result was an agreement to keep eight hundred men on the job for a year.

At that important June, 1864, directors' meeting in Sacramento, the company also assessed its experience in building the first thirty-one miles and decided that if construction were divided among many contractors, as had been tried during the last thirteen miles, labor would become unmanageable; its price would mount, and work would be seriously impeded. The directors decided that the company must have more control over construction than was possible when work was let out in comparatively small units. Labor was scarce, money scarcer. Individual sections must be built as nearly as possible in consecutive order so that, as each section was completed, railroad operations could be extended to yield constantly increasing revenues. Crocker would proceed at prices paid him for the two sections below Newcastle, although lack of money compelled him to cut working forces to the bone.

It was characteristic of the Big Four that from the day ground was broken, each day showed some progress in building the road. If they lacked the means for 500 workers, they employed 100; if they could not employ 100, the force was held to 10. They limited their work strictly to what they could pay for.

Huntington returned to his task of scheming and pleading for money from all possible sources in the East. When not trying to borrow money, he bargained with manufacturers, foundries, and ship owners to get the maximum value from what money there was to spend.

In 1887, attorney Alfred A. Cohen told the Pacific Railroad Commission: "I have seen Mr. Huntington trudging about from office to office in New York trying to get people to lend him money. For months—almost for a year if not more—he was traveling at night between Washington and Boston trying to raise money to send to California. They were put to terrible straits to get money to get over the mountains."

Huntington also kept in touch with his associates, from time to time making the hazardous and tiresome journey to California by stage to help them battle the obstacles—financial, physical, social—that plagued the Central Pacific. In a few days he would turn around and make the grueling trip back to New York.

San Francisco bankers would obviously have been useless as credit references in coaxing loans from eastern bankers, so Huntington had to depend largely on his own eloquence—and such collateral as he and his associates could scrape together. Cohen later told the Railroad Commission: "I have sat here in bank parlors in San Francisco and heard bankers say 'Don't have anything to do with those men—Stanford, Hopkins, and Huntington. Don't you put any money into their schemes. They are bound to come to grief. Nobody in the world could get that road through.' "

Although the Central Pacific had welcomed the Pacific Railroad Act of 1862, operating under some of its provisions was proving difficult. The government's first mortgage on the road prevented the company's bonds, automatically in second place, from being either sold or used as security. When the Thirty-eighth Congress convened in Washington, Huntington tried to secure conditions more favorable to expedite the work, if not save the railroad from total failure. On March 6, 1864, a bill was introduced to amend the act of 1862; it was passed four months later. In a telegram to his partners, Huntington outlined its significant portions: "Railroad bill passed. It gives one more year on first fifty miles, twenty-five miles thereafter. Forfeit is removed. No percentage is to be kept back. Gives double amount of land. Allows a first mortgage on the road of equal amount to the government, making the government mortgage second. Old law regarding bond as before. I was not able to do anything for the road between Sacramento and San Francisco."

As advantageous as these changes were, they did little to help the Central Pacific until either the first fifty miles were completed or the state and county aid, still entangled in litigation, could be made available.

Word of C.P.'s financial condition and the resultant cut-back in construction forces above Newcastle soon reached the railroad's enemies, who moved rapidly to capitalize on the situation. A pamphlet, *Dutch Flat Swindle,* was issued anonymously in San Francisco on August 18, 1864. Given wide circulation, it was effective propaganda and for a time interfered seriously with the railroad's financial plans, for it concluded "that the directors do not intend to prosecute the enterprise to the state line but only a sufficient distance to feed the wagon-road enterprise, owned by a portion of the board of directors." It also charged "that the whole concern is a closed corporation instituted, conducted and managed to enrich the directors and impoverish the stockholders."

Placer County and San Francisco interests opposed to the venture did everything possible to prevent local court actions favorable to the company. Official "investigations" were promoted in Placer County, where it was declared that the company had no intention of building a line beyond Dutch Flat, the point from which their newly opened Dutch Flat and Donner Lake Wagon Road ran.

The report was sufficiently truthful to make it dangerous; but still the railroad moved, slowly but surely, toward the Sierra, as outlined in October by Miller and Montague in separate reports. Miller, in his secretary's report, said in part:

"Trains for the transportation of freight and passengers commenced running to Newcastle on the 6th day of June last; since that time the business of the road has been steadily increasing. The earnings for the first three months were $47,917.74 in gold coin.

"The expense of operating the road, for employees on the trains and at depots, and for wood, water, oil, etc., for the engines, has been less than three thousand dollars per month.

"Surveyed line of the road to the eastern boundary of the State cost $66,740.66.

"Work on the line between Newcastle and Auburn, amounting to over $50,000, already has been done. . . .

"The work on the heavy cut of Bloomer Divide, sixty-three feet in depth, and upon the cuts and fills immediately above and below that point, has been steadily pressed forward by the Company for the last four months, with all the force that could be advantageously employed, and is now nearly completed. The work between Bloomer Divide and Auburn will be comparatively light."

Montague's report dealt with the road already completed, grading already under way, and surveying of the route in Nevada Territory:

"Gentlemen:

"I present herewith a report upon the progress of the surveys, work of construction and equipment of your Road to the present date:

"As the report of your Chief Engineer, the late T. D. Judah, Esq., made in July, 1863, contains a detailed description of the several lines surveyed up to that time, I have deemed it unnecessary to embody a similar description in this report.

"First Division of Fifty Miles. No changes were made in the line between Sacramento and Newcastle [Judah's Survey], but from the thirty-first to the forty-eighth section almost an entire relocation has been made, resulting in a material reduction in the cost of the work, and several important improvements in the alignment on sections 35 and 43; the changes being made without any increase of grade.

"The most important changes were upon the line through Dutch Ravine (Sections 32 through 35), from Lime Point to the head of Rock Creek (Sections 38 to 40, inclusive), through Clipper Ravine to Wild Cat (Sections 44 and 45), and at Baney's Ranch, by which the contemplated tunnel at that point is avoided, reducing the cost of a single section (47) more than $70,000.

"By the present location no tunneling will be required on the first division.

"As much of the heavy work on your road occurs in crossing the depressions or gaps in the Divide along which the line runs, it has been deemed expedient in some instances to substitute trestling for embankments.

"Trestling, properly constructed of Puget Sound pine and redwood, will last from eight to ten years, and can then be replaced with embankments, by transporting the material on the cars, at much less than the present cost.

"At Newcastle Gap, Lovell's Gap, and at two points near Clipper Gap, trestling has been designed, and timber for the structure at the former place is now arriving.

90

"There have been purchased for use upon the first division, and are now in daily use upon the road, 5 locomotives; 6 first-class passenger cars; 2 baggage cars; 25 box freight cars; and 25 platform [flat] cars.

"In addition to which there have been received one heavy freight locomotive, and 20 freight cars not yet put together.

"There have been purchased and shipped 4 first-class passenger cars; 2 mail and express cars; 24 freight cars; 20 dump (or gravel) cars.

"Two more heavy freight locomotives have been contracted for with Messrs. Danforth, Cook & Co., of Patterson, New Jersey, and are now in course of construction. Extra axles, car wheels, locomotive tires, etc., have been purchased and shipped.

"The rolling stock is all of the best class used on eastern roads. The locomotives, with one exception, were built to order, and have thus far given perfect satisfaction. Those now under construction are designed particularly for service on heavy grades.

"The work of grading above Newcastle was commenced in April last, and has been steadily progressing since that time.

"The cut through Bloomer Divide, which is the heaviest . . . on the First Division, being 63 feet in depth, and 800 feet in length, through a hard indurated [cement-like] gravel, is now fully completed [October, 1864] and the grading on other portions of the line is in a favorable state of progress. . . .

"All of the unfinished work between Newcastle and Clipper Gap, a distance of 12 miles, is of such a character as to admit of its rapid prosecution, and the work upon this portion of the line can easily be completed within four months."

Montague went on to report that the total cost of grading, masonry (including the bridge over the American River), ties, and track-laying for the first eighteen miles of the road had been $400,000. The cost of grading, masonry, bridging, ties, and track-laying for the next thirteen miles was estimated at $505,658, with the total cost for the first section as far as Newcastle more than $900,000. The cost of grading, masonry, bridging, ties, and track-laying of the next nineteen miles of the first division was estimated by Montague at $1,330,238, the work above Newcastle being very heavy. Total cost for construction of the first division of fifty miles was $2,235,896.

In December a pamphlet, *The Pacific Railroad: A Defense Against Its Enemies,* was issued in response to the *Dutch Flat Swindle,* the polemic of the previous August. The Central Pacific had invited a group of Placer County supervisors and San Francisco County Supervisor H. De La Montanya to make a first-hand inspection of the books and property, and to make their findings public; their conclusions were detailed and vigorous:

"A pamphlet entitled 'The Dutch Flat Swindle', containing among other pettifogging statements equally baseless, the minority report of J. H. Rogers, one of the Board of Supervisors of Placer County, having been recently published and extensively circulated, would seem to demand some notice from the friends of the Pacific Railroad.

"The author very prudently conceals his name, as few citizens in the state would voluntarily peril their reputation as truthful and honorable men by signing a publication containing so many gross misrepresentations, demagogue insinuations, willful fabrications and unmitigated slanders.

"Before proceeding to notice the absurdities in the pamphlet, we beg to call attention to the sources from whence emanate the bitter, reckless and malignant personal opposition of the interested few, to the progress of the Pacific Railroad, which has developed itself in San Francisco.

"At the time Congress passed the Act granting the franchise for a Pacific Railroad, with the subsidies which attended it, not a man on this coast could be found who was not, and had not been for years, a zealous friend of the work. Every newspaper in the State advocated the passage of the Bill, and had been for a long time urging and demanding, in the name of the People of California, the passage by Congress of a bill to secure the construction of a Pacific Railroad. After the Bill became a law, the Company to which was entrusted the building of the Road in California, entered vigorously upon the gigantic work before them; and we may add that up to this time the California companies are the only ones which have laid a rail of iron, or put in operation a single mile of the Pacific Railroad, from the Missouri River to the navigable waters of the Bay of San Francisco. But as soon as the Central Pacific Company sent into the field its engineers, opposition, founded on self-interest, began to develop itself.

"The route was selected by the late Theodore D. Judah, then Chief Engineer of the Company, and who was conceded to be one of the most eminent of American railroad engineers. But the route he decided the best did not meet the approbation of those living on other lines, which their self-interest considered superior to the one adopted. The location of the railroad on that line would injure the stock of the Sacramento Valley Road and the capital invested in wagon roads on the Placerville route, and, therefore, those owning said stock and wagon roads, determined to oppose, to the extent of their ability, the progress of the Pacific Railroad. . . .

"The individuals representing these interests, have, of course, produced noisy, active, factious and unscrupulous opposition to the progress of the Pacific Railroad. Unless the Sacramento Valley Railroad could interpose obstacles to the advance of the Pacific, until it could extend its line further into the mountain region, its stock would become comparatively valueless. The wagon road owners on the Placerville route, collected

Progress halted at Newcastle (left), waiting for funds. Then two thousand laborers and three hundred wagons went to work in January, 1865, and the Newcastle Trestle (below) was completed by May of that year.

in tolls on the Nevada business, by estimate, over a million dollars in 1863. The Pioneer Stage Line of Louis McLane & Co., received for the transportation of express, passengers and treasures a sum which must have nearly, if not quite, equaled another million. The completion of fifty miles of the Pacific Railroad would divert the freight, travel, express matter and Overland mail from the Sacramento Valley Railroad and the Placerville line to the Dutch Flat and Donner Lake Line; and hence it was a matter embracing hundreds of thousands a year, if not millions, to those companies, to keep back, as long as possible, the Pacific Railroad.

"When the bills to authorize certain counties to subscribe to the stock of the Road were before the Legislature, they encountered this opposition; when the question was submitted in each county, a marked influence from the same quarter was exerted to defeat the proposition.

"Not content with the popular verdicts in the counties, the interested opponents resorted to the law's delays to hinder and obstruct the Pacific Road. . . .

"The administration of the affairs of the Company by its officers, is fully vindicated by the steady progress of the road, and by the confidence manifested by the stockholders.

"We ask the enemies of the enterprise to point to a single railroad in the United States, commenced since this war was inaugurated, which has been as successfully managed. . . .

"Another of the weak devices of the enemy, is the assertion that the officers only intend to complete the Pacific Railroad as a feeder to the wagon road which has been built from that point over the mountain, by a few of the stockholders.

"To build that wagon road as an auxiliary to the railroad was a necessity. Without it, the railroad would have found no outlet for its business, while being constructed on the mountains. The road is conceded to be superior in grade and work to any ever built over the Sierra Nevada, and over its smooth surface passengers are conveyed to and from Virginia, in from three to four hours less time than by any other route. Up to this time the proprietors have expended all its earnings in improving the road, though it was built with the expectation that it would prove good property until it was superseded by the advance of the railroad. The idea that the Pacific Railroad is to terminate at Dutch Flat—that it is a Dutch Flat Swindle—is a very silly invention of the enemy. Its course will be steady onward, and literally upward, as the road at Newcastle is a thousand feet above the level of Sacramento. . . .

"One of the grounds of complaint against the Company by enemies of the road, is that the officers of the Company refused to permit them to examine and make such extracts from their books, as would suit their

*On its maiden trip the locomotive "Conness"
at Griffith's Station, March, 1865.*

purposes. The books of a Railroad Company are not, like those in public offices, open to the inspection of the public. The law, however, provides that the book containing 'the record of corporation debts', and 'the book of stockholders', shall, at all times, be open to the inspection of stockholders and creditors; thus implying that the others are private, and may or may not be permitted to be examined, as might be determined by the officers of the Company. The provisions of the law have always been complied with by the Company, but it has properly refused to permit those hostile to the work in which they are engaged, and who were neither stockholders nor creditors, to take possession of its books, place them in the hands of an expert employed by them, to search for items for publication, which, unaccompanied with explanation, were calculated to injure those dealing with the Company and the enterprise in public estimation. The books of the Company, however, have been examined by the Supervisors of Placer county, with the full consent of the officers. The members of that Board occupied ten days in the work, and made a thorough and searching investigation of the affairs of the Company, and a majority, consisting of Supervisors Scott and Madden, submitted a full report to the people of Placer, in which they bore ample testimony to the fidelity, energy and good faith with which the affairs of the Company had been managed. . . .

"This hue and cry about the refusal of the Company to permit its books to go into the hands of its enemies, is well illustrated by rebel sympathizers, when they charge the National Government with depriving them of the right of free speech, because they are not permitted to preach treason. It is only heard from those hostile to the Pacific Railroad, and, therefore, entitled to no particular attention or consideration.

"The charge made in the pamphlet that the people of San Francisco were bribed to vote for the Pacific Railroad proposition [a $600,000 bond issue in 1863], will be disposed of in a few words. It is too absurd in itself, and too insulting to the people to require any formal refutation. The slander was not uttered by strangers but men claiming to be citizens of San Francisco, who in their frantic efforts to defeat a great public enterprise, and put money in their purse, do not hesitate to propagate infamous charges against their fellow-citizens. . . .

"The Road is a National one, fostered and sustained by the Federal, as well as the State Government, and the Company deserve, and should receive the encouragement and support of every lover of his country."

On December 1, 1864, the company's secretary, E. H. Miller, Jr., issued a "business of the Road" statement, detailing the first freight and passenger revenues recorded. His statement contained some revealing items covering the first ten months of rail operation:

"On the 26th of April, 1864, track was completed from Sacramento to Junction [now Roseville], a distance of 18½ miles, and trains were run daily over the road to that point. Little freight, however, passed over the road until the 10th of the following June, when it was opened to Newcastle, 31 miles from Sacramento, and regular freight and passenger trains commenced running to that point.

"The following is a statement of the number of passengers transported each month, and the amount received therefor:

	Passengers	Amt. Received
April 26 to 30	298	$ 354.25
May	8,906	4,291.25
June	7,329	9,364.30
July	7,687	11,047.35
August	6,508	10,107.14
September	4,726	8,801.22
October	7,615	10,089.90
November	6,870	9,347.74
	48,941	$63,403.15

"The following statement shows the amount received for transportation of freight each month:

April 26 to 30	$ 183.25
May	160.50
June	3,993.86
July	5,002.70
August	6,393.72
September	7,668.04
October	8,110.82
November	7,154.00
Total	$38,666.89

"There has been received for transportation of Express matter and Messengers: $ 1,487.50

"The expenses of operating the Road from April 25th to December 1st have been as follows, viz.:

For repairs of Locomotives	$ 3,089.95
For repairs of Cars	3,234.47
For repairs of Track	9,520.41
For repairs of Buildings	251.95
For repairs of Bridges	1,343.64
For Locomotive service	3,666.73
For Train service	3,634.49
For Station service	6,953.54
For fuel and water	5,746.12
For oil, waste, etc.	842.38
For stationery and printing	565.00
For advertising	836.75

For office expenses 75.95
For damage to freight 141.67
For miscellaneous damage 137.00
For taxes 10,051.61
For United States Revenue Tax...................... 1,060.14
For Incidentals (fixtures for trains, depots, etc.).......... 449.18
For telegraph expenses 8.00
    Total $51,608.98
November payroll not yet distributed 4,680.19
    Total operating expenses $56,289.17

RECAPITULATION

Passengers .... $ 63,403.15
Freight 38,666.89
Express 1,487.50
    Gross Receipts $103,557.54
Operating expenses ....$ 56,289.17
Net earnings in gold coin ....$ 47,268.37

"Miles run by passenger trains, 14,016; miles run by freight trains, 19,468.

"Average rate of speed of passenger trains, including stoppages, has been 22 miles an hour. Average rate of speed of freight trains, including stoppages, has been 15½ miles an hour.

"There has been but one accident to persons on the road during seven months running. Frank Brady, an employee of the Company, in attempting to get on a construction train in motion, was injured so as to cause his death in a few days.

"The Earnings will be increased fully 50 per cent by the further extension of the road, soon to be completed to Rock Creek or Neilsburg station, 42 miles from Sacramento, while the expenses for operating the road to that point will not be materially increased."

"The *Alta Californian*," said the Sacramento *Union* of December 3, 1864, "is the origin of the enemies of the Pacific Railroad. It pretends to favor the road, but opposes the administration of it. It supports the idea of having a road, but opposes every effort made to develop it. It labors with all its vigor and with intensely bitter feelings to deprive the managers of the road of the means to accomplish the work, to deny them the 'sinews of war' which the people of San Francisco have voted them; and by all the strategy which cunning and recklessness can suggest, it endeavors to embarrass and delay the execution of the work with a view to its final defeat."

Secretary Miller that same month apparently felt compelled to issue another "Dutch Flat Swindle" defense: "It has been stated that the Company intended only to construct the Road to Dutch Flat, a distance of about 70 miles from Sacramento. There is not the least foundation for this assertion, yet many have been led to believe it. The immense trade to Washoe and the profit to be realized from its transportation, is alone a sufficient inducement to urge us to as speedy a completion of the work as possible. But the further fact that by the 17th section of the Pacific Railroad Act the Company will lose its road, and all the means we have invested in it, and that the same becomes forfeited to the Government unless the road is completed as required by the Act, is sufficient to urge on the work to its full completion. Of course no such suicidal policy will be pursued, and no interest could induce the Directors of the Company to fail in completing the work."

DUTCH FLAT WAGON ROAD.

This new route over the Mountains, by way of Dutch Flat and Donner Lake, can now be traveled by Teams without load, and will be open for loaded Teams

JUNE 15th, 1864.

IT IS

The Shortest, Best and Cheapest Route to Washoe, Humboldt and Reese River.

Its grade going East at no place exceeds ten inches to the rod, and it is wide enough for Two Teams to pass without difficulty. All teams coming West, without load, can travel the New Road FREE OF TOLL until further notice. All those taking loads at Newcastle, the terminus of the Central Pacific Railroad, three miles from Auburn, can travel the New Road going East, Free of Toll, up to July 1, 1864.

Teams starting from Virginia City will take the Henness Pass Road to Ingram's, at Sardine Valley, where the New Road turns off to the left.

CHARLES CROCKER.

Sacramento, June 6, 1864   Pres't of the Co.

SEVEN

CONSTRUCTION MOVES
INTO HIGH GEAR: *1865*

THE WINTER OF 1864/65 was exceptionally mild in California. It could have seen rapid progress in constructing the Central Pacific through the Sierra. But opposing interests managed to tie up state railroad aid funds in extended litigation, and the C.P. could afford to keep only 300 men on the job that December—compared with the 13,500 they would have two years later.

The resulting delays hurt not only the railroad but the entire Pacific Coast. Governor Stanford told the Pacific Railroad Commission in 1887 that, had the funds already voted been available for work that winter, "we would more easily have met the Union Pacific at Cheyenne than we did at Promontory." This more easterly terminus, he pointed out, would have given San Francisco control of the business of Utah, Wyoming, Montana, and Idaho.

But on January 3, 1865, the Sacramento *Union* heralded the news that all those connected with the C.P. had longed to hear: "On the second day of January the Supreme Court, in an able decision, sustained the validity of the state law granting aid to the Company. . . ." That decision reaffirmed the constitutionality of the legislature's act providing for payment by the state of interest on $1,500,000 of Central Pacific bonds at the rate of 7 per cent for twenty years. This made the Central Pacific bonds equal to state bonds and thus immediately saleable. In exchange, the railroad guaranteed free transportation for all stone for state public buildings, as well as free transportation of all state troops, animals, "lunatics, and paupers."

The rate of construction promptly increased. But constant pressure to

100

move forward soon depleted the treasury, in spite of the favorable decision on the bonds, and Central Pacific officers again had to exert every effort to raise funds sufficient to continue work. The most difficult and costly part of the line lay ahead, and they still had to transport all their materials around Cape Horn. Many difficulties and many arduous miles lay between them and the eastern base of the Sierra.

Moreover, the new year of 1865 also saw the "Dutch Flat Swindle" controversy reappear. The legislature of the newly-admitted state of Nevada had before it a proposal for a subsidy for the Pacific Railroad, which was opposed by the same interests that had opposed such aid from California and its various counties. The struggle developed there as to which route would receive aid from Nevada—that through Donner Pass and Dutch Flat via the Central Pacific, or that through Johnson Pass via Placerville and the Sacramento Valley Railroad. For a time, it seemed that the Central Pacific had a powerful rival for Nevada's subsidy in the so-called "San Francisco and Washoe Railroad," which was projected over the Sierra along the general route of the Placerville wagon road. This route, its supporters said, offered a much more feasible way across the Sierra than that by way of Dutch Flat and Donner Pass. Its chief proponent was none other than L. L. Robinson, with whom Judah had been connected in constructing the Sacramento Valley Railroad.

Robinson had alleged that his company had hired Judah to explore various passes through the Sierra for a wagon road, and that the Donner Pass route had been discovered during these explorations. Because of a dispute over the ownership of this discovery, the engineer had been summarily discharged under rather unpleasant circumstances. Whatever the truth of these charges, Robinson remained a bitter critic of Judah during the last few years of his career. In a letter to the Nevada legislature written in January, 1865, he commented caustically upon the dead engineer's work. Robinson declared that Judah had never examined the Placerville route and that he had never made anything but the roughest preliminary examinations of that over Donner Pass. He stated that difficulties on the latter were so great that he "couldn't conceive any set of men would seriously undertake to construct a railway over such a country," adding that "a railway across the Semmening Alps, from Vienna to Trieste—is a bagatelle as compared with the projected line via Dutch Flat. I can see no obstacles in the way to Illinoistown [Colfax]; but from there it is so heavy, reports and newspapers' publications to the contrary, that even Mr. Judah became convinced that the route was a hopeless one, and on his return from Washington, after the franchise was granted, urged the advisability of not fixing the route of the road until he or the company could examine other routes; and he opposed the location as it now exists.

Fixing the route of the road where it is was the cause of his leaving the service of the company; for when he went to New York the last time, he had left the service of the company, and never intended to re-enter it. They gave him $100,000 of their first mortgage bonds in order that he should not state what his examination led him to know was the facts; that the Dutch Flat Route was a hopeless one. Judah possessed no interest in the Wagon Road; the directors did; and the Wagon Road ruled the location, regardless entirely of the merits of the route for a railroad."

Robinson went on to charge that beyond Illinoistown [Colfax], Judah's surveyors had "found the work so heavy that they dare not make public the results of the location." He added that he himself was so much in favor of a Pacific Railroad that he "would gladly advocate any route which could be built," but that he favored an examination of all routes. He urged the Nevada legislators to offer financial aid to "any railroad that first reaches your state line." Such action, he said, could "hurt no interest except the Central Pacific Railroad."

Robinson also declared that if Judah's cost estimates were trebled, they would "still be below the result," because his surveys "were not of a character to base any estimate of cost upon." After giving statistics as to the cost of numerous other railroads, he concluded, "My firm conviction is that the Central Pacific Railroad will cost $250,000 to $300,000 a mile before it is completed to the Truckee, stocked and equipped as a first-class railroad."

F. S. Bishop, a trained and experienced engineer who had surveyed much of that mountain area, supported Robinson and the Johnson Pass route. He told the Nevada Legislature, "Johnson Pass differs from most of the passes in the Sierra Nevada Mountains in having no broad elevated plateau. Some of the sources of the Truckee River on the east side and the south fork of the American River on the west side leave the main summit at the Johnson Pass and vicinity so abruptly that the main divide is very narrow. Consequently, the deep snow belt is on the crest of the divide when but a short distance from it on either side, the snowfall is very light.

"It seems then," he continued, "that the method which would most naturally suggest itself for avoiding this obstacle would be to pierce through the crest at as low an elevation as possible with a tunnel, by the construction of which the deep snow is avoided. Constant working of the road is insured and lighter and more uniform grades secured. It is readily admitted that a tunnel through this ridge is an undertaking of considerable magnitude, but greater works of the same character are already in the process of construction, and it must be remembered that the commercial interests of our whole country are more or less affected by the location of the Continental road."

The Central Pacific was not long in replying. On January 12, 1865,

*The completed Newcastle Trestle (above and below)
was a necessary link for work trains hauling rails,
timber, and other materials north to Colfax.*

the railroad issued a pamphlet, which, in part, declared that Judah was "one of the most eminent and experienced railroad engineers of the time." It asserted, too, that during August, 1862, the Central Pacific had advertised in the Sacramento *Union* for eight weeks in an effort to secure information as to better routes, but to no avail. The Central Pacific also observed that building two railroads over the mountains was completely out of the question.

After reading Robinson's letter, Stanford wrote a reply to the Nevada Legislature: "Recently and since the death of T. D. Judah, Esq., the late Chief Engineer of this Company, I have heard rumors of a similar character, and emanating from the same and kindred sources, but this is the first time they have appeared in a tangible form, so that they could be fairly met. Lest your committees, who may not be aware of the true facts, should be misled by the numerous falsehoods in that letter, and especially as a matter of justice to the memory of Mr. Judah, it is proper that it should not be suffered to pass without notice.

"Contrary to the impression which Robinson attempted to convey," Stanford continued, "Judah regarded Mr. Robinson as his bitterest enemy. Moreover, Judah has never opposed the route of the Central Pacific as located, but always recommended it in the strongest terms." Stanford explained that it was on the strength of Judah's recommendations that the route was selected, following personal examination by several of the directors, of this and various alternate routes mentioned in Judah's report.

As to Robinson's implication that Judah's silence was bought, Stanford insisted that Judah would have made every effort to keep it a secret, especially from "his deadliest enemy." Furthermore, "Mr. Judah's character as an engineer, respecting which he was particularly sensitive, and as a man of integrity, stands too high to be reached by such infamous assaults. His friends will read these charges with astonishment, if they can be astonished at anything coming from such a source. These charges were made after he had been laid in the silent tomb. They never would have been made if he was living."

Robinson's motive in attacking the Central Pacific, Stanford suggested, was wholly due to his pique at not having been unable to unload the bankrupt Sacramento Valley Railroad. He also emphatically denied the charge that the wagon road determined the location of the Central Pacific.

"In making the charge, he again betrays his ignorance of facts, for the wagon road was not commenced, nor the wagon road company organized, until long after the railroad was located. It was constructed because it was necessary for the railroad. Without it, the railroad, until completed, could only have done a local business. With it, the Central Pacific is already fully prepared to compete successfully for the Washoe trade."

Teamster camp at Colfax.

Bridge at Long Ravine (length, 1,050 feet).

In a statement appended to Stanford's letter, Charles Crocker declared that Judah, before his death, had shown him a letter from Robinson demanding that the Central Pacific purchase the Sacramento Valley line and threatening opposition of every sort if his terms were not met.

Robinson's letter to the Nevada Legislature was widely circulated by the company's enemies. When word of the charges in it reached former Congressman A. A. Sargent, who had been so influential in obtaining passage of the Pacific Railroad Bill, he wrote an indignant letter to Stanford on February 18, 1865, saying that Judah had repeatedly expressed his firm belief in the desirability and practicability of the Donner Lake route across the mountains. Sargent's defense, he said, was made in justice to the memory of Judah, who had been one of his "dearest friends," and "to avert the imputation that he countenanced and assisted what he must have known to be a gigantic swindle if Robinson's statements of his views are not erroneous. Whether or not Judah would have preferred another route, I am not prepared to say. I only know that he firmly believed that the route he explored and recommended was feasible."

A few days later, Robinson renewed his attack with a second letter to the Nevada Legislature, in which he protested that he had not charged Judah with fraud or corruption, but that "Judah simply protected himself when he found that, under the wagon road management, he could earn neither credit, money nor fame." As to Stanford's declaration that Judah remained chief engineer until his death, Robinson wrote that if this were true, Mr. Huntington would be placed in an unpleasant position "as I saw letters in New York stating just the reverse; and Mr. Holmes, Street Commissioner and Trustee of the City of Sacramento, told me but a short time since, that Mr. Huntington had given him the same information."

Robinson then reiterated the charge that the Sacramento Valley Railroad had paid for Judah's explorations, and declared that the "Dutch Flat Route" was "impracticable," and would never be anything other than a "wagon road feeder." Moreover, Judah had, he said, been personally in favor of purchasing the Sacramento Valley Railroad.

This exchange of denunciations was the last open fight between Robinson and the Central Pacific; it ended in what might be called a "draw." The state of Nevada never did vote funds to help either railroad. The legislature did pass a resolution on February 27, 1865, urging their senators and congressmen to work for the passage of a law awarding the sum of $10,000,000 to whoever completed a railroad across the Sierra, but Congress ignored the resolution.

"The Central Pacific Railroad Company advertises for 5,000 laborers to work upon the road between Newcastle and Illinoistown [Colfax]," the Shasta *Courier* reported on January 21. "It is the intention of the company to employ at once as many men as can be advantageously worked on the distance between these points—twenty-three miles. The iron for laying this additional amount of track is already in Sacramento and it is expected that the cars will run to Illinoistown by August next. The above opportunity affords a chance for those out of employment."

The base camp for the construction crews was in Auburn. The heavy cut at Bloomer had been ready for the laying of iron since the previous October, and new men were hired and put to work completing the unfinished grading of the twelve miles between Newcastle and Clipper Gap. This was slated for completion by April so that crews could begin laying track.

The Sacramento *Union* recorded another victory for the Central Pacific on April 5, when they announced that two days earlier, the Supreme Court had handed down a decision favorable to the company following two years of litigation. It ordered the San Francisco Board of Supervisors to pay the Central Pacific $400,000 in bonds and the Western Pacific, $200,000. C.P.'s bonds were delivered to Stanford one week later (April 12).

The two-year litigation had cost Central Pacific more than $100,000. Of the bonds received, 315 were sold at $751.60 each ($1,000 bonds), bringing in $236,754. The remaining 85 were disposed of at par in payment for rolling stock. The aid granted Western Pacific accrued to that firm prior to its acquisition by Central Pacific and thus did not benefit C.P.

On April 12, 1865, E. B. Crocker (brother of Charles) wrote the following letter to his long-term friend, Cornelius Cole, who was retiring from Congress and returning to his home in California. In this letter Crocker gave the first indication that Central Pacific had hired a large number of Chinese to fill its work force:

"Friend Cole—

"Yours of the 11th inst. just received. I hesitated when to write, not knowing but you might be on your way to Cal. But I must congratulate you on your success in getting through Congress some of the most important measures for Cal. especially that bill for the Pacific [the Act of 1864].

"It has removed the great obstacles we found to our progress and we can now go on with confidence. I can assure you that we will redeem all the promises that you made on us. We have now about 2,000 men at work with about 300 wagons and carts and I can assure you they are moving the earth and rock rapidly. We are now on some of the heaviest work in the mountains, but so far we have been very fortunate in meeting very little hard rock. You will be astonished when you come back to see the amount of work we have done.

"A large part of our force are Chinese and they prove nearly equal to

*Trestle building was a frequent and
expensive interruption, requiring heavy
timber and huge construction forces.
Below, the long span at Secrettown.*

white men in the amount of labor they perform, and are far more reliable. No danger of strikes among them. We are training them to all kinds of labor, blasting, driving horses, handling rock, as well as the pick and shovel. We want a body of 2,500 trained laborers and keep them steadily at work until the road is built clear across the continent, or until we meet them coming from the other side. I tell you Cole we are in dead earnest about this R. R. and you take 6 or 8 men in real earnest, and if they have any brains and industry they will accomplish something. We are now laying track, and expect to lay 12 miles before stopping, then we shall have to wait a couple of months to get the next section of 12 miles ready for the tracklayers, and then we shall finish up 55 miles this fall—and next winter finish to Dutch Flat 15 miles further. Then a bold push for the summit in the summer of 1866. . . ."

Charles Crocker had conceived the idea of employing Chinese, against the opposition of J. H. Strobridge, construction superintendent, who gave in only after a series of trials demonstrated the worth of the Oriental worker. Strobridge objected because they "were not masons." Crocker countered that the Chinese had to their credit the greatest piece of masonry in the world—the Great Wall.

Strobridge finally agreed to the hiring of fifty Chinese on a trial basis, and soon employed fifty more. Before the road was finished there were about twelve thousand on the payroll, and as the Chinese increased in skill and numbers, the ascent of the summit gathered speed in spite of increasing construction and supply difficulties.

Shovel and pick and black powder were the only aids to grading, and "horsepower" meant horses pulling small carts. Speedy construction under such conditions required employment of many men, and in 1865 nothing was scarcer in California than labor. Such Caucasians as were not employed on ventures of their own found it more profitable to work in the mines or follow agricultural pursuits than to face the hardships of hand-carving a railroad right-of-way up the steep slopes and between the granite spires of the Sierra. At the same time, many thousands of Chinese had been drawn to California by gold fever, and were eager for employment.

Chief construction engineer Montague, in his annual report of 1865, said, "It became apparent early in the season that the amount of labor likely to be required during the summer could only be supplied by employment of the Chinese element in our population. Some distrust was at first felt regarding capacity of this class for the services required, but the experiment has proved eminently successful. They are faithful and industrious and, under proper supervision, soon become skillful in the performance of their duty. Many of them are becoming very expert in drilling, blasting and other departments of rock work."

The industry of the Chinese was in large measure responsible for the speed with which construction of the Central Pacific proceeded. The Asian workmen in the camps were divided into small groups, each of which had a cook, whose duties required that he not only prepare meals but also have a large boiler of hot water ready each night. When the Chinese came off the road, they filled their little tubs made from powder kegs, took a hot sponge bath, and changed clothes before their evening meal. Strobridge pronounced them "the best in the world. They learn quickly, do not fight, have no strikes that amount to anything, and are very cleanly in their habits. They will gamble, and do quarrel among themselves most noisily—but harmlessly."

Stanford, in a report to President Andrew Johnson on October 10, 1865, wrote of the Chinese:

"As a class they are quiet, peaceable, patient, industrious and economical. Ready and apt to learn all the different kinds of work required in railroad building, they soon became as efficient as white laborers. More prudent and economical, they are contented with less wages. We find them organized into societies for mutual aid and assistance. These societies can count their numbers by thousands, are conducted by shrewd, intelligent business men who promptly advise their subordinates where employment can be found on most favorable terms. No system similar to slavery, serfdom or peonage prevails among these laborers. Their wages, which are always paid in coin each month, are divided among them by their agents who attend to their business according to the labor done by each person. These agents are generally American or Chinese merchants who furnish them their supplies of food, the value of which they deduct from their monthly pay.

"We have assurance from leading Chinese merchants that, under the just and liberal policy pursued by the company, it will be able to procure during the next year not less than 15,000 laborers. With this large force the company will be able to push on the work so as not only to complete it far within the time required by the Acts of Congress but so as to meet the public impatience."

The difference in the eating and drinking preferences of the Chinese and Caucasian workers building the Central Pacific was as great as their other living habits. The Chinese menu included dried oysters, abalone and cuttlefish, dried bamboo sprouts and mushrooms, five kinds of vegetables, pork, poultry, vermicelli, rice, salted cabbage, dried seaweed, sweet rice crackers, sugar, four kinds of dried fruit, Chinese bacon, peanut oil, and tea. Conceivably, this was the forerunner of the modern American well-balanced diet. The fare of the Caucasian laborers consisted of beef, beans, bread, butter and potatoes.

The work involved in such enormous fills as this at Sailor's Spur required a small army of hand laborers.

The demands of labor were filled by the employment of Chinese, over twelve thousand eventually entering the rolls. They were hired by Crocker's Contract and Finance Company through agents who supplied the workers with food and distributed the monthly pay.

On the grade, the Caucasians relieved their thirst with water, not always the purest and, at times, despite all precautions, a source of illness. The Chinese drank lukewarm tea, which stood beside the grade in thirty- and forty-gallon whiskey barrels, always on tap. Several times daily, the barrels were replenished by fresh tea brought in powder kegs suspended from each end of a bamboo pole balanced on the shoulder of a Chinese mess attendant.

While construction forces laid rails above Newcastle, surveyors and locators were working far beyond, plotting the route. On April 28, 1865, the Central Pacific filed with the Secretary of the Interior a map showing the general route of the proposed line from the eastern boundary of California to Great Salt Lake. The Secretary notified Central Pacific on May 12 that the government had withdrawn the land from preemption, private entry, or sale from Salt Lake to the eastern boundary of California, as indicated on the map.

On May 13, 1865, the railhead for freight and passengers, which had been at Newcastle for eleven months, was moved to Auburn, five miles beyond Newcastle and thirty-six miles from Sacramento, and trains began daily operation to that point. That same day, Stanford received good news from Huntington in New York: "I received yesterday twelve hundred and fifty-eight thousand dollars ($1,258,000) United States bonds for account of Central Pacific Railroad of California."

Secretary E. H. Miller, Jr. announced that during the month of May, 1865, the railroad earned about $665 daily. This, he said, would be increased to $1,500 daily when the line was opened to Illinoistown [Colfax], and earnings could even be greater if C.P. reached that point by September.

Because of good weather, Strobridge was able, by June, 1865, to establish his advance construction camp at Cisco, niney-two miles from Sacramento. For the next three years, this was to remain his advance camp for heavy tunnel and mountain construction at the summit of the Sierra. On June 10, C.P. announced that trains were running to Clipper Gap, seven miles from Auburn. Track crews had laid the rails in just one month. Now forty-three miles from Sacramento, the force, which by July had grown to more than four thousand men, began in earnest its assault upon the mountain barrier. Not until July 10 did the Union Pacific far to the east, lay its first rail.

That year also saw the incorporation* of a railroad running from the Oregon border to Los Angeles, the California and Oregon Railroad Com-

---

*Incorporators were Alpheus Bull, Simon C. Elliott, Thomas Bell, C. Temple Emmet, William E. Barron, and Joseph Barron.

114

pany. C & O filed incorporation papers with the secretary of state in Sacramento on June 30, with $15,000,000 capital stock, for the purpose of building a rail line from Marysville to the Oregon state line, an estimated 278 miles. The directors of the Central Pacific doubtless viewed the formation of this rival with more than passing interest, and would enter the scene actively later in the year.

In the meantime, the Central Pacific succeeded in eliminating its chief rival for the Sierra trade, the Sacramento Valley Railroad. Little had been heard from this line or from Robinson since the early part of the year, when the two companies had clashed head-on before the Nevada Legislature. Fate was against this independent, scrappy, chip-on-the-shoulder outfit from the start. Interest rates on money borrowed in 1865 to build the line were so high that, although the S.V.R.R. operated with success before the entry of Central Pacific into the field, most of its earnings went to creditors for interest. When Central Pacific built enough track to make its Dutch Flat and Donner Lake toll road the fastest and most comfortable route to the silver mines of the Comstock Lode, the Sacramento Valley Railroad was finished.

Huntington, Hopkins, and Stanford, as individuals, announced purchase of the 22½-mile line from Sacramento to Folsom in August, 1865, for $800,000. It was operated as a separate railroad until consolidated as part of the Southern Pacific—not the Central Pacific—on April 19, 1877. The extension of the S.V.R.R.—the Placerville and Sacramento Valley Railroad, which was operated under lease to the older line—was sold at foreclosure to Wilborn Alvard in 1869. He conveyed the line to Stanford, Huntington, and Hopkins in 1877.

Strobridge announced from his advance camp at Cisco that while track-layers were busily working above Clipper Gap, grading crews had, on August 1, begun the difficult job of carving out the road bed above Colfax. Camps, he reported, were established at all the tunnels and heavy construction points to the summit, and construction forces grew daily. Work was begun at both ends of the summit tunnel.

In two and one-half months, track-layers put down rails to Colfax— twelve more miles, and fifty-four from Sacramento. Beginning on September 1, trains would operate to Colfax, the Central Pacific announced. The town, formerly Illinoistown, had been renamed in honor of Schuyler Colfax, speaker of the House of Representatives and later Vice-President under Ulysses S. Grant. The settlement of Colfax remained the C.P. railhead for the winter of 1865/66, while the company made a drive to accomplish as much advance grading as possible above that point before winter weather would force a halt in construction.

On October 10, 1865, the C.P. directors issued the following report on operating expenses from January to October, 1865:

Repairs of Locos., incl. alterations	$ 7,564.67
Repairs of cars, incl. alterations	5,942.77
Repairs of track, ordinary & extraordinary	23,378.32
Repairs of bridges	9.38
Locomotive service (engineers, firemen, wood, water, oil and waste)	15,883.87
Station service (agents, clerks, laborers, etc.)	18,828.02
Wharf service	2,155.61
Mail transportation	400.00
Stationery and Printing (incl. Advertising)	1,533.35
Loss and damage to freight	341.12
Damage to persons and property	761.77
Overcharges and Commissions on Freight	2,489.24
U. S. Revenue Tax	5,666.02
Office expenses	619.21
Train service (Superintendents, Contractors, etc.)	6,850.42
Repairs of Buildings	25.00
	$93,448.77

With the railroad now running over 54 miles of track, operating expenses stood at less than 30 percent of gross receipts.

On that same date, October 10, Leland Stanford wrote to President Andrew Johnson and Secretary of the Interior James Haran:

"The work of grading has been continued without cessation from the commencement, in February, 1863, up to the present time.

"The grading between Newcastle and Colfax was very difficult and expensive, increasing as the line was pushed up the mountain slope. The cuttings have been deeper, the embankments higher, and more rock work encountered, as the line has progressed eastward.

"One cut [Bloomer Cut, west of Auburn] is 63 feet deep and 800 feet long, and several others are from 40 to 50 feet deep and from 800 to 1,200 feet in length, all of which were through rock or hard cement, requiring to be blasted.

"Several expensive trestle bridges have been constructed across deep ravines, some as high as 100 feet in the center. Some of the embankments are over 70 feet high.

"Time is required to complete such heavy work. The first fifty miles was completed prior to the 1st day of September, 1865, and several months within the time required by the Acts of Congress, as extended by the 5th section of the amended Act, passed July 2, 1864—an extension which was found necessary on account of the difficult character of the work. . . .

"On the first day of January, 1865, the prospect of a speedy close of the war, and favorable decisions by our state courts of several matters

Ties stacked along the line at Secrettown.

The cut at Dixie Spur, 64 miles from Sacramento.

*Engines of empire building: Cylinders on such locomotives varied from
17 x 22 or 18 x 22, to 18 x 24 inches. Steam pressures ran from 110 to 125 pounds.
Drivers varied from 28 to 54 inches in diameter. The locomotives weighed
from 62,000 to 75,000 pounds. They had tallow-pot oilers, crosshead feed
pumps, wooden cabs, hemp lubricators on driving axles; used pine or fir for
fuel and had coal oil head lamps. Tractive efforts varied from 12,000
to 18,000 pounds, according to variations in steam pressures, sizes of
cylinders, and diameter of drivers. The locomotives had no brakes.*

which had been in litigation, placed the affairs of the company in such a position that we felt justified in putting forth all our energies.

"A call was issued for 5,000 laborers, and from that day to the present, every able-bodied laborer that could be procured has been employed and kept constantly at work in the construction of the road. . . .

"With the force of laborers which we are confident can be procured, if the National Government shall promptly issue to us the bonds granted by the Acts of Congress, we shall be able to complete the railroad over the Sierra Nevadas to the Truckee River, a distance of 120 miles from Sacramento, attaining at the Summit an altitude of 7,000 feet above tide water, during the year 1866.

"Thence to a point 50 miles east of the Great Bend of the Truckee River, during the year 1867, and to Salt Lake in two years thereafter, where we hope to meet the road building from the East. We feel confident of being able, after reaching the Truckee River, to construct the road eastward as rapidly as the track can be laid.

"The construction of a railroad over so high a mountain range, is necessarily slow and expensive, but it is the determination of this company to press on vigorously, and to employ all the men and means they can command to complete the road as early as practicable.

"We have encountered and are now laboring upon the most difficult and expensive portion of the line entrusted to us. This, too, at the very commencement of our efforts.

"But another year will enable us to extend the road over the long dreaded Sierras. We have gone far enough already to convince the most incredulous, not only of the entire feasibility of the route, but that the work can and will be accomplished within the time stated.

"The rails used being of extra weight, and the high grades requiring powerful locomotives, all these have to be manufactured specially for the company, and have to be paid for upon delivery on board ship, a full ten months before they can be placed upon the road.

"In addition, large disbursements are required to grade the road in advance of the completed line.

"Thus it follows that the company are compelled to spend generally over $4,000,000 in advance, before receiving the Government bonds, upon the different sections of completed road.

"It will be seen that any great delay in receiving the means provided by Congress will necessarily cause a serious derangement of our plans and hinder the progress of the work."

Another name appeared on the growing list of California railroads when on December 2, 1865, the Southern Pacific Railroad Company was incorporated with capital stock of thirty million dollars to build a line from

San Francisco Bay, through the counties of Santa Clara, Monterey, San Luis Obispo, Tulare, and Los Angeles, to San Diego, whence it was to proceed east through San Diego County to the Colorado River. [Incorporators were listed as: T. G. Phelps, San Francisco; Charles N. Fox, San Mateo; Benjamin Flint, San Juan; C. I. Hutchinson, San Francisco; B. G. Lathrop, San Mateo; W. S. Rosencrans, Cincinnati, Ohio; J. B. Cos, B. W. Hathaway, John F. Sears, William T. Coleman, and J. W. Stephenson, all of San Francisco.] This company did little beyond acquiring the San Francisco and San Jose Railroad before it was taken over in 1868 by the Big Four. Eager to expand, they acquired the S.P., eliminating a potential transcontinental rival.

At the end of the year, chief engineer Montague was able to report "most satisfactory progress" on the C.P. line. Earlier in 1865, little work had been accomplished above Newcastle, except for the heavy cut at Bloomer Divide, every foot of which had to be blasted with gunpowder. This cut, just below Auburn, and now on the westbound track, was one of the most backbreaking jobs of the early construction. The steep sides of this strait through solid rock stand today just at the builders of the road left them. They show no more signs of disintegration than if the cut had been carved from solid granite. It was here that Strobridge lost an eye in a blasting accident, an injury from which he soon recovered sufficiently to continue work.

Montague reported that original plans called for timber structures to bridge the deepest ravines and gaps between Newcastle and Colfax. Whenever possible, however, embankments were built instead. In an entire stretch of twenty-five miles over broken country, the only wooden structures were the Newcastle trestle, 60 feet high and 400 feet long; two of the same size at Lovell's Gap; one 50 feet high and 400 feet long near Clipper Gap Station; two 59 feet high and 350 feet and 500 feet long respectively in Clipper Ravine; and one trestle of four bents at Lower Illinoistown Gap near Colfax.

George E. Gray, who had been chief engineer of the New York Central, inspected the line in operation at the end of 1865. He declared that it compared "most favorably in every respect with any railroad in the United States" and that "the roadbed and mechanical structures are well constructed, ample provision being made for drainage, the cross ties are of redwood and the whole laid with a rail of 60-pound weight per yard and wrought iron chairs. Locomotives, cars and machinery are all of the first quality and of the best material and are maintained in good order."

Weather, so kind the previous winter when lack of money had made it impossible to work on a large scale, hampered work seriously during the winter of 1865/66. Snow in the mountains stopped work on the tun-

"The cuttings have been deeper, the embankments higher, and more rock work encountered as the line has progressed eastward." Bloomer cut was 63 feet deep and 800 feet long.

nels; heavy rains made the roads below the snow lines impassable for wagons. Supplies for the men at work on the grades had to be transported by pack trains. The end of the track remained at Colfax.

Under normal conditions, passengers for Virginia City made the journey from Colfax by stage; however, the rain converted the clay soils of the foothills into a mire that made staging impossible. One stage was stuck in the mud in the streets of Gold Run and remained there for six weeks. Consequently, passengers for Nevada points continued their journeys from Colfax to Dutch Flat by saddle train. At Dutch Flat, the wagon road previously finished by the company furnished good footing for the stages.

The railroad between Dutch Flat and Colfax met many obstacles, and was one of the more difficult portions to build. These segments included Long Ravine Bridge, Cape Horn, and Secrettown Gap Bridge, none of which was completed until the next spring.

The winter was unprecedented for severity and duration. Though the first snow fell on September 24 and disappeared by October, which remained comparatively mild and pleasant, November brought violent southwest winds sweeping dense, dark masses of snow and storm clouds over the mountains. The storms continued throughout November, and by December 1 the whole countryside was covered with five feet of snow.

After New Year's Day, as is common along the Pacific Coast, skies remained comparatively clear and calm, for this was the interval between the early and late rains. The thermometer, seldom ranging low, recorded temperatures for days at a time that made it unnecessary to light daytime fires except for cooking. This was the condition until March, 1866, when again the southwest winds appeared, bringing new snow and sleet. March, April, and May were long remembered, for drifting snows obliterated all the narrow trails across the summit. Even the wagon road could hardly be traversed in many places. From May 20 until June 1 was virtually one constant snow storm. J. H. Strobridge later described the situation: "The winter of 1865–66 was a very wet one, making the roads on the clay soils of the foothills nearly impassible for vehicles. Large numbers of pack animals had to be brought into use, and on them were carried nearly all supplies, even hay and grain, over steep mountain trails, to the construction camps. The building of the railroad was prosecuted with energy but at a much greater cost than would have been the case in the dry season. . . .

"Account the very wet and terribly muddy conditions, it was impossible to have the goods needed for use. Obliged to use pack horses for the mountain trails—had to pack even bales of hay distances of 25 miles and for four or five miles all supplies were taken over this way. All work between Colfax and Dutch Flat was done during this winter in the mud."

EIGHT

SAILING SHIPS, PROSPERITY, AND PACIFIC RAILROAD PUNCH: *1866*

T HE STEADY GROWTH of the Central Pacific Railroad effected many changes in the operation of the trans-Sierra stage lines, according to the Sacramento *Union* of January 1, 1866: "Since 1853, the California Stage Company has furnished the largest proportion of the accommodation for stage travel throughout this state and adjacent territories—their various lines extending more than eleven hundred miles. For many years, Sacramento was the grand focus, where all this immense stage interest centered. The railroad interest from time to time pressed the stages into the mountains, and so separated the various lines that the control of such large business could not be managed economically, and the California Stage Company sold out their lines to individuals, so that in our resumé of staging this year we have more proprietors than formerly."

The California Stage Company, which the *Union* was too polite to call a monopoly, had been the giant of California transportation for nearly fifteen years. Curiously, its monolithic control was broken by the still-young Central Pacific, which would become a giant in its own day, a hundred times more powerful than the company it destroyed. The Central Pacific was beginning to feel its oats—in more ways than one.

Spring came late in 1866; the mountains were still capped with snow in May, streams held fast in ice, the giant pines draped with icicles. Still, the weather affected but slightly the tide of adventurers and gold seekers, who returned to the mountains about the first of May. It was estimated that no less than four thousand persons arrived in the gold mining district during May and June, and it appeared for a time that the excitement of

Virginia City a few years earlier was to be repeated in the Meadow Lake area near Cisco.

In the early summer of 1866 Collis P. Huntington, still busy in the East, checkmated the Union Pacific in the purchase of 66,000 tons of rail which U.P. needed badly. To get the rails to California, Huntington needed a large number of vessels, so he went to E. B. Sutton, a New York shipping agent, to charter the necessary bottoms. He later told this story:

"I said 'Well, I want to get a good ship, a good steady ship—safe. You can go out and run around and give me a list of what you can find.' He came in with three or four. Sutton said, 'You can have this one for so much and this one for so much.' 'Such a price is too high,' I said. 'I can't take one of those ships. I am in no hurry, ships are coming in all along.' Well, he came back. He went out three times and came back with 23 ships. I got them down whilst talking. 'Well,' I said, 'I'll take them.' 'Take them,' said he, 'take what?' I said, 'I will take those ships if they are A-number-1.' 'Well,' Sutton said, 'I can't let you have them. I thought you wanted only one. I will have to have two or three of them myself.' I said, 'Not those you won't.' Those ships took about 45,000 tons of rail. Mr. Sutton told me afterwards, 'Huntington, you would have had to pay $10 a ton at least more if I had known you wanted all those ships.' That would have been $450,000."

On May 8, 1866, the Secretary of the Interior withdrew land from preemption, private entry, or sale on the first fifty miles of the line, as shown on the Central Pacific's definite location map, which the company had filed March 26, 1864. One month later, Charles Crocker was quoted by the Sacramento *Union* as saying that Central Pacific was then "working between 9,000 and 10,000 men, and 1,000 horses, and will employ more if they offer."

While the construction crews were attacking the Sierra, Huntington was busy persuading Congress once again to modify the 1862 Pacific Railroad Act. He accomplished his goal when on July 3—almost four years to the day after Lincoln had signed the original act—Congress amended the previous acts of both 1862 and 1864. Largely as a result of Huntington's vigorous lobbying, the Railroad Act of 1866 cleared the way for the race that followed between the Central Pacific and the Union Pacific. It authorized the Central Pacific to "locate, construct and continue their road eastward, in a continuous, completed line, until they shall meet and connect with the Union Pacific Railroad." This act did not specify where they should join. From the presidents down to the spikers and gaugers, every man on the competing lines set out to advance that point as far into the territory of the competitor as possible.

As soon as the act was passed, chief engineer Montague sent Central Pacific surveyors working under Butler Ives to run lines north of the Great

Salt Lake and east of Ogden in the Wasatch Mountains. By spring of 1868, Central Pacific crews would be working alongside the flags of the Union Pacific survey near Fort Bridger, Wyoming. General Dodge's Union Pacific surveyors staked out a line clear across Utah and Nevada to the California border.

Two provisions in the 1866 amendments helped speed construction. One permitted the companies to grade three hundred miles ahead of the end of track. The other permitted the railroads to draw two-thirds of the government subsidy bonds upon completion of acceptable grade and before track had been laid.

On Independence Day, 1866, the C.P. rail line was completed to Dutch Flat—jumping off point for the Big Four's fine wagon road, and subject of so much vituperation the previous year. Rather than run a special train from Sacramento to celebrate the opening of the line to that point, the company brought a large delegation of Dutch Flat's foremost citizens to Sacramento by a special on that July 4.

Dutch Flat did not long remain the railhead. On July 21 the Sacramento *Union* told of the completion of the road to Alta, nearly seventy miles from Sacramento, and of the ten-car excursion train for the directors and invited guests that Central Pacific made up to celebrate the occasion: "In addition to the food on the table, the excursionists were supplied with cold water, lemonade and a stronger beverage which may be called Pacific Railroad Punch. Among the men, the last named drink seemed to be the favorite. When Pacific Railroad Punch is freely circulated, speechmaking is almost sure to follow. The addresses were all impromptu and brief, and of course had reference, either directly or indirectly, to the rapid progress of the road, to the difficulties encountered at the beginning of the enterprise, to the prospects of its early extension to the summit, the energy and determination of those who are engaged in its construction, to its importance to the state and the whole country. During the brief period allotted to this purpose, Judge Clark, Charles Crocker, L. Stanford, E. H. Heacock, M. M. Estee, Judge Foote, Judge Sawyer, M. D. Boruck, Mark Hopkins, and others were called upon and responded. Three cheers were given for C. P. Huntington, absent at Washington, three for E. B. Crocker, absent at Washoe, three for Lauren Upson, an early editorial friend and advocate of the road, and three more for the Sacramento *Union*. The memory of T. D. Judah, the original projector of the road, was proposed and drunk in silence."

Alta remained the railhead for six months, while heavy cut and fill work, tunnels, and bridges were completed. Meanwhile, the Sacramento *Union* reported on August 6, 1866, that both companies had received the grant of federal bonds: "The fourth section of twenty miles of the Pacific

Long Ravine, July, 1866.

Railroad, eastern division, having been completed, and a report to that effect having been made by the Commissioners, General J. H. Simpson, W. M. White and William Prescott Smith, the Secretary of the Treasury has ordered the issue to the above company of bonds to the amount of $320,000, to which they were entitled on completion of this section of their road. The Secretary has also ordered the issue of bonds to the amount of $640,000 to the Central Pacific Railroad Company of California, which had fallen due owing to the completion of one quarter of the work on a section of twenty miles of the road, the cost of which has exceeded $1,015,000."

While the Central Pacific continued to enjoy its first year of real prosperity, the daily work of building the railroad went on, the sometimes grueling task of conquering the forbidding Sierra. Two reminiscences from 1866 portray vividly the details of a job the demands of which were often beyond belief.

The first of these is the recollection of J. O. Wilder, who retired on August 1, 1920, after fifty-four years of continuous service with the Central Pacific–Southern Pacific railroads, and who started with the line as a lowly "back-flagman" on a surveying team in the mountains:

"On May 30, 1866, I left my home in San Francisco, a mere youth of 16 with my blankets and carpetsack, with canvas pants, high-top boots, and with seven dollars and a half in my pockets, to find myself among strangers, to take my place in the employ of the Central Pacific. I left San Francisco at 4 o'clock in the afternoon by the steamer *Capitol,* that being the only route to Sacramento at that time. Reached the Capital city the next morning. After eating breakfast I went to No. 54 K Street, the main office of the Central Pacific at that time. Being there first, I sat on the steps with my blankets and carpetbag and awaited the coming of Mr. S. S. Montague, who was chief civil engineer and to whom I had a letter of reference. He arrived with Fred Steiner, his chief draughtsman.

"It was fortunate for me that Mr. Montague was going up to the front that morning. So with my blankets on my back we walked to the depot, which was on Front, J and K Streets. The train consisted of two passenger coaches and a baggage car. . . . The main line turned into I Street, leaving I Street at Fifth, along the levee, crossing the American River east of what was known then as Rables tannery. Our first stop was Rocklin, and our last Gold Run, which was the end of the track.

"Here Mr. Montague took his span of horses with a light wagon and drove up the dusty road to Dutch Flat to what was known as Chinnie Ranch, now called Alta. Here Mr. Montague was met by Mr. L. M. Clement, assistant chief engineer. I was invited to dinner with them. Tin plates and cups were used but the food tasted good, even if it was my

In July, 1866, the line was open to Alta, 69 miles from Sacramento.

Superintendent J. H. Strobridge and family at their temporary home in Alta.

first experience in a railroad eating house. After dinner Mr. Montague and Mr. Clement inspected the roadbed, which was then about completed to this point.

"After the inspection they started up the line. I was told to ride Mr. Clement's white mule, and what that mule didn't know was not worth knowing. For instance, he knew that he had something of a lightweight and seemed to enjoy it, but not so with me, for I had been in the habit of riding on the back of wagons or a street car. While he trotted along with his nose close up to the light wagon I would have given my last five dollars for a pillow. When we reached a watering trough near Emigrant Gap I found myself standing in the stirrups and was glad to get off his back to unloosen the check rein on the horses. I then led His Muleship to get his drink. He would drink and then take a sniff at me, as much as to say 'what have I had on my back?' In fact, he had never seen a boy before.

"As we passed along up the line of construction, every now and then we would hear some gang foreman sing out 'fire', then the explosion, with rocks flying in all directions. Mr. Montague had some trouble with his horses, but to my surprise and delight His Muleship didn't seem to care half so much about those rocks as I did. At Emigrant Gap, the wagon road leaves the rail line under construction and up through a small valley to the top of a mountain, then commences the down grade to Crystal Lake, where we arrived about sundown. This was the headquarters for Mr. Clement and for the party headed by Engineer McCloud, to which I was assigned for a time, doing cross section work. . . .

"Later, I was assigned to the locating party east of Crystal Lake. The camp was about half a mile east of the town of Eatonville on the Donner Lake Wagon Road. This town is now known as Cisco. With my blankets and carpetbag, I boarded a fast freight wagon to make another new start on life's journey.

"At the new camp I found one man, the German cook. He asked me where I was from. I told him from San Francisco, which seemed to strike him just right, as he was from there himself. The sun was fast sinking in the West when the party returned to camp. I presented my letter of introduction to C. H. Guppey, engineer and transit man. He introduced me to the members of the party by saying 'Boys, this is our new back-flagman'. The party included Guppey; John Currier, leveler; Arthur Ledley, leveler's rodman; Chauncie Brainard, head chainman; John Harding, back chainman; and M. N. Denton, stake agent. The cook they called 'Haunse'. I never knew his right name. Myself and a little dog called 'Tip' completed the party.

"I was assigned my sleeping room in one corner of the tent. Mr. Ledley gave me a small hand axe and went with me to find a small fir tree from which to cut boughs to make a mattress for my bed. The ends of the boughs I stuck into the ground, laid my canvas on them, then my blankets and my carpetsack for a pillow. Supper was served in an old log cabin a few feet from the tent, and included dried apple sauce, coffee and brown sugar, eaten from tin plates and cups. Everyone seemed to enjoy the meal. I know I did.

"The first thing I heard in the mornings was 'Haunse' blowing his horn, the signal for us to get up. I was always the first up, and after putting on my canvas pants, leather boots with hob nails and short spikes in the heels, would go to the river, take a wash and return ready to eat. After breakfast the first morning, I was shown how to hold the red and white rod with sharp point on one end and was then sent to turn the grindstone for Mr. Brainard and Mr. Harding to sharpen their axes before going up the line.

"My hands were soft and I was soon changing from one to the other and had blisters on both. We started up the mountain to commence work where they had left off the day before. We went through the underbrush, over rocks, and I was not slow in finding out what the spikes were for in my boots, for they saved me more than once from falling. We picked up the line about two miles east of what was known as Butte Canyon.

"Mr. Guppey set his transit on the first peg with a tack in it, I set the next one back with a stake driven beside it marked C. T. with red chalk. We had not gone more than 1,000 feet when the line struck a big pine, which meant it must come down, and it was here that Brainard and Harding came in with their axes. After two hours work the giant fell, which meant another turn at the grindstone the next morning. We did fairly well that day, which brought us up to about opposite Eatonville.

"Nothing more of interest happened until we were about a mile above the present town of Cisco. Here we came to a deep gorge where the sides were so steep that we had to use a rope to get down to the bottom. To get up the other side was a problem, but Mr. Guppey was equal to it. He sent Mr. Brainard and 'Long John' [Harding] to a place where it could be crossed, taking with them their axes to fell a tree across at some point where it could be found. They worked their way up the other side, which was no easy task, there being much underbrush to contend with. The water was deep for that time of the year, and Ledley, Denton and myself were sent to find from whence it came.

"At the top of the mountain we found a lake, about a mile and a half wide. At the outlet, we found a deserted log cabin which at one time had been the home of a trapper. Having found what we went for we returned to the line and made our report. Brainard and Harding had come up from the other side, hitched a rope around a tree and were then ready to go ahead with the line. It consumed all of one day to cross this outlet. About

*Another formidable cut was
made at Prospect Hill.
Thousands of tons of rock
were hauled out by Chinese
laborers with horse and cart.*

one mile east, we came upon another stream not quite so deep as the first.

"These gorges we called 'Kidd's Outlets'. They were later known as the Cascades. We were not five miles above our camp, so we spent one day moving to Driver's Creek, about two miles northeast of Tinker's station. This move was a bad omen for our party, for when nearing Summit Valley, we met with our first accident. Mr. Guppey fell and his leg was broken. He was sent to Sacramento for treatment.

"While we were waiting for the new engineer to come up, we visited Soda Springs, also Castle Peak. This was the hardest climb we had undertaken. It was now the first of August, but there was still snow on the north side of the mountain. We were compelled to cross over some of the patches, which nearly cost Mr. Ledley his life, for he slipped and fell and finally brought up against a big rock, none the worse for his slide. We reached the top, ate our lunch, wrote on a piece of paper who we were, signed our names, placed it in a bottle, corked it tightly, and placed the bottle, big end up, with rocks around it.

"With the coming of Engineer Stevenson, we completed the survey to the summit. Here the party was broken up, some to return to their homes, others to Kidder's party in Nevada. I remained with Stevenson and helped him lay out the heading in the shaft of the Summit Tunnel. From here, I was sent to join Joe Wilkinson at Cisco to lay out the town and sidings.

"The construction crew was at work on the main line. Wilkinson would barely get his transit set before some 'China' herder, as they called them, would sing out 'fire', and he would then have to take up his transit and make a run for a pine tree shelter. I was with him about a week. When this work was completed I returned to the Summit and Wilkinson went to Sacramento to take charge of the building of the shops, which were then under construction. About this time, Mr. Clement moved his headquarters and also Mr. Strobridge, and I saw much of the latter.

"At times the Chinamen would strike and refuse to take their shifts in the tunnel, but Strobridge was ever on the job. They feared him in their hearts as much as they did the Chinese devil. He was a fine general. He had a mild but firm way, which was in the form of a pick handle, in dealing with these fellows. He had but one eye, yet he could spot the ring-leaders at one glance and would bring his persuader into action and was not particular where it landed, for he was a past master in this line. Inside of five minutes you could not find a Chinese in camp, and could hear them say 'muckahigh' as they went to their work with Strobridge acting as escort, for many times he was called upon to settle discords and confusion. . . ."

Henry Root also went to work on the Central Pacific in May, 1866, although in a somewhat more elevated position. He left his own recollections of that year in the Sierra:

"On May 2, 1866, I commenced work for Mr. S. S. Montague, being assigned to help J. R. Wilkinson around Sacramento and up the line as far as Rocklin. The line was then in operation to Colfax but was soon extended to Secrettown. On July 5, 1866, I was sent to Polley's Station at Crystal Lake from this time until December 23, when I moved with McCloud's party to Camp 41 to go into winter quarters to give lines and grades in Tunnels 3, 4 and 5 and to work on estimates.

"That summer was a strenuous one. Montague, acting chief engineer, was in control of all engineering work. His office was upstairs at 54 K Street, Sacramento, but he went wherever necessary to supervise the business under his control. A. Steiner was chief draftsman and J. R. Wilkinson, also a fine draftsman, was in charge of the local work within easy reach of Sacramento. L. M. Clement was resident engineer of the work from Alta to Truckee, with A. R. Guppey under him as locating engineer; on the subdivisions were George Johnson at Emigrant Gap, McCloud at Crystal Lake and Guppey at the Summit, as soon as the location there was finished. . . .

"The entire construction was done by contract in the name of Charles Crocker & Company and the engineering department was required to make a monthly estimate as the work progressed and to make a final one when completed. The culverts and other masonry work were sublet by Charles Crocker or his representative, J. H. Strobridge, to stone masons like Quinn and Scobie, but the engineer on the division had to lay out and approve the work.

"During the summer of 1866, Mr. Strobridge resided at Alta most of the time, but moved to the Summit later and had his real quarters there during the construction of the Summit Tunnel—No. 6 as it was called. Mr. Strobridge had assistants who traveled over the work and were known as 'riding bosses.' . . . More powder was used by the rock foremen than was economical, but time was the essential of all operations, so there was a good reason. But the frequent and heavy blasting made it very difficult to keep the work to correct lines, and when the rock cuts were completed, there were a large number of fills uncompleted. The calculation was that the material removed from a cut would be used to make the nearest fill, but that was impossible when it was blown away by heavy blasts, so it was necessary to use a large number of horses and carts for the long haul required to get material to complete the fills as the track-laying gang was approaching.

"When mountain construction was at its height more than 500 kegs of powder a day were used. When the work began, powder cost $2.50 a keg. During the period that the greatest quantity was being used, the price advanced to $15 a keg.

"In the vicinity of Cisco, the rock was so hard that it seemed impossible to drill into it a sufficient depth for blasting purposes. Shot after shot would blow out as if fired from a cannon. A nitroglycerin factory was established near the summit tunnel, glycerine, nitric and sulphuric acids being hauled by teams to the factory from Cisco. Some of this nitroglycerin was used on the Summit tunnel and the two tunnels to the eastward. Its use was abandoned after a disastrous explosion, and Charles Crocker ordered them to 'bury that stuff.' Dynamite was invented in 1866, but was never used on the Central Pacific."

The rapid progress in construction that had marked the spring, summer, and fall of 1866 slowed down abruptly with the first storms of what would prove to be another rigorous winter; J. O. Wilder described the early months of that winter in his memoirs:

"Winter was now fast approaching, for the grouse would get on a log and hammer with their wings, and it proved to be a very severe winter. The snowfall was heavy and it was very cold. There was one large snowslide at Strong's Canyon known as Camp 4. In this camp were two gangs of Chinese for Tunnels 11 and 12, also a gang of culvert men. The slide took it all, and one of the culvert men was not found until the following spring. At our camp, the snow was so deep we had to shovel it from the roof and make steps to get to the top of the snow. We were snowed in, and our provisions got down to corn meal and tea. Had it lasted one week longer we would have been compelled to eat horse meat, for there were two hundred or more men in this camp. We broke a road to the main wagon road where there was a store known as the Donner Lake Post Office.

"There was a complete blockade east of Blue Canyon, and all construction work had to stop with the exception of the tunnels. Between Blue Canyon and Cisco, the cuts were filled by landslides, which had to be removed by gangs of Chinese. A Push Plow loaded with pig-iron to hold it to the rails, with three engines behind, would back up and take a run at the snow and keep going until it got stuck, and then back up and take another run."

In October, 1866, in New York, the Central Pacific issued a printed report of the "Character of the Work, Its Progress, Resources, Earnings, and Future Prospects," over the signature of C. P. Huntington. It was, not surprisingly, rather self-congratulatory in tone: "The portion of the road between Colfax and Alta was the most expensive part of the whole line between Sacramento and the eastern boundary of the state. During the recent month [October, 1866] the road will be opened to Cisco, 21 miles above Alta and 94 miles from Sacramento, a point where the company will control nearly the entire business crossing the Sierra Nevadas. [The line actually did not open to Cisco until December.]

"The construction work is also progressing at several of the most difficult points on the line; among which are included a tunnel at the summit

*The station at Gold Run.
A cut was made below
the town, and a flume
constructed to run
along side the track.*

Excursion train at Cape Horn.

Rounding Cape Horn, road to Iowa Hill in the distance.

American River and Canyon from Cape Horn.

of the Sierra Nevada mountains 1,600 feet in length, and one of 800 feet, seven miles east of the summit, on which laborers are working night and day.

"Work has also been commenced on all the other tunnels, which are being constructed wide enough for a double track, which it is confidently believed will be required in a few years to do the business of the road.

"Suitable machinery and a steam engine have been shipped from the Eastern States for a large repair shop. There has been constructed at Sacramento, on the lands granted by that city, a wharf with steam engine, derricks, etc., together with suitable freight and passenger depots for the transaction of the business of the road.

"The road, so far as completed, will compare favorably with any railroad in the United States. The rails are of the best quality of American iron, weighing at least 60 lbs. per yard. The chairs are of wrought iron; the cross ties, numbering 2,400 per mile, are 6 x 8 or 10 inches and 8 feet long, of redwood, which is quite equal to red cedar or locust for durability.

"The culverts are all of granite, or other hard rock, except a few of hard-burnt brick in the valley, where stone could not be procured.

"The bridges are made of the best quality of Puget Sound timber, with foundations of masonry.

"The drainage is ample and complete, and the roadbed is well ballasted with gravel or broken stone. The alignment is remarkable for its directness in such a broken, mountainous country. The least radius of curvature is 573 feet or 10 degrees.

"The highest grade is 116 feet per mile, of which there are three and one-half miles on the present completed line. No serious difficulty is found in operating this portion of the road, running the regular passenger trains thereon at the rate of twenty-five miles, and the freight trains twelve miles per hour. A greater speed could be obtained by the motive power of the road, but thus far it has not been found necessary.

"The whole cost of the work done, and material purchased, amounted on the 10th of July, 1866, to the sum of $8,596,476.80. . . .

"The officers in charge of the construction of the road are very sanguine that they will be able to complete the railroad over the Sierra Nevada to the state line, a distance of 156 miles from Sacramento by July, 1867; thence to a point 50 miles east of the great bend of the Truckee River, a further distance of about 82 miles, and 238 miles from Sacramento, during the year 1867; and to Salt Lake, about 675 miles from Sacramento, in two years thereafter, where it is hoped to meet the road being built from the East. . . ."

The road had reason for a certain amount of satisfaction. The net profit for operation of the line then open to passenger and freight business from

January, 1865, to September, 1866, had been nearly three-quarters of a million dollars, a cheerful harbinger of future prosperity. Moreover, the mighty Sierras were steadily succumbing to the ingenuity of Yankee engineers and the diligence of Chinese labor, as the Sacramento *Union* reported November 5: "Central Pacific railroad track is now laid to Emigrant Gap, a distance of fifteen miles from Alta, and a point 5,000 feet above the level of the sea. In order to reach to summit it will be only necessary to go 2,000 feet higher, and a distance of about nineteen miles. The rails will be laid to Cisco, seven miles distant from Emigrant Gap, in about ten days. On November 3, after the rain on the plains and in the foothills, there was no snow on the summit."

A. P. Partridge, a veteran Central Pacific construction worker, later explained in part the delay incurred in achieving Cisco, which they had hoped to reach in October: "Two miles west of Cisco, we put up a high trestle [Butte Canyon] bridge, 100 feet in height. With a heavy storm and a big fall of rain there was a lake on the hill above the bridge and when it filled it broke loose. Down everything came and swept away four bents from the center of our bridge. That bridge had to be replaced, with the road blocked to Blue Canyon. Well, we went to the woods and hewed the timber, hauled it to the track by main force, then got some ox teams and hauled it to the bridge and repaired the break."

At this point Central Pacific started its tunneling operations. Tunnels 1 and 2 were both located west of Cisco. The first, called Grizzly Hill Tunnel, was one mile west of Blue Canyon and seventy-seven miles east of Sacramento. Completed in the summer of 1866, it was 498 feet long, 232 feet of which were timber lined. The second, known as Emigrant Gap Tunnel, was just east of Emigrant Gap and eighty-four miles from Sacramento. Completely lined, the 271-foot bore was completed in September, 1866.

"The Central Pacific is now completed and in daily operation from Sacramento to Cisco," the *Union* announced triumphantly on the last day of the year, "a distance of niney-two miles, reaching within twelve miles of the summit of the Sierra Nevada mountains and 5,911 feet above the level of the sea—a higher altitude than is attained by any other railroad in America. The work of construction has been vigorously prosecuted during the year with an average of about 10,000 men. Much of the masonry and heavy rock excavation has been done beyond Cisco, toward the eastern boundary of the state. Twelve tunnels, varying from 800 to 1,650 feet in length, are in process of construction along the snow belt between the summit and the Truckee river, and are being worked night and day by three shifts of men, eight hours each, every twenty-four hours — employing in these tunnels an aggregate of 8,000 laborers. These tunnels will be com-

Bear River Valley.

pleted by next spring, except the 1,650-foot tunnel at the summit, which is to be ready for the track in September. A large force of laborers is also employed during this winter east of the mountains, in Truckee canyon. It is expected that during the year 1867 the road will be completed and in operation to the eastern line of the state, from which point the work of construction toward Salt Lake is comparatively light and can be prosecuted at all seasons of the year at the rate, it is believed, of a mile a day, and to reach Salt Lake City of the 1st of January, 1870."

Things were looking good—but winter had just begun.

NINE

THE CP DIGS IN:
WINTER, *1866-67*

T HE CENTRAL PACIFIC met its greatest test in the Summit Tunnels, after the line was opened to Cisco. To breach the summit of the Sierra, eleven tunnels, Nos. 3 through 13, must be built within a twenty-mile stretch between Cisco and Lake Ridge just west of Cold Stream Valley on the eastern slope. Three years later civil engineer John R. Gillis, who worked on these tunnels, told the American Society of Civil Engineers of the construction problems during that rugged winter:

"The line here [summit of the Sierra] lies on steep hillsides, in some cases being, for long distances, on bare granite, more or less broken by projecting ledges and boulders, but with an average slope often greater than 1 to 1. In such places embankments were almost impracticable; the hills were too steep, and most of the rock from cuts were thrown far down hill by heavy seam blasts. On these accounts, the line for two miles east of Donner Pass was thrown further into the hill than on original location, thus adding to the depths of cuttings and increasing the number of tunnels, but saving retaining walls, and where tunnels were made, enabling the work to be carried on in winter. Another important object was the saving of snow-covering where tunnels were made, and giving a good foundation for it where they were not. It is within thees two miles that seven tunnels are crowded.

"During the fall of 1866 the track reached Cisco, and as fast as the gangs of Chinese were released they were hurried to the summit to be distributed among the tunnels in its vicinity. The year before [August, 1865] some gangs had been sent to summit tunnel No. 6, and commenced the cuts at its extremities; winter set in before the headings were started, and the work had to be abandoned. To avoid a repetition of such delay, the approaches to all the tunnels were covered with men, [who] worked night and day in three shifts of eight hours each. Thus time was saved, and the tunnel organization started at once. As an illustration of the hurry, I may mention walking two miles over the hills after dark, and staking out the east end of No. 12 by the light of a bonfire; at nine o'clock the men were at work.

"In November and the early part of December there were several snow-storms, just enough to stimulate without denying the work. The rough rocky sides of Donner Peak soon became smooth slopes of snow and ice covering the trail that led from tunnel 8 to 9; it remained impassable until spring, and communication had to be kept up by the Dutch Flat and Donner Lake wagon-road, five or six hundred feet below. From the pass the descent toward the lake was over very rough ground, requiring heavy side cuts and retaining walls with numerous zig-zags to gain distance.

"From this road the scene was strangely beautiful at night. The tall firs, though drooping under their heavy burdens, pointed to the mountains that overhung them, where the fires that lit seven tunnels shone like stars on their snowy sides. The only sound that came down to break the stillness of the winter night was the sharp ring of hammer on steel, or the heavy reports of the blasts.

"By the time winter had set in fairly, the headings were all under ground. The work was then independent of weather, except as storms would block up tunnel entrances, or avalanches sweep over the shanties of the laborers. Before tracing the progress of the work underground, it will be well to see the character of the weather outdoors.

"Snow storms, forty-four in number, varied in length from a short snow squall to a two-week gale, and in depth from a quarter of an inch to ten feet —none less than the former number being recorded, nor had we occasion to note any greater than the latter. This, the heaviest storm of the winter, began February 18th, at 2 p.m., and snowed steadily until 10 p.m. of the 22nd, during which time six feet fell. The supply of raw material was then exhausted, but the barometer kept low and the wind heavy from the south-west for five days more, by which time a fresh supply of damp air came up from the Pacific, and then . . . was ground up without delay. It snowed steadily until March 2nd, making ten feet of snow and thirteen days of storm. It is true that no snow fell for five days, but it drifted so furiously during that time the snow-tunnel at the east end of tunnel No. 6 had to be lengthened fifty feet.

"These storms were grand. They always began with a fall in the barom-eter and a strong wind from the southwest, hurrying up the tattered rain-clouds or storm seed in heavy masses. The barometer, which averaged twenty-three inches, would drop sometimes as low as twenty-two and a half. The thermometer was rarely below twenty degrees at the beginning of a storm, and usually rose to thirty-two degrees before its close, so that the last snow would be damp and heavy, sometimes ending in a rain. The storms ended, and clouds were scattered by cold winds blowing over the eastern range of the Sierra Nevada. These raised the barometer and dropped the temperature at once. The lowest temperature of the winter . . . from a wind of this sort [was] five degrees above zero.

"Our quarters were at the east end of Donner Pass, but still in the narrow part. About the second or third day of a storm the wind would be a gale, sometimes ten pounds per square foot; and would plough up the new fallen snow to heap it in huge drifts beyond the east end of the pass. About thirty feet from our windows was a large warehouse; this was often hidden completely by the furious torrent of almost solid snow that swept through the gorge. On the cliff above, the cedar trees are deeply cut, many branches of the thickness of a man's wrist being taken off entirely by the drifting snowflakes.

"No one can face these storms when they are in earnest. Three of our party came through the pass one evening, walking with the storm—two got in safely. After waiting a while, just as we were starting to look up the third, he came in exhausted. In a short, straight path between two walls of rock, he had lost his way and thought his last hour had come.

"Of course these storms made the road impassable even for sleighs. They were opened by gangs of men, kept there for the purpose, with heavy ox sleds. The snow when new fallen is very light, so that a man without snowshoes would sink to his waist or shoulders. Into this the oxen would flounder, and when they lay down, worn out, be roused by the summary process of twisting their tails. I saw three in one team so 'fortunate' as to have theirs twisted clear off, none left to be bothered with. The men were as regardless of themselves as of their animals. They took life easily in fine weather, but were out nearly all the time when it stormed. Late at night they could be seen shovelling on a bad drift at the corner of the warehouse, where the wind heaped in the snow faster than they could dig it out, and then a denser mess of flying snow would hide them altogether.

"We started with Canadian snowshoes, but soon abandoned them for the Norwegian, each a strip of light wood ten to twelve feet long, four inches wide, and an inch and a quarter thick in the center; they taper in thickness towards the end, are turned up in front, and grooved on the bottom.

"There is a broad strap in the middle to put the foot under, and a balancing-pole to steady, push, and brake with. The latter will be seen as all-important, as a speed of twenty-five to thirty miles an hour is often

*Most of the tunnels had to be made through solid rock, a slow process
of digging, blasting, and hauling away the smashed debris.*

attained on a steep hillside. During several winters the mails were carried across the mountains by a Norwegian named Thompson, on these shoes. It is said he made sometimes forty or fifty miles a day on them.

"Snowslides or avalanches were frequent. The storm winds being always from the southwest, form drifts or snow-wreaths on the northeast crests of hills. Then these become too heavy, which is generally towards the close of the storms, they break off, and in falling start the loose snow below. This slides on the old crust.

"Near the close of one storm, a log house with board roof, containing three Scotsmen, brothers, and sub-contractors with their gang, some fifteen or sixteen men in all, was crushed and buried up at daybreak. The storm ended at noon. Towards evening a man coming up the road missed the house and alarmed the camp, so that by six o'clock the men were dug out. The bulk of the slide had passed over and piled itself up beyond the house, so that it was only covered fifteen feet. Only three were killed; the bunks were close to the log walls and kept the rest from being crushed. The snow packed around the men so closely that only two could move about; they had almost dug their way out; over the heads of the rest little holes had been melted in the snow by their breath. Most of them were conscious, and, strange to say, the time had passed rapidly with them, although about 14 hours under the snow.

"This event startled us, for at the top of the cliff, in front of the camp, was a snow-wreath forty or fifty feet long, projecting twenty feet, and of about the same thickness. We were uncertain when it would come down and where it would stop. A keg of powder was put down behind it next morning and fired. A white column shot up a hundred feet, and then the whole hillside below was in motion; it came down a frozen cascade, covered with glittering snow-dust for spray. It was a rare sight, for snowslides are so rapid and noiseless that comparatively few are seen. They were so frequent across the trail leading to tunnel No. 9 that it had to be abandoned for some months. At tunnel 10, some fifteen or twenty Chinese were killed by a slide about this time. . . .

"Before the snow had acquired depth enough to interfere much with the work, the tunnel headings were all started. The cuts at their entrances soon filled up with snow, but drifts were run through them, in some instances large enough for a two-horse team. Through these snow-tunnels, whose lengths varied from 50 to 200 feet, the material excavated was hauled in carts or on sleds to the waste banks. These snow-tunnels kept settling at the crown, so that they had to be enlarged from time to time, otherwise they were perfectly satisfactory.

"The most remarkable snow-tunnel was made to connect the two ends of Tunnel 8. The spur through which this is made terminates in a vertical

148

bluff of granite a hundred feet high. To get around it during the fall, a rope was fastened to the rocks at a point where there was a deep descent of thirty or forty feet. During the early part of winter a snowdrift formed on the face of this bluff, descending in a deep slope from its top to the wagon road, two hundred feet below. On this slope a trail was cut and used for a month or two.

"Later in the winter, when the accumulation of snow made it practicable, a snow-tunnel was excavated through the drift, and around the face of the bluff. Windows were made at short intervals for light, and to throw the material out in excavating. Steps were cut where a descent was necessary. One flight of these led down to the blacksmith's shop, buried still deeper in the snow, while the main passage led into one already excavated at the east end of Tunnel 8. The snow kept settling down hill and away from the bluff, so that there was an open space of three or four feet between it [the drift] and the rock towards the close, which was far from inspiring much confidence in the route. . . ."

Gills went on to outline general techniques used in constructing the tunnels:

"Most of the work was through solid rock, which did not require lining, and the following dimensions were adopted: Bottom, a rectangle, 16 x 11 feet; arch, a semicircle, 16 feet in diameter; grade at center of tie, and one foot three inches above subgrade.

"Tunnel 11 was partly, and Tunnel 13 wholly lined with timber in the following manner: 12" x 12" sills were placed on each side, and posts 12" x 16" mortised into them. The latter support arches, each composed of three thicknesses of 5" x 12" plank, breaking joints, and bolted with ¾-inch iron bolts, thus making a solid arch of 180 square inches sectional area. The distance from center to center of arches varies from one-and-a-half feet to five feet, according to material. Over the arches, and, where the material required it, on the sides also, split lagging about two and a half inches thick was put in. The width at subgrade inside of posts is seventeen feet; at springing line inside of arches, nineteen feet; giving a batter of one foot on each side. Height of crown above grade, nineteen feet nine inches, thus leaving room for masonry inside the temporary wooden lining.

"Tunnels 1 and 2 were lined in a similar manner, except that the batter of side posts was only six inches.

"In these tunnels, through soft material, the heading was supported by temporary timbers. Chambers were then excavated at the sides to below subgrade, for the sills, and the central core left to support the shores which held the material above in place. As the timbering advanced, the core and false work were removed. . . .

"In all the tunnels on curves, allowance was made for elevation of the

To speed up construction before the snow set in, the tunnels were worked from both sides. Above, east portals of Tunnels No. 6 and 7.

outer rail, so that the top of cars would remain in the center of opening. As soon as each heading became sufficiently advanced, the center line was secured, generally by small holes drilled in the roof, with wooden plugs and tacks. These points were placed as far apart as the length excavated would permit, and from them the line produced as the work advanced. In most cases the entrances were afterwards so blocked up with snow that it was impossible to accurately refer to the line outside, and the tunnels were completed from the points first put in. . . .

"Most of the tunnels are on curves, No. 13 being on one of 575 feet radius, with 87 degrees of curvature inside the tunnel. In this, as in No. 11, the usual difficulties of working with instruments by candlelight were much increased by the numerous temporary timbers in the headings. The lines met in the center of the tunnel, parallel to each other, but two inches apart. In the other cases the discrepancies were too slight to notice.

"With the exception of a few white men at the west end of tunnel No. 6, the laboring force was entirely composed of Chinese, with white foremen —the laborers working usually in three shifts of eight hours each, and the foremen in two shifts of twelve hours each. A single foreman, with a gang of thirty to forty men, generally constituted the force at work at each end of a tunnel; of these, twelve to fifteen worked on the heading, and the rest on bottom, removing material, etc. . . .

"The Chinese were as steady, hard-working a set of men as could be found. They were paid from $30 to $35, in gold, a month, finding [maintaining] themselves, while the white men were paid about the same, but with their board thrown in. The force at work on the road probably averaged from six to ten thousand, nine-tenths of them being Chinese. . . .

"Nitroglycerine was introduced on the work early in 1867, to expedite progress of the summit tunnel. It was made on the spot by Mr. James Howden, and used the four headings of Tunnel No. 6 from February 9th . . . In the headings of summit tunnel the average daily progress with powder was 1.18 feet per day; with nitroglycerine, 1.82 feet, or over 54 per cent additional progress. In the bottom of summit tunnel, average daily progress with powder, full gangs, was 2.51 feet; with nitroglycerine, 4.38, or over 74 per cent in favor of nitroglycerine. The same number of men were used with both explosives. . . .

"The cost of nitroglycerine made at Donner Pass, according to Mr. Howden, was about 75 cents per pound. It was considered there to be about eight times as powerful as the same weight of powder, which would make it the cheapest, viewed simply as to expense of producing a given effect. Wherever practicable, I have no doubt that it is safest to manufacture nitroglycerine on the site where it is to be used, and from day to day as required. At Donner Pass, I only recollect two accidents, and these would have happened with powder. The conclusion we may safely come to, from the Central Pacific work, is that in hard rock tunnels, with the same number of men, over fifty per cent additional progress can be made by using nitroglycerine in place of powder, and the expense will be reduced proportionately. . . ."

Summit Tunnel No. 6 is parallel to, and about four hundred feet north of, Donner Pass. Its length of 1,659 feet takes it 124 feet below the surface (measuring from grade) through medium quality granite crossed by seams in every direction. To speed construction, as the tunnel was being worked from both directions, an 8 x 12 x 72.9-foot shaft was sunk at about the center. Work started on the shaft on August 27, 1866, and for the first thirty feet it was sunk at the rate of one foot daily. Then, delay in hoisting the material with a common hand derrick slowed progress; a steam hoist was considered necessary, and thus began one of the more intriguing tales in the annals of the Central Pacific—how the *Sacramento,* California's first locomotive, was taken out of mothballs and transported to the summit of the Sierra. J. O. Wilder recalled the details:

"The officials wanted a locomotive to work the drum and rock-cage in the shaft at the summit tunnel, and it was up to the Motive Power Department to get it there as soon as possible. The Department at this time was in charge of I. H. Graves, its first Master Mechanic. He found that the Sacramento and Placerville Company had an engine that would answer the purpose. It was a small Hinkley Four Driver and Poney Truck. The engine of which I speak, the *Sacramento,* was dismantled at Sacramento, everything taken from her to lighten her weight. The cab and tank and stack were left at Sacramento, and then it was pulled up the line to Gold Run, which was the terminal. Here she was jacked up, wheels taken out, and by the use of traveling jacks was moved 14″ at a time to a logging truck, with wheels 24″ wide. This truck later did service at Tunnel 13, as did Missouri Bill and his ox team from whom I learned this story of the transportation of the first locomotive to reach the summit of the Sierras, though not under her own power. With the engine on the truck, securely bolted and braced to the same, Missouri Bill made ready to start with what he termed 'the black picked goose;' and with ten yoke of oxen, wagon-master Pratt in charge, and several teamsters to assist, they got under way. All went well till a half-mile east of Dutch Flat. It was here the engine received its first cussing, for she had been the cause of stampeding a ten-mule freight team. Anyone familiar with mules knows that when they start something they usually finish it to the Queen's taste, with broken harnesses and tug-chains. This happened every day while on her way up the mountain; even the stagecoach horses would balk at the sight of her, and it finally became necessary to blindfold teams of mules and horses to get them to pass, for they would leave the road and take to the hills or the ravines, whichever looked best to them; and they weren't particular, either, about what they took along with them. They would endeavor to kick themselves loose of everything before starting for the bushes.

"Another problem was caused by many soft places in the road, some of them from 10 to 25 feet in extent. Wagonmaster Pratt had small trees cut and laid crosswise, others lengthwise, with heavy brush matting. This all consumed much time. Where a grade was too heavy for the oxen, Pratt would stop one of the Company's fast freight teams to give him a lift up a grade, and in such a manner reached the divide above Emigrant Gap. From here to Crystal Lake, it is down grade—the largest problem of all, for Pratt had to make assurance doubly sure, taking into consideration the heavy weight. This part of the locomotive's journey was fraught with fear, for one mishap meant loss of time and perhaps engine. With heavy logging chains and chain tackle made fast to big pine trees, they would let down as far as the tackle would permit, then block it. This was repeated time after time until the bottom of each grade was reached."

With such painstaking effort, the old *Sacramento* finally made it up to Tunnel No. 6, where it was housed in a shack over the tunnel's vertical shaft and put to work, six weeks after departure from its namesake town.

The *Sacramento* also figured in a sidelight on the construction of Tunnel No. 6. Apparently in an effort to speed up work, the company decided in early 1867 to try steam-powered drills, using some of the power from the newly-installed *Sacramento*. Strobridge vetoed the idea, much to the disgruntlement of at least two of the company's officials.

On April 1, 1867, Stanford received a letter from Hopkins, which read in part: "Also rec'd today from Crocker a letter from the man who went up to attend the drilling machines. He says Strobridge says that the present engine cannot be stopped to make the necessary connections for steam. Mr. Moore says it will not take over two hours at the most. Now, if they get out rock so fast as to pile up at the shaft, and what they would raise in two hours could not be got out of the way, then it would seem that the drilling machines would be of little benefit, because it would seem that already our progress had reached a point at which it was equal to the capacity to raise. But I have bought an engine and will have sent up what is necessary to connect it with present boiler."

The same day, April 1, 1867, E. B. Crocker had written the following letter to Mark Hopkins, which doubtless led to Hopkins' letter to Stanford: "Stanford got a letter from Charles, or rather from Fleming from the Summit. Strobridge's refusal to let steam be taken from the boiler there now and Charles' apparent indorsement surprises me. It looks as though both were set against drilling machines. It seems to leave no other way but

Workers at the East Portal of the Summit Tunnel.

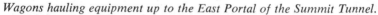

With the exception of a few white men at the west end of Tunnel No. 6, the laboring force was entirely composed of Chinese, with white foremen. A single foreman, with a gang of thirty to forty men, generally constituted the force at work at each end of a tunnel; of these, twelve to fifteen worked on the heading, and the rest on the bottom.

Interior of the Summit Tunnel—No. 6.

Wagons hauling equipment up to the East Portal of the Summit Tunnel.

*The rockbound wilderness through which the wagon road to the
Summit Tunnel was carved, as seen above, indicates the profound labor
involved in chipping away across the Sierra Nevada.*

to buy a separate boiler and engine here and send it up."

The situation was not quickly resolved. On April 15, E. B. Crocker wrote Hopkins: "Yours of yesterday to Stanford is rec'd and it puts me out of all patience to see how that drilling machine matter is mismanaged. I sat right down and wrote the inclosed letter to Charles. Perhaps it is not just right, but I believe it is the truth, every word of it. If you think best send it up to him. The truth is things have got to such a pass that there can't be a thing done unless it suits Strobridge. Whenever a man gets Charles' confidence, he swears by him and all he says or does is right."

After the first exchange of letters on the subject, early in April, Stanford decided to make the trip to the summit and investigate the matter at first hand. On his return April 16, Stanford wrote Hopkins: "Your letters of the 13th & 15th inst. rec'd. I fear the drilling machines will prove useless. There does not appear a will that they should succeed, and usually where there is no will there is no way."

Drilling machines or no, work in the tunnel progressed until, in August, 1867, the Sierra had been pierced.

TEN

RAILS TO THE SUMMIT: *1867*

WHILE THE MAJORITY of the Chinese workers—about eight thousand of them—continued to hand carve their way through Tunnel No. 6 during the winter of 1866 and on into the summer of 1867, a crew of about three thousand more Chinese was sent ahead to grade as far as the state line during the winter months. Central Pacific vouchers indicate that a locomotive, car parts, and a few rails were hauled to Coburn's (Truckee) in July, 1867. Ultimately, they show a total of 33 track miles (66 linear miles) of rail were hauled over the summit during August, September, and October.

"The Judge [E. B. Crocker] says Charley says to wait until we reach the Summit before we haul iron over to the Truckee," Stanford told Hopkins in a letter of February 5, 1867. A few months earlier, after moving the *Sacramento* to the summit, Crocker and Strobridge had decided to wait until the rails were laid to the summit before attempting to lay any rail or move any locomotives and construction cars to the Truckee area. The winter of 1866/67 was proving to be the hardest the builders had yet experienced, and Crocker feared such an undertaking would prove disastrous. By the summer of 1867, crews were laying rail, and the movement of iron and equipment to the eastern side of the Sierra was put aside until the following winter.

By March, 1867, there was still fifteen feet of snow in Summit Valley. When that began to melt, workers faced the danger of slides, which carried away a number of buildings above Alta and completely destroyed the large trestle near Cisco. Efforts to keep the road open to Cisco amid the hardships of that winter convinced the associates that some form of protective covering would be necessary. One day, while Crocker and Stanford discussed the problem at lunch, Stanford took out his pencil and began estimating the cost of covering the track with snowsheds. Before the conference ended, the two associates agreed that before another winter passed, Central Pacific's line must be protected. The job was assigned to Arthur Brown, superintendent of bridges and buildings.

Because the planning and construction of railroad bridges and, to some extent, other railroad structures, was of a specialized nature, the Central Pacific had made field construction the sole responsibility of one man as early as 1865. Now that man, Arthur Brown, undertook the task of planning and supervising the building of nearly forty miles of snowsheds during five working months each summer. "Although every known appliance," he later said, "was used to keep the road clear from snow that winter of 1866–67, including the largest and best snow plows then known, it was found impossible to keep it open over half the time and that mostly by means of men and shovels, which required an army of men on hand all the time at great expense.

"It became evident from our experience then that the snow problem had become serious and it was decided after various discussions on the subject by the directors of the company that the only positive means of protecting the road was by snowsheds and galleries. Although the expense of building a shed nearly forty miles in length was almost appalling and unprecedented in railroad construction, there seemed to be no alternative. . . ."

In the summer of 1867, some experimental sheds were built. The winter of 1867/68 proved that the experimental structures would have to be modified considerably. Not until the summer of 1868 would permanent construction begin.

The Huntington-Hopkins partnership in the hardware store at 54 K Street, Sacramento, ended in the spring of 1867 when the store was sold to their longtime employees. On March 29, 1867, Huntington expressed somewhat mixed emotions in a letter to Hopkins:

"As to selling out our store or a portion of it, I quite agree with you, and think we have too much to do to do it well—at least I will speak for myself. I do not know of any other parties that I had rather sell it to than Foye, Miller and Gallatan. I think with you that it would be well (at least for a time) to keep one-fourth interest ourselves. And if you wish to sell one-half or three-fourths interest, do so. As to the plan for the stock and the manner of payment, I shall leave entirely with you, feeling that my interest is as safe in your hands as in my own. While I would like very much to go to Sacramento and take you by the hand and talk over matters as in years gone by, but if I should sell all my interest at 54 K, I think that I had rather you would do it while I am here, than do it myself. I do not think I could sell all my interest there and walk out of the old store without dropping a tear on the threshold, for the old place is somehow dear to me with all my losses there by fire and flood."

By that spring of 1867, the Central Pacific surveyors were east of Great Salt Lake, working up through Weber and Echo canyons, across the Wasatch and on to Fort Bridger on the eastern slope of the Utah-Wyoming range. They set their flags and stakes beside those of the Union Pacific, which was then striking westward at the rate of more than a mile of track daily. The Union Pacific boasted it would meet the struggling Central Pacific at the California line.

In reply, Crocker concentrated in the Sierra Nevada a force of 11,000 Chinese, 2,500 Caucasians, and 1,000 teams; he recalled crews from the upper Truckee, and with every pick and scraper, spade, crowbar, and plow, launched a fresh and final attack on the tunnels and grades. However, it was June of that year before the men were finally back in the mountains—and the grade still lay beneath ten to twelve feet of snow. They wasted no time waiting for it to melt, but shoveled it by hand from the sides of cuts and banks and resumed grading.

In the meantime, Central Pacific surveyors had located at least a portion of its line to the east of the Sierra, and on April 25, 1867, the company filed with the Secretary of the Interior a map of location from the Big Bend of the Truckee River to Humboldt Wells (now Wells), Nevada.

"During the past year," said the Sacramento *Union* of June 22, 1867, "the Central Pacific Railroad Company had their surveying parties running lines in all directions between the Wasatch Mountains [Nevada] on the west, the Snake River on the north, and the Overland mail route on the south, in order to determine the best route for their railroad. Lines were run both north and south of Great Salt Lake. These surveys have demonstrated the great superiority of the route by the *north end of the lake*. One great obstacle to the location by the south end is the great salt mud plain, about seventy miles in width, which is destitute of fresh water and will require to be piled, and which is entirely avoided by the northern route. The company therefore located their line, commencing at the Big Bend of the Truckee thence to Humboldt Lake, thence up the Humboldt River to the Wells near the head of that stream, at which point the East Humboldt Mountains terminate, and the line can be located easily to the Wasatch Mountains, by the north end of Great Salt Lake.

"Under the law, this location required the approval of the Secretary of the Interior. The maps, profiles and reports were laid before him, and after a full examination he has finally approved. It enables the Central Pacific Company to proceed early with the necessary location surveys, and to prosecute the work to the Humboldt Wells without delay. The distance from the state line to the Humboldt Wells is 370 miles."

Looking west across Blue Canyon, 78 miles from Sacramento.

Rounding Emigrant Gap, the Yuba Mountains in the distance.

On October 28, 1867, one of the most controversial acts in the history of the Central Pacific took place when the Big Four formed the Contract and Finance Company, incorporated under the laws of the state of California with a capital stock of five million dollars to construct the railroad from the eastern boundary of California to its junction with the Union Pacific.

The Big Four had been unable to interest outside capital in the construction firm of Charles Crocker & Company. Stanford later testified before the Pacific Railroad Commission:

"By this time [October, 1867], our means were very limited. Under act of Congress we had mortgaged the road and issued bonds 100 miles in advance of construction, and they were all consumed, together with the county aid and all the aid that we received, and it was doubtful if we could possibly go on.

"We thought that by forming the Contract and Finance Company and agreeing to give it the stock of the company, that the new company might be able to interest capital. Of course this was practically giving the contractors all the assets of the Central Pacific, but it was better for us to do that than to fail.

"We organized the Contract and Finance Company in the hope of inducing capitalists to come in and take a part. We did not succeed in any quarter in interesting others and finally gave it up.

"Then I think each of us subscribed for a fifth, Mr. Hopkins, Mr. Huntington, Charles Crocker, E. B. Crocker and myself."

Huntington also testified before the Commission telling of his efforts to interest eastern money in investing both in California and in the Contract and Finance Company:

"These strong men in New York did not like to come in under an unlimited partnership; but William K. Garrison said if we would organize a company, by which they would know the extent of their liability, he thought he would get his father in for one; that was Commodore Garrison. I had a talk with William E. Dodge, whom I knew very well, and Moses Taylor; but more particularly Mr. Dodge. After the organization I spent a good deal of time with a dozen men, perhaps, in New York, endeavoring to get them to come in with us, but I did not get any of them in. D. O. Mills I talked with a great many times, but he said the risk he thought was too great."

The C.P.'s advisor, Roscoe Conkling, later testified to the contractor's difficulties: "When the work on the mountains commenced, Mr. Crocker saw that he had probably assumed a task beyond his financial strength. Crocker appealed to the Directors for help. Stanford investigated and found that in the absence of precedent there were no rules that could govern between contractors that would answer the purpose of rapid construction, that sacrifices would have to be made, which the company could afford, but which the contractor, looking for profits could not, so they told Crocker to go on with the work without regard to the terms of the contract and that the Directors would see him through."

Because of the many difficulties and extraordinary capital outlays, Crocker's construction firm was exhausted financially, if not physically. The Contract and Finance Company came to the rescue. Emulating the example set by the Union Pacific's Credit Mobilier, it had been organized and duly incorporated by the four builders and Edwin B. Crocker, the road's attorney, to carry on construction. The new company agreed to build and equip the road from the state line through to Salt Lake City for $43,000 a mile in cash and an equal payment in C.P. stock. At the completion of the line, the four principals held some $52,000,000 in company stock and assumed from $3,000,000 to $4,000,000 in company debt.

It was when the group organized the Contract and Finance Company that Huntington wired Hopkins to "Take as much as you are forced to but as little as you must."

A. P. Partridge, who was a member of one of Arthur Brown's bridge and building crews, tells of that work during the last half of 1867:

"In the summer of 1867 we were sent back eight miles to Emigrant Gap and framed the two Cascade bridges. The lumber, 16 x 18 and 20 inches, and from 40 to 60 feet long, was split by whip-sawing. After the bridges were framed and the road opened, after the snow was cleared, [the timbers] were shipped by cars to Cisco, then hauled by teams on sleighs seven miles to the bridge-building site and were left there until October 1867. Then I was transferred to that outfit of framers. The bridge was framed and piled up and covered until time to raise it. We also framed the other two bridges and finished them about the last of June. In the latter part of July a raising gang was started under a foreman by the name of John Haton. His crew was sent east of the Summit to the Truckee River canyon to construct the bridges where the grading had been completed the previous winter. We first raised the Little Truckee and Prosser Creek bridges, and then went to the first crossing of the Truckee River.

"Then we backed up towards the Sierra Nevadas and about one mile west of Truckee we framed and raised a four-span bridge across Cold Stream. That brought us to the last of September. We then went for the Cascade bridges and raised them before the winter snows. That about finished October and November. Then attention was turned more eastward."

By the close of the year, C.P. track had crossed the California-Nevada line. In the spring, the energies of the company were centered upon seven

By the end of 1866, track had been laid to Cisco, two views of which are shown at left and right, below. Above, left and right, engines of progress start the long climb from Cisco to the summit.

*Cutting timber along the way to build their bridges,
they crossed the upper Cascades, 95 miles above Cisco.*

miles at Donner Gap, where the building of the Cascade bridges was the last obstacle west of the summit. The rail was laid and the line opened to the summit in November, 1867; the first scheduled train from Sacramento arrived on November 30.

In December, also, the sale of the Huntington-Hopkins store was completed. On December 8, 1867, Huntington wrote to Hopkins: "I am satisfied with the sale that you have made of the four-fifths of our stock and hardware, and if the boys do the best that they know (as I doubt not that they will) they ought to make their fortunes by giving the business their undivided attention. Now I hardly think it is for the interest of Huntington, Hopkins & Company that I should do the buying now. I will not turn my back to anyone as a buyer when I have the time, but the first is the business of the different railroads that I represent which is enough for any one man to do."

The "different railroads" are a story in themselves.

ELEVEN

AN INTERLUDE OF EXPANSION: *1867*

Not only did the Big Four conquer the mighty Sierra in 1867, but they also began reaching out to expand their interests, and by the end of the year owned not one but five railroads: the Central Pacific, the Western Pacific Railroad, the California & Oregon Railroad, the California Central Railroad, and the Yuba Railroad; and they were considering the acquisition of the Southern Pacific Railroad. There is no doubt that by then these four had been repaid the loans that they had made to get the Central Pacific started while awaiting government aid. The sale of the Huntington-Hopkins hardware store at this time undoubtedly provided extra cash also, as the Yuba Railroad was purchased by Huntington himself at a bankruptcy sale.

While Charles Crocker and the construction crews eliminated the last obstacles at the summit of the Sierra, and Huntington, in the East, purchased supplies and kept them moving west, E. B. Crocker and Leland Stanford had been kept busy elsewhere negotiating for the purchase of these railroads which were needed to give the associates a north-south line. Now they would have routes running the entire length of California from the Oregon border to the Arizona border at Fort Yuma. They had secured little finished construction, but in the case of the California & Oregon and the Southern Pacific, the purchase at least brought federal land grants.

The four associates, separated by many miles, wrote a series of letters that outline the negotiation process, letters which are part of the collection on file at Stanford University. It is a curious fact that these railroads were acquired in the same period during which the company was too short of funds to prosecute construction to its fullest, the period of difficulty that resulted in the formation of the Contract and Finance Company.

On February 5, 1867, Stanford wrote to Hopkins:

"I rec'd a letter this morning from the Judge [E. B. Crocker] stating that he and Montague were intending to start for Benicia to determine what surveying is necessary to locate the most direct line to Goat Island. Now my idea is that we should at once extend our line to Goat Island and announce the fact. But it is useless to talk of a route by the way of Benicia, first, because the ground is already occupied [by the California Pacific Railroad then underway to Sacramento], 2nd, because to cross the straits by bridge is so costly as to render it substantially impracticable. Besides, if the straits were not crossed by a bridge, a steamboat starting from here would reach Benicia as quickly if not quicker than you could go by rail and two ferries."

The associates moved quickly, as evidenced by the comment in the Sacramento *Union* of March 22, 1867, that the "Central Pacific Railroad filed in the office of the Secretary of State a preamble and resolution adopted by the board of directors expressing their intention to extend their road to Goat Island. The proposed route was thus outlined: Starting at Sacramento, proceeding on a line about two miles east of Freeport and Richland, between Walnut Grove and Mokelumne City, crossing the Mokelumne River at its south fork and the San Joaquin River via Antioch, to a point on Los Juntas Creek about three miles south of Pacheco, and thence to Goat Island."

It is not certain whether the Big Four actually intended to build this line to Goat Island, or whether they used the proposal to depress the price of the Western Pacific Railroad, then under construction from Sacramento to Oakland and San Jose via Stockton. However, one week later Leland Stanford and E. B. Crocker apparently were in San Francisco to acquire the Western Pacific and the California Central railroads.

On March 29, 1867, E. B. Crocker wrote Hopkins:

"I have been busy reading contracts and papers relating to matters here, so as to find out the snags, and have them got out of the way. So far as I have discovered any, the parties are confident that they can be removed. They are at work at it. I think we will prefer a new construction contract directly to ourselves and made by the present Board.

"Tevis told Stanford that Wilson [Col. C. L. Wilson of the California Central Railroad] or Pixley had made no arrangements with the Nav. Co. [California Steam Navigation Company] for money, that if there had been he would have known of it, that he had no talk with Wilson yet but probably would soon, that he thinks W. is trying other parties. S. [Stanford] told Tevis [Lloyd Tevis, a San Francisco promoter] that we would prefer to have the debt paid rather than take the rolling stock.

"McLaughlin has some trades to make before he can close with us [Western Pacific Railroad], so it may take some time before I can get back. Mills tells Stanford that we ought to own the Western & San Jose RR to have it all right, that the San Jose [Southern Pacific Railroad formerly called the San Francisco and San Jose Railroad] is the butt end of all railroads coming directly into San Francisco, that the owners of the San Jose don't know how to manage it, etc. Mills is director in the San Jose, and it looks like it was a feeler."

Judge Crocker again wrote Hopkins on April 1: "Yours of Saturday with inclosed draft of contract is rec'd. As I do not understand by your letter that you will refuse to unite in the purchase of the W.P.R.R. I shall go on with the trade, avoiding however incurring liabilities that cannot be met with the assets of the W.P.R.R. and with plenty of time to meet the payments with the assets.

"McLaughlin and Carr [previous owners of the W.P.R.R.] are hard at work clearing up difficulties and it would seem as though they were going to succeed. I am not so much struck after the thing as to overlook possible events. I am taking great pains in looking into matters and in drawing the papers, but still some matters may fail to ferret out everything. I am drawing the papers so as to provide for every event I can think of as likely to happen.

"Neither Stanford or I have seen Col. Wilson [California Central Railroad]. Tevis says that Pixley told him they were going to pay us off, but Tevis didn't have faith. Tevis don't know who they are negotiating with. I suppose he will not come to us until all other things fail."

And again on April 6 Judge Crocker sent a letter to Mark Hopkins: "Railroad matters are stewing and boiling here [San Francisco]. We have settled pretty much all the points with McLaughlin, but papers not signed yet; they are examining them. I hope to be able to go up this evening, but can't until Monday. Have Charles [Crocker] there [Sacramento] Tuesday morning to sign papers. I think we are making a big point in buying the WP. Nobody here suspects it. But RR & Steamboat combinations are working here. Some moneyed man or men . . . want to buy our judgt. vs Wilson and are negotiating for Oroville RR [California Northern Railroad], to pay cash for latter. We say if the party is the right sort, will work in harmony with us, clear of W we would sell out all we have in Cal. Central, Cal. & Oregon & in the judgt. They are not prepared to pay the judgt. today but expect to Monday. Luning [Nicholas Luning, a prominent capitalist of that day] would sell us today the Oroville RR & give long time, say 2 years at 1 p.c., that would effectually head off all parties trying to control that northern trade. If moneyed men go into that, then the purchase of WP is the key to that trade, unless they go in and build the

*Castle Peak (above) and American Peak (below) in
the late spring are still crowned with snow.*

Vallejo RR [California Pacific Railroad] and a road from Sacto. to Lincoln, a heavy load just to control that northern trade. I would give a good deal if Huntington could only be here for a few days to consult. It is a strong temptation to buy the Oroville RR and checkmate them all." [Central Pacific finally did buy both the California Pacific and the California Northern Railroad in the 1880's.]

During that same week, on April 6, 1867, Stanford also wrote Hopkins: "I telegraphed you yesterday for the amount of the judgment against Wilson, also for the acknowledgment of Tevis that he held it for our benefit. It seemed then that we were to be paid. Ralston [William C. Ralston, of the Bank of California] was to advance the money, but today it is to wait until Monday. Ralston will not disclose for whom he is acting. But he says he represents a party abundantly able to buy. I have been following up the thing and find the party had obtained the refusal of the Oroville RR [California Northern Railroad]. Emmett [probably C. Temple Emmet, a San Francisco attorney] tells me that they want the Oregon RR [California & Oregon Railroad] he thinks. I find from Ralston that he has investigated the assignment of the Oregon Co. to us of the lands and is advised that we have forfeited by non-compliance. [The land grant rights were later extended by another act of Congress.] Ralston is the agent. From various sources I conclude the Project embraces Wilson's Road, the Oroville Road and the Oregon Road with a project of building from Lincoln to Sacramento. There is an attempt at arrangement of the Steam Ship interests. It was supposed to have been accomplished, but yesterday afternoon there was found some obstacle, but today the matter is again being considered. Whether this has anything to do with the RR matters or not I cannot say. . . . Ralston says he thinks the arrangement will be injurious to us, but that he controls nothing and only pays out the money as directed. He did not say a word about the Oroville Road. I got this latter part from De Ro this morning who says that he only gave the refusal until yesterday. I of course take the ground that we want our money and want to build east and are content to let others do as they please. Luning told me that nothing less than $450,000 will buy the Oroville RR, that any less sum than that cannot prevent it from going into his hands. In other words it takes that sum to clear it. L. said he would give two years time for payment. I only pretend to give you the outline of what is said. Much of my information has been given confidentially and please guard all this as such. We want the money from Wilson but we don't want that northern business controlled and against us. In your dispatch of last night about the judgement you do not say anything about the receipt of Tevis. If you have not sent it please do so Monday."

Arrangements to purchase the Western Pacific were completed, and

E. B. Crocker took the papers to Sacramento to get the signatures of Charles Crocker and Mark Hopkins. But the ever cautious Hopkins, who held the power of attorney for Huntington, would not sign without consulting his absent partner. So Judge Crocker returned to San Francisco without their signatures, while Hopkins telegraphed Huntington for his decision:

STANFORD ARRANGED FOR WESTERN SUBJECT TO YOUR VOTE WHICH WILL CONTROL MINE. ANSWER YES OR NO IMMEDIATELY.

After Judge Crocker's return, Stanford wrote to Hopkins on April 12, somewhat testily:

"Yours of yesterday rec'd. The Judge has reported somewhat of the difficulties he encountered. His report took me somewhat by surprise. Before going to Sacramento to announce the result of negotiation, I agreed that it should be a trade if my associates approved. After submitting the matter I certainly thought the negotiation was approved, and when the Judge and I came down here we so stated, and proceeded at once upon investigations and statements of what was necessary to be done.

"One of the first things to be done was for McL. to get rid of the Houston Claim, and to do so he paid off $10,000 down and gave Carr's obligation for $12,500 more in thirty days or forfeit the $10,000. McL. has straightened other matters none of which he would or could very well have done except upon the assumption that if he complied with our terms the trade was definite and certain. We are in honor bound to stand by the trade and I certainly cannot do otherwise than make the trade good to McL. and shall in any event as far as in my power individually. But I do not doubt that Huntington will approve the trade, in which case we shall certainly have a good thing and I shall be relieved from embarrassment.

"If the trade is perfected we shall do as you suggest, have a schedule of assets."

That same day, Judge Crocker likewise wrote to Hopkins:

"We are waiting your action about the Western Pacific. I shall feel terribly mortified if after I have spent 2 weeks in arranging details of contract got McL. to settle up several matters he intended to contest, and pay out a good deal of money on it, to have it fall through because you and Charles [Crocker] were opposed to purchasing on any terms. It makes the biggest kind of fools of the Governor and I. But I have not the least doubt but that H. [Huntington] will say buy.

"In reading over the letters from him I brought down, I see how anxious he is to buy the northern roads, and yet he is not half as emphatic on that as on a San Francisco or Goat Island road.

"One point I want your view on, shall we buy out Wilson [California Central Railroad], or let Emmet and his friends buy him out, and we sell

*In the early winter of 1866, Donner
Lake lay sleeping below the snow-capped
summit where men were altering a wilderness reflected in the lake's placid mirror.*

out our interest to them or put it in with them jointly? Is it best in your opinion to get a friendly Co. to buy and build the northern line or we to do it ourselves? As soon as Emmet gets back the point will come up, so let me know. I am decidedly in favor of buying the WP & selling out all our interest in the northern line to a friendly Co. I fear we cannot carry both, and as the WP is the butt end of all the lines, and has a big slice of Govt. Bonds I prefer that. But if you should insist on carrying the northern line too, I will give it due consideration, thought I doubt the policy.

"It seems to me important that I remain here for a while to assist Stanford in these negotiations unless they are likely to last too long."

Five days later, on April 17, 1867, he again charged Hopkins: "I am very impatient to get back home, but as that telegram though unaccountably delayed, may come at any moment, I am for the present tied fast here. But I am putting in my time to good advantage in several matters.

"McLaughlin seems to take matters patiently, though I am afraid he will come across other parties who may talk him out of it.

"We have proposed to Emmett who has been requested by Wilson to see us about getting an extension of time, that we will give him until the 1st of July, if he will put up as collateral all the stock of the Yuba RR except the $28,000 held by Pixley, and the 100 2nd mortgage bonds. Then if he don't pay when due we have got the control in our hands. Emmett is to see Wilson about it."

A week had passed, and on April 19 Stanford again tried to induce Hopkins to move:

"Yours of the 17th rec'd this morning. We are waiting for answer from Huntington with such patience as we can command. If he fully understands that we get 20 miles completed road, rolling stock worth about $50,000 with no incumbrance but gov't bonds and that we get other value for our money, besides the advantages of gov't aid to build a road to San Francisco, I do not think we can hesitate to say yes. As to the matter of advances of money immediately it could be raised on the rolling stock piles up here and for which there is no immediate use. And that without interfering with our sources of loans for the CP. I am the more impatient because McLaughlin's cousin does not like the trade and would gladly break it up. I have to take up $60,000 on the 22nd but I have got it arranged to satisfaction by a new loan."

On that same day, Crocker rejoined the assault:

"Expecting as I do every moment to receive a telegram from you to close that trade, I still am waiting. Not altogether idle however, for I am pushing forward that matter of letters from capitalists.

"How long do you expect to have me wait here before you decide? It is now more than a week since I came down. It seems to me you might

Strobridge on the roof of the snow-gallery at Crested Peak.

View of Crested Peak from Grant's Butte.

as well telegraph me to go ahead, for there is no doubt that that will be Huntington's answer. As he wants us to buy out Wilson, there can be no doubt he will say yes to buying out McLaughlin, a matter he has been trying to do for a year past. What is the use then of keeping me waiting here and away from urgent business at home? I suggest therefore that as soon as you receive this you telegraph back immediately 'Go ahead' and we will close the trade at once. Do it, and if Huntington's reply should induce you or Charles to recede, Stanford and I will agree to take the whole thing off your hands, and give you our personal guarantee secured by all we have to save you harmless, you to assign all your interest in the trade to us. Now that's fair. I do it to bring the thing to a focus and not remain sitting here like a fool with nothing to say. By the way, has it occurred to you what a ridiculous position Stanford and I will be placed in if you should stop the trade? I do not see any other way left for us but to tell McL. here, rather than you shall be fooled now the thing has gone so far, if you will take us in place of the whole, we will close the trade in that way. If we should, you and Charles, in less than 6 months would be willing to pay us well to be let in. But the shortest and best way is to telegraph us 'Go ahead' without waiting any longer, and let it drop into our hands if you should afterwards recede."

No telegram arrived from Hopkins, and Judge Crocker went to Sacramento to continue the argument at close range. Stanford, beleaguered in San Francisco, wrote Judge Crocker on April 22 concerning some apparent new developments:

"Your dispatch saying 'Charles & Hopkins opposed to any outside operation by either of us' rec'd. It is not a question of an outside operation by either you or myself except as they may force us into the position. We have made a trade with their consent in which they with us were to be equally interested, now they are unwilling to carry out the trade. I consider all are bound in honor to stand by that trade. But certainly you and I cannot escape in honor if we can legally. That McLaughlin has assumed obligations in consequence of the trade more strongly urges us to go on and perfect it as far as in our power, or suffer an imputation that we can't afford to bear, however good we may know our intentions to have been. It is not a question of outside operation by us, but it is whether they by refusing to carry out the trade leave us with an operation on hand in which they have no interest. For my part I shall carry out the trade as far as may be in my power.

"As McLaughlin must on the first of the month pay Houston $12,500 or forfeit the $10,000 already paid, the time in which to determine what is to be done is short. I shall tomorrow look for the means to carry out our undertaking. This is necessary in any event, though it should finally be decided that we will all go on together."

Crocker evidently returned to San Francisco and, on April 29, again wrote to Hopkins:

"Yours and Charles' letters of last Friday were rec'd, but yours I did not get until Saturday evening after the boat left.

"Carr interposed some difficulties when I first came down, but they were soon disposed of. Before signing the papers we insist that Houston shall be got entirely out of the way. They had made a contract with him by which he sold out on certain terms. Saturday they went to pay him off and comply with the terms but he claimed that they were to do certain things which were not in the contract and that matter has to be arranged. Now you ask, 'why don't you say the trade is at an end because of these things?' I am inclined to do so if we can honorably, because I don't like to go on with a trade, even as advantageous as I deem this to be, while you and Charles are so strongly opposed, though I deem your fears groundless. But they waited patiently for us to hear from Huntington, and we are in honor to give them a reasonable time to clear away their obstacles. They have a clear distinct contract with Houston, and he cannot escape it, but during the delay, caused by us, he has probably heard that we intend to buy out, and he thinks he can squeeze more out of McLaughlin. I understand from Huntington's letters that if we can buy the franchises of the WP without paying money it would be well. That is substantially the trade, for all the money payments are for property consisting of RR materials delivered over to us as soon as the trade is closed. For the franchise we let McLaughlin keep the lands."

More than a month elapsed, and on June 8 Judge Crocker wrote to Hopkins that the deal was finally consummated:

"We have finally completed the trade with the WP. The papers are all signed, the stock has all been transferred except that of Mr. Dooley who is absent at Stockton, but will assign when he gets back. The directors now stand Leland Stanford (President), Mark Hopkins (Treasurer), A. P. Stanford, E. B. Crocker, Charles Crocker, C. W. Sanger (Secretary), Dooley. When Dooley returns he will resign and C. P. Huntington appointed in his place.

"A. P. Stanford was appointed so that we could make up a full Board here, until matters are settled down. Monday we settle up and arrange the claims and take poss. of the property. I hope to go up Monday night but may be detained until Tuesday. We have telegraphed to Huntington that the trade is closed and to pay the interest on the 211 bonds. So far all seems right and I think it will come out right."

Now affairs once again began to move, and on June 18, 1867, Stanford hurriedly wrote to Hopkins:

With a free day in his heavy schedule, Strobridge
takes the family boating on Donner Lake.

"Carr called to me this morning and said Mr. Conness thought if we did not intend to apply for State aid on the WP that it was desirable to say so to the public. As things are now agitated I have no idea we will ask for aid. I think it best to take the ground that we are abundantly able to build the road with present means and that we won't ask for that but what is absolutely necessary. I expect the Judge down tonight. Telegraph early tomorrow morning your views and Charley's too if he is in town. No time to add more."

A. N. Towne, general manager of both the Central Pacific and the Southern Pacific for many years, later stated that there may have been differences of opinion at the outset between these four builders of the Central Pacific, but after carefully weighing circumstances and conditions surrounding a business proposition, they always voted unanimously.

"The Central Pacific Railroad Company have purchased the Lincoln and Marysville Railroad [Yuba Railroad], and will complete the work without delay," the Shasta *Courier* announced on September 28 of that year. "The purchase of this railroad was recorded with the Secretary of State in Sacramento one month later on October 28."

The California Central Railroad, from Folsom to Lincoln, came into their possession at about the same time, and that purchase was recorded four days earlier. The stage now was set for acquisition of the fourth and final portion of the proposed rail line to run from the Oregon border to the Arizona border. This was the California and Oregon Railroad, which was not yet under construction, but which held land grants in Northern California.

The California & Oregon Railroad, incorporated in San Francisco on June 30, 1865, was to extend north from Marysville to the Oregon boundary. It was capitalized at fifteen million dollars, aided by land grants through an act of Congress, July 25, 1866. The Big Four, as individuals, acquired this railroad in November. However, it was not until January 16, 1868, that formal notice was filed with the secretary of state to consolidate the C. & O. with the Yuba Railroad.

A company that just two years before had appeared to be in serious danger of collapse now was the major railroad power in the state of California.

TWELVE

FORTY FEET OF SNOW:
WINTER, *1867–68*

In August, 1867, with the last of the summit tunnels completed, thousands of workers were released for the drive to the Nevada state line. Now the job of hauling locomotives, cars, and iron over the summit began.

Construction worker Partridge has left a chronicle of that effort:

"We had hoped that the storms would hold off until late, to enable us to get through with the grading east of the summit, but the heavy fall of snow came on early and drove the crews out of the mountains. There were about 4,000 men working there in the mountains, 3,000 of them Chinese, and they all had to get out. Most of the Chinese came to Truckee and they filled up all the old buildings and sheds that were in Truckee. With the heavy fall of snow the old barn collapsed and killed four Chinese. A good many were frozen to death. There was a dance at Donner Lake at a hotel, and a sleigh load of us went up from Truckee and on our return, about 9 a.m. next morning, we saw something under a tree by the side of the road, its shape resembling that of a man. We stopped and found a frozen Chinese. As a consequence, we threw him in the sleigh with the rest of us, and took him into town and laid him out by the side of a shed and covered him with a rice mat, the most appropriate thing for the laying out of a Celestial.

"In November, 1867, the Company hauled an engine [overland] from the Summit, or near the Summit, to Truckee, with seven or eight flat cars and set them up there. They also hauled over 20 miles of iron. The ties were handy. In the winter, early in 1868, they also hauled over from Cisco two more engines and about ten flat cars and set them up at Truckee.

"In the meantime, they had started the bridge on the Second Crossing of the Truckee, and the gang that I was with was putting up some buildings in Truckee and shipping the lumber from there as fast as it was sawed. That bridge was a two span bridge of 150 feet each span. The First Crossing was a 204-foot span, with arches. The Third Crossing was also a 204-foot span, the same as the Cascade Bridges, and was put up in February and March.

"Some time in March, we (the gang that I was with at that time under M. J. Healey) were sent to frame the bridge at the Fourth Crossing. After we had framed the bridge we were sent back to put the arches on the Third Crossing. That was seven miles from the Fourth Crossing and one night about 9 p.m. there came word for us to come to the Fourth Crossing and help to raise the bridge the next day, the occasion being a heavy rise in the river. We got there at 3 a.m., went out on our bridge, got our tackle and some bars and carried them seven miles, and arrived there before 7 a.m. To make a long story short, we raised that bridge and had it swinging by 5 o'clock that evening, then walked back home; a good day's work for a man."

Both Charles Crocker and J. H. Strobridge later gave similar accounts of that winter in the Truckee area: "The total snowfall of the season was about forty feet," Crocker said, "and the depth of hard, settled snow in midwinter was eighteen feet on a level in Summit Valley and Donner Pass, over which we hauled on sleds track material for forty miles of railroad, three locomotives, and forty cars from Cisco to Donner Lake, where all was reloaded on wagons and hauled over miry roads to Truckee, a total distance of twenty-eight miles, at enormous cost. In this way the road was forced to the east slope of the Sierra Nevadas."

According to Strobridge's report, crews were at work many miles ahead of the line. "It was necessary," he said, "to have the heavy work in Palisade Canyon done in advance of the main force, and 3,000 men with 400 horses and carts were sent to that point, a distance of 300 miles in advance of the track. Hay, grain and all supplies for the men and horses had to be hauled by teams, over the deserts for that great distance. Water for men and animals was hauled at times forty miles."

Crocker's report indicated that twenty-five saw mills were constructed around Truckee to saw lumber for the line through Nevada.

At the close of 1867, the end of track had moved past Cisco, over the summit, and two miles beyond to Tunnel 12; sixteen miles of track had been laid after completion of the last tunnel in August. Heavy snow then halted track laying east of Tunnel 12 toward Truckee, where the line was being built westward and eastward. Such progress was made that on December 13, 1867, the first construction train, moving east from Truckee,

Snow became a major problem in movement. The Bucker plow, seen at work on this page and at the bottom of the facing page, required several wood-burning locomotives to push it and an army of shovels to clear the way. It was later replaced by the more efficient rotary plow, which could eat up in one hour the distance that previously took a whole day.

poked its nose across the Nevada line. Twenty-four miles of track had been hauled over the summit and laid in the Truckee region from Cold Stream to Camp 24, near the state line. But there still remained a seven-mile gap east of Tunnel 12 in the Donner Lake area, where crews could not return to work until the weather broke in the spring. Also, the rails between Cisco and summit, having been hastily laid without ballast, had to be abandoned for the winter; for the second winter Cisco remained the railhead.

By the end of 1867, a total of thirty-nine miles of track had been laid, and all summit tunnels had been completed. The roadbed had been graded for twenty more miles, beyond the state line into Nevada, and was awaiting the iron and raising of the bridges across the Truckee, to be completed in the spring of 1868.

Assistant engineer Joseph M. Graham, who was in charge of construction from the state line to Reno, later recalled:

"While on the work along the Truckee River, the Indians used to come into our camp. The squaws brought in berries and things. One day an Indian came to the cabin we had and wanted whiskey. He rolled on the floor and made out that he was in great pain. I came in with Mr. Montague and yelled at the Indian and he got up and was all right. He left.

"This cabin we had was used as my office. It was 200 yards east of the California-Nevada state line . . . set back in a little ravine out of the winds. We passed the winter there in '67 and '68. And while on that location, my wife became fairly well acquainted with Mrs. Strobridge. They became quite chummy and that resulted in an arrangement that my wife would live in the superintendent's car, when it was built finally. I had one of the rooms in it for an office."

Graham went on to say that the Big Four and other officers of the road were active in numerous outside projects, but not always successfully. One such enterprise was an ice business:

"When they wanted to start such a project, they usually selected me to make the survey and do the construction. They organized the Summit Ice Company for filling their ice houses. They built the ice houses at some little lakes south of Summit Valley and struggled for about three winters to make ice, but the snow came so heavy that when a few inches of ice formed, the fallen snow would cover it and then they discovered that the ice would thaw, and so they scraped the snow off and after struggling for three years getting no marketable ice, they found that it was an unprofitable business.

"During that time, I had learned that the temperature down the Truckee River near Boca was some 20 degrees lower than it was registered at Summit. I then made surveys of Prosser Creek near Boca and found that we could build a dam 35 feet in height. It would give them a reservoir of 42 acres, which was more than sufficient for their ice house. The Summit Ice House immediately abandoned all their works in Summit Valley and constructed ice works at Prosser Creek.

"They were also interested in getting out wood for use of the railroad and they chose me to make a survey for a flume to bring the wood in down the Truckee River to near Truckee Station. I had experience in building flumes in order to bring wood down to the Truckee River. Strobridge and other railroad men got interested in a saw mill near Prosser Creek and they were wondering how best to get the lumber down from there. They selected me to locate the flume line to transport the lumber from the saw mills some 15 miles up Prosser Creek.

"The conditions given me were that this flume should carry 14-inch square timbers 40 feet long. We were all inexperienced in that line of work, but I figured out curves for this flume which I believed would carry the timber successfully and when they first tested it, these 14-inch timbers came down to Prosser Creek Station very successfully."

Portions of a report issued in New York by Collis P. Huntington on August 1, 1867, give, as he put it, "the character of the work, its progress, resources, earnings and future prospects" of the company, which would soon, in 1868, begin the dash across the Nevada desert.

COST OF CONSTRUCTION AND EQUIPMENT

"Ten thousand men, mostly Chinese laborers, and 1,300 teams are now employed on the work, the heavy parts of which are in a forward state; and it is confidently believed that in January next the locomotive will be traversing the plains of Nevada.

"The original estimated cost of building the road across the Sierra was but slightly above that of the most expensive railroads in the country where the right of way had to be purchased at considerable cost. Up to the 1st of January last [1867] the Central Pacific Company had expended in building the ninety-four miles in operation, together with about a third of the preparation upon twenty-five miles additional, and for a liberal equipment of rolling stock, nearly $15,000,000 [$14,558,714]. Fifty-three miles additional, or about one hundred and fifty in all, will, it is confidently expected, be running by October next, which brings the road to the comparatively smooth ground. The total construction cost of this mountain section will be about $15,000,000, or at the rate of $100,000 per mile. The rest of the distance to Salt Lake City, five hundred and seventy-five miles, can be constructed for about $60,000 per mile. The difference in the prices of labor and iron, sufficiently accounts for the increase upon the original estimate. About $5,000,000 more will have been expended by midsummer for labor, rails, and equipments, most of which is either on the other side or enroute. The bulk of the engineering difficulties, it will be observed, has already been overcome; and by far the most costly and rugged resistance left behind. Rails are already being laid east of the summit, ready for the advance when the tunnel is opened.

SURVEYS AND ESTIMATES FOR THE EXTENSION TO SALT LAKE

"The general route for the road after leaving the Big Bend of the Truckee River is northeastwardly to the Sink of the Humboldt River, which stream it follows for upwards of 250 miles, through a fertile valley, abounding in wood and water, to Humboldt Wells, 507 miles distant from Sacramento; to this point the route has been officially designated by the Secretary of the Interior. From Humboldt Wells the country has been thoroughly explored to Salt Lake City, in all directions. Two practicable lines were found, one running round the south end of Salt Lake, and the other skirting the north end. The former, however, passes through a rough and desert country destitute of wood and water, and involves, besides a longer distance, the necessity of crossing the famous Mud Flats of the Great Salt Lake Desert, which would require piling for 25 miles. The more northerly route proved to be very favorable in alignment and grades, and with plenty of wood and water, both for fuel and construction. More than half the distance can be built with grades varying from 0 to 25 feet per mile, while none of them exceed 75 feet per mile, for short distances.

"The line, as surveyed from the Eastern Base of the Sierras to Salt Lake, gives such a favorable location that it is confidently believed the remainder of the line can be built on such easy terms as to keep the Company's interest liabilities down to the ratio of the first 150 miles, or less than two and a half per cent upon the total cost. The assistance from the national government for this distance is $32,000 per mile; while a great proportion of the distance can be built for $50,000 per mile. . . .

"This will give the Company a Great Trunk Line across the Continent, following the isothermal belt, nearly 800 miles in length, at a cost for construction and equipment of less than sixty millions of dollars; but worth in earning power a very much greater sum.

"The Company hopes to increase its force of ten thousand men to fifteen thousand during the present season, when progress over the plains will be very rapid."

In an "Exhibit of Earnings and Expenses" for 1867, Huntington showed that the line already in operation was, to say the least, a money-maker, and would seem to justify the years of struggle and uncertainty that had created it:

1867

Month	Gross Earnings	Operating Expenses	Net Earnings
January	$ 38,169.22	$ 21,564.79	$ 16,604.43
February	51,831.38	23,867.79	27,963.59
March	60,029.14	20,115.16	39,913.98
April	81,156.31	21,242.76	59,913.55
May	98,828.59	23,184.44	75,644.15
June	121,702.59	22,689.53	98,013.01
July	174,812.05	30,973.89	143,838.16
(est.) August	181,000.00	30,885.00	149,180.00
" September	200,400.00	35,000.00	175,400.00
" October	212,109.00	37,000.00	175,109.00

THIRTEEN

HEAVEN BEFORE
AND HELL BEHIND: *1868*

WHILE GRADING GANGS and track-layers attacked the Nevada desert east of Reno, Arthur Brown, superintendent of bridges and buildings, began constructing snowsheds to shield the tracks in winter. Brown wrote later of this undertaking:

"It was not until June, 1868, that construction began. Owing to the short season in which the work had to be done (less than five months), it was decided to cover all the cuts and the points where the road crossed the great avalanches beyond the summit, with the idea that the high embankments on the road could be kept clear of snow.

"As the road was then rapidly progressing up the valley of the Humboldt, it became a matter of the most vital importance that the sheds should be so far finished that the supplies and building materials for construction ahead should not be interrupted.

"We therefore had to gather men from all quarters and pay high wages —carpenters $4 per day, and suitable laborers about $2.50 to $3. We employed about 2,500 men, with six trains with locomotives distributing material.

"The expense was considerably increased by the fact that we had to keep the road clear for the traffic, which was great, owing to the large amount of building material forwarded to the front, and to avoid accidents, which consumed about 30 per cent of the time. Besides, we had, by commencing early in the spring, to shovel from 6 to 8 feet of snow before we could put in foundations for sheds.

"Two types of construction were adopted; the shed for localities where the weight of the snow had to be supported, and the gallery for such places as were exposed to the terrible avalanches of snow and ice from the steep and rocky slopes. Some of these galleries extend back up the slope of the mountain several hundred feet from the center line of the road. The galleries were built along the side of the mountains where the slope of the roof conforms with that of the mountain, so the snow can pass over easily. In other places massive masonry walls were built across ravines to prevent the snow from striking the sheds at right angles. It was necessary to build sheds and galleries of enormous strength by bracing them against the mountain side, framing them and interlacing them with beams and cross beams.

"The snow sheds and galleries were finished in the fall of 1869. In them was used 65,000,000 feet of timber and 900 tons of bolts and spikes, etc. The total length of sheds and galleries when finished was about 37 miles, at a cost of over $2 million. [For several years the loss from fires was considerable, and several miles of sheds were burned down and had to be rebuilt. In 1870 water trains were installed to fight fires and for sprinkling down the sheds twice a week, thus helping to protect them from fire.]

"On the east side of the summit of the Sierra where the snow lay in drifts 80 feet deep, it was impossible to build snow sheds. Under such pressure even the best selected timber of the mountains snapped. Sheds were crushed in, requiring constant shoveling of snow during the remainder of winter. It was therefore decided to build heavy retaining walls and to fill in the back of the wall with rock and other convenient material, forming a slope or incline about equal to that of the mountainside."

At the beginning of 1868, a gap of twenty-three miles still separated Truckee and Cisco. Of this segment, sixteen miles had been laid from Cisco to the summit the previous fall and abandoned without ballast when the heavy snows came. This stretch had to be cleared by hand because the hard-packed, ice-cemented drifts defied the plows. There was no time to wait until it melted, for seven miles still awaited the rail-layers.

Charles Crocker announced as a New Year's resolution "a mile a day for every working day in 1868." Apparently the other associates were of the same mind. On January 26, 1868, Collis P. Huntington wrote to Crocker, "I consider it of the most vital importance that we build to the Wasatch Mountains for many reasons which I have given before. I would build the road in the cheapest possible manner then go back and improve it at once, because the Union Pacific have built the cheapest kind of road."

In January the Secretary of the Interior approved the proposed Central Pacific line from the Big Bend of the Truckee River to Humboldt Wells. On January 20 the land was withdrawn from preemption, private entry, or sale.

In February, 1868, the Sacramento *Union,* which had been one of the

*Snowsheds and galleries of enormous strength were built
to withstand the heavy snow. By 1869
they were completed, using 65 million feet
of timber and covering over 37 miles.*

strongest supporters of the Central Pacific and its builders, suddenly became one of the bitterest foes of the railroad company, and remained so until the newspaper changed hands a few years later. A sample of the new policy is an item of March 10, 1868: "The Central Pacific—poor, starving, frozen thing which the credulous public warmed into life by its charities—is about to prove a very Egyptian asp and sting the hand that nourished it with a more deadly venom than slave lords ever possessed." Among the many reasons for this break, apparently, was the newspaper's failure to get the printing business of the railroad. Instead, H. S. Crocker & Company, a firm in which Charles Crocker was interested, did all the printing for the railroad. Huntington in later years deplored this action and stated that had he been consulted, he would have recommended giving the business to the newspaper.

With or without the newspaper's support, the line pushed ahead into Nevada. Joseph M. Graham, engineer, told of laying out the new townsite of Reno:

"As I was moving my outfit forward to Wadsworth after having been placed in charge as Engineer of Construction on the building of the road eastward from the California-Nevada State line, I measured and staked out what was later to be the city of Reno. On the first day of April, 1868, I set the first stake of the survey of this boundary for Reno on the bank of the English Ditch.

"The original townsite comprised about 35 acres extending for about a quarter of a mile between the Truckee River as the south boundary and English Ditch as the north boundary. The site was donated to the Contract and Finance Company, Central Pacific contractors, by a Mr. Lake who owned a bridge across the river and a short toll road. With the establishing of a station at that point, Mr. Lake planned to profit from the tolls collected from travelers over his bridge and road leading to Virginia City, Washoe, and Carson country, I understand he collected more than $60,000 in tolls during the year and a half before the Virginia and Truckee railroad was built and opened for traffic in December, 1869.*

"The townsite itself was named for Jesse Lee Reno, a Civil War general. Lots in the townsite were sold at auction. As Reno was to be the trade center for the Virginia, Washoe and Carson country, there was a rush for town property and some of the choice 25-foot lots sold for $1,200."

On May 1, 1868, the Central Pacific line from Reno to Truckee was completed, and the crews were working their way back into the Sierra, clearing the snow so that the track-layers could re-lay the track between

---

*The Virginia and Truckee railroad was completed to Carson City, Nevada, in 1869, but did not reach Reno until 1872.

Hauling timber along the Truckee River at Boca, 127 miles from Sacramento.

Cisco and Tunnel 12, and complete the last seven-mile gap to open the line through to Reno.

"I notice that you write that everybody is in favor of a railroad until they get it built and then everyone is against it unless the railroad company will carry them and theirs for nothing," Huntington wrote Hopkins on April 14, 1868. No doubt Hopkins had alerted Huntington to the change in policy by the Sacramento *Union*. Huntington continued, "I have about made up my mind that it is about as well to fight them on all the railroads in the state as on our road, as it is not much more fight and there is more pay. I wish you would send me the names of all the railroads in California, the length of them, and the names of the officers, stating starting point and terminus of each."

"Keep right on laying rails just as though you did not care for the snow, but we're bound to get to Weber Canyon before the Union Company," said Huntington in a letter to Crocker of April 15, 1868, "and if you do that I will forever pray that you will have your reward."

Surveying parties, working well in advance of construction crews, had finished staking the line; and the maps were drawn. On May 15, 1868, the Central Pacific filed with the Secretary of the Interior a map of the definite location of their proposed line from Humboldt Wells to Weber Canyon. The Secretary's approval was needed before the construction crews could start clearing the grade in advance of the track-layers.

On June 15, 1868, the gap between Cisco and Truckee was finally closed. Three days later the first passenger train eastbound left Sacramento for Reno—a distance of 154 miles—and a reporter for both the *Alta California* in San Francisco and the *Territorial Enterprise* in Virginia City, Nevada, was aboard:

"On June 17th, learning that the Pacific Railroad Co. was to run their first through train across the mountains on the following day, we hastened to secure a ticket from the agent and learning that the train was to depart at 6½ A.M., in the morning, we were on hand early. . . . The train consisted of one box car well stocked with freight, one baggage car also well filled with freight and the U.S. mails, and three of the railroad Co's new cars just out of the shop.

"The locomotive engine that was to draw our train up the steep slopes of the mountain was the fine *Antelope* from the work shops of McKay and Aldus and she was in fine shape and had just been overhauled and painted and presented a pretty picture with her bright red wheels, walnut cab, shiny bright brasswork and a picture of an Antelope painted on the headlight case. Hank Small, our engineer, was on hand oiling up and looking over his iron steed with a critical eye to see that all was well. Our time being now short we took our seat in the cars and shortly afterward there was a shriek from the locomotive whistle and we pulled slowly out amid the shouts of the crowd that had gathered to see us off.

"After skirting the shores of Lake Sutter we proceeded out the "B" St. levee some three miles when we came to the fine new bridge across the American River. After slowly crossing that stream we headed due East and our first stop is at Junction [now called Roseville] where the line crosses the line of the California Central RR from Folsom. After a brief stay we proceeded on our way and now the mountains appeared so close that it seemed that we could put our hand out of the window and touch them, and the snow on the mountains could be plainly seen. . . . Now we enter the foothills and we commence to ascend more rapidly, the great mountains before us seem to sink down until we lose sight of them altogether and we do not see the snow fields again for a long time.

"The engine blows and wheezes, with short, sharp aspirations and the feeling of weight as we lean back in our seat tells us that we are ascending a steep and increasing grade.

"Newcastle, Auburn (a pretty little and somewhat active place), Clipper Gap and New England Mills, all more or less important mining and trading posts are passed and at 9:50 a.m. we have ascended 2,448 feet and reach Colfax, fifty-four miles from Sacramento, where stage roads lead off to Grass Valley, Nevada City and other mining towns. . . .

"Soon after passing Colfax the cars pass on a high embankment around Cape Horn and nervous passengers begin to look around anxiously peering with evident trepidation into the depths below. Eight miles from Colfax we pass the mining town of "Secret Town" and look back into the valley from an elevation of 2,985 feet. Up and up, onward we climbed skyward. At sixty-seven miles from Sacramento we look down on the well nigh exhausted placers of Dutch Flat. Two miles further on we reach Alta, at an elevation of 3,625 feet above the sea. . . .

"Passing Shady Run station we reach the first tunnel, 500 feet long, seventy-five miles from Sacramento, and 4,500 feet above the sea. The mountains are growing more rugged and the snow levels come down to the road. We are in the heart of the Sierras, a barren, dreary desolate country. At Emigrant Gap we meet the down train eighty-four miles from Sacramento and the road is open before us at last. . . .

"Chinese are swarming all along the road. They have nearly finished their work in this vicinity and are packing their traps preparatory to passing on over the summit into the great interior basin of the continent.

"One hundred and two miles from Sacramento we stand 6,800 feet above the sea. Two miles more and the cars reach the entrance of the great summit tunnel, 1,659 feet in length. We have scaled the great Sierras at last and a plus ultra might be written on the granite walls of the great tunnel before us. We are 7,043 feet above the sea.

"A swarm of Chinese are busy at the other end of the tunnel shoveling away the snow, which has come down in great slides bringing with it huge granite boulders upon the tracks. The water pours down in torrents from the numberless crevices and seams in the granite walls and roof of the long, dark, cavernous tunnel, but we struggle through on foot and anxiously inquire after the prospect of getting through.

"Two or three hours will clear the tracks. We wait with what patience we may and at four o'clock the prolonged whistle of the good locomotive *Antelope* which has drawn us up the steep slopes of the Sierra is heard. 'All aboard', shouts the conductor, George Wood, who has had the honor of taking the first passenger train across the mountain, and the train moves slowly on. A halt for another slide, another start, another halt, and so we go slowly and carefully. The snow banks come down so close to the track that the eaves of the car rake them on either side.

"We have descended 600 feet and as we emerge from the last one the conductor exclaims: 'By heavens, we are over the mountains. This is new road built this summer and we will have no more snow slides'. It is true, indeed; the mighty task is accomplished at last after years of toil and the expenditure of millions of money. Words cannot describe it, we will not attempt to do so.

"And now the train at accelerated speed moves downward the valley of the Truckee. The steam is shut off, the brakes put on and as the Eagle sets his wings and floats . . . [we roll] swiftly and smoothly down the mountains into the great basin of Nevada.

"The road winds around the precipitous mountainside, almost encircling Donner Lake as it descends, and following around a long canyon, making a circuit of seven miles to gain not more than a quarter of a mile, we reach the outlet of the lake. Now we descend rapidly on one of the most beautiful, smooth and solid roads on the continent into the romantic valley of the Truckee. As the first through passenger train sweeps down the eastern slopes of the Sierras, John [meaning the Chinese laborer] comprehending fully the importance of the event, loses his natural appearance of stolidity and indifference and welcomes with the swinging of his broad brimmed hat and loud, uncouth shouts the iron horse and those that he brings with him.

"John with his patient toil, directed by American energy and backed by American capital, has broken down the great barrier at last and opened over it the greatest highway yet created for the march of commerce and civilization around the globe. . . ."

Now that the end was in sight, both Stanford and Charles Crocker spent most of their time in Nevada and Utah in order to speed construction.

From the base of the Sierra, Reno lies before the long desert.

Freight wagons await loading at the Reno Depot, shortly after the line opened in 1868.

Stanford journeyed to Salt Lake City five times in 1868 in search of man-power. On June 9, 1868, he wrote Hopkins from Salt Lake City:

"We have been pretty industrious and at last it appears as though we may get help from President Young [Brigham Young of the Mormon Church] without waiting until he can man the work he has undertaken for the U. Pacific.

"I start tomorrow morning with Mr. Gray [Geo. E. Gray, consulting engineer for the C.P.] to examine Weber canyon. To make the arrange-ment will cost big money or a big contract. I am inclined to make an arrangement by which Brigham's son shall undertake to furnish the men and to help push the work. . . .

"Brigham was cold and close, but I have I think got pretty near to him. He and everybody here was dead set for the southern route. How to meet this bothered me a good deal, but this afternoon being pressed I was able to find good reasons why they would be most benefited by the northern route. They do not seem, any of them, to be aware of the location from Humboldt Wells to the north end of the Lake [the survey already accomplished by the C.P.]. I have not thought it advisable to enlighten them.

"Col. Seymour [of the Union Pacific] told me they expect to be at the mouth of Weber by the first of January. They lay track night and day.

"Have Charley [Crocker] double his energy and do what is necessary to secure what labor is required to push the road to its utmost. Anything less than the utmost that can be done will likely end in defeat and, fore-warned as we are, anything less than the utmost that can be done will merit it."

"It is all important we build to Weber Canyon, we all understand that," Huntington wrote Stanford on June 15, 1868, "but I have been sorely troubled about iron. It sometimes seems as though the fates were against us from the mills that have burned and broke, hands striking, etc. But all great enterprises of this kind must have their mishaps. I only hope the Union may have as many as we do."

Meanwhile, work progressed in Nevada, as engineer J. M. Graham recounted:

"In the spring of 1868, I was given charge as Engineer on Construction of the work from the Cal-Nevada state line on east past Reno. After measuring and staking out the new town of Reno on the first day of April, 1868, we went on to Wadsworth. We had a number of miles of rather difficult construction, including rock work west of Wadsworth. I might add right here, I set the stakes where the town of Wadsworth is on the first day of July, 1868. We did many things at that time without consuming any drawing paper.

"For instance, Charles Crocker came to this town site of Wadsworth and with him we walked over the ground and after about one-half hour located the site of the engine house and station buildings for Wadsworth, which became the sub-terminal. I then made a detailed location of this yard and town site and it was rapidly built."

The Union Pacific by this time was coming west at full speed. Both lines were awake to future benefits that every additional mile would mean, and from all sides came the demand for haste. In their effort to meet this demand and to acquire mileage each for itself, the Union Pacific and the Central Pacific levied on every available resource.

"A humorous incident occurred when we got east of Reno," Graham continued. "The Central Pacific found it desirable to increase the grading forces considerably so that they brought several hundred Chinese direct from China and organized them into construction gangs. The Piute Indians got among these Chinese and told them some big stories about enormous snakes out on that desert large enough that they could swallow a Chinaman easily. That alarmed these Chinamen to the extent that four or five hundred took their belongings and struck out to return direct to Sacramento. Crocker & Company had spent quite a little money to secure them and they sent men on horseback after them. These men handled these Chinamen like a cowboy would cattle and herded most of them back again. These Chinamen kind of quieted down, and after nothing happened and they never saw any of the snakes, they forgot about them."

From New York, Huntington wrote to Crocker on July 1, 1868:

"There has left this port in all up to this time, 60,146 tons of rails. I shall continue to ship on fast ships until I have on the way 90,000 to 100,000 tons. I think all the iron that we lay on the Central Pacific (except for repairs) will be laid between this and the first of next February. So work on as though Heaven were before you and Hell behind you."

With the same urgent reasoning, Huntington wrote Stanford on July 17, 1868, "Hurry up with all possible speed to reach within 300 miles of Echo Canyon, as it is all important that we make that point." Progress of the track-layers was picking up so that in one month the line reached Wadsworth, thirty-five miles beyond Reno. The first service to that point was announced on July 22, 1868.

By the time the road reached Wadsworth, surveys had been made far into Utah, and the Central Pacific builders knew exactly what was ahead of them. The mountains through which the grade had until now been driven provided a boundless supply of pure water for all purposes; timbers and boards for ties, bridges, and other structures; wood for use as locomotive fuel; and rock for retaining walls and other masonry.

The country east of Wadsworth was a desert and would contribute

Indians come down to the Reno station to watch a train depart.

nothing to construction of the railroad. With the exception of a few cords of wood from stunted pine and juniper trees, fuel would have to be hauled from the Sierra. There was not a coal bed anywhere on the line of the Central Pacific. There was not a tree that would yield a board for more than 500 miles along that desert section of the road. Beyond the Truckee and Humboldt rivers there was no water. Tunnels, bored into the hills by the Central Pacific in an effort to develop small springs, may still be seen in the mountains east of Wadsworth. Thousands of dollars were spent here and farther east in well-drilling. When water was located, it was carefully protected and piped over miles of desert to the rail line. Most of the water used in desert construction had to be hauled in water trains to the end of track, and from that point in tank wagons to graders working in advance of construction. About 3,000 men, working 300 miles in advance of the track to Palisade Canyon, were supplied by wagon teams, that crossed waterless stretches of desert up to 40 miles long.

The remaining forces handled the grading from Wadsworth east. Ties were hauled from the Sierra, hundreds of miles into the desert. Canvas towns, springing up overnight in sandy wastes where "a jack-rabbit had to carry a canteen and haversack," lived but a few days, disappeared, and reappeared elsewhere as the speedway for the iron horse forged its way eastward.

The *Alta California* pictured such a town in motion: "Camp equipage, work shops, boarding house, offices, and in fact the big settlement literally took up its bed and walked. The place that knew it at morning knew it no more at night. It was nearly ten miles off and where was a busy town of 5,000 inhabitants in the morning, was a deserted village site at night, while a smooth, well built, compact road bed for traveling stretched from the morning site to the evening tarrying place."

The work in Palisade Canyon was done with great dispatch. One twelve-mile stretch through the canyon was graded in six weeks and another, of five miles, in three weeks, a rate that wins the respect of today's builders.

In the interests of speed, a force of engineers went ahead to make location surveys for a distance of about one hundred miles west from present-day Ogden, Utah. A contract was let to local Mormon residents to grade this segment of the line so that the track-layers would lose no time. About a carload of supplies and materials was transported by wagons across the desert from Wadsworth to Promontory, on the northern rim of the Great Salt Lake, reportedly at a cost of $5,400. The grading was completed under the contract, and the roadbed and supplies were ready when the track reached that point from the west.

By August 21, 1868, the road was open and operating to Browns,

Nevada, after forty-six miles of iron had been laid from Wadsworth in one month, an average of one and one-half miles a day. While the track-layers increased the tempo of their advance across the desert, many miles to the rear other crews installed facilities necessary to operation of the railroad.

In August, 1868, the Big Four added yet another railroad to the growing list. To obtain a franchise to bring their railroad into Oakland, they purchased from A. A. Cohen a majority of the stock of the Oakland Railroad & Ferry Company (also called the San Francisco & Oakland Railroad), which operated a ferry from the foot of Pacific Street in San Francisco to San Antonio (East Oakland), across the Bay).

In September, the railroad commissioners journeyed to inspect the new track. Caxton, pen name for San Francisco *Chronicle* correspondent W. H. Rhodes, gave the following account of the inspection trip:

"We left Sacramento on the 3rd of September [1868], and a jollier set of good fellows never set forth on a trip of pleasure. How it happened that I came to be of the party, was after this fashion. The Railroad Commissioners, Messrs. T. H. Henley and Frank Denver were called upon to examine the track and certify to the condition of the last twenty mile section completed, in order that the company might draw the government bonus of $30,000 per mile; Hoft, Baldy Johnson, of Sacramento, and myself were appointed by the proper authority to supervise the Commissioners and see that they perform their duty between the public and the owners of the Pacific Railroad. The beauty of the whole affair was, that the Commissioners never suspected our true characters, but looked upon us simply as invited guests, regular 'dead heads' booked for the round trip, and of course were completely off their guard in their intercourse with ourselves. Mr. Charles Crocker, Superintendent of the road, and Mr. Marsh, of Nevada, were likewise of the party.

"Shortly after leaving Sacramento, we were informed by Mr. Crocker, that it would be quite a difficult matter to overtake the end of the road before it reached Salt Lake, as he had just placed upon the work all the Indian tribes living in the great basin of the Humboldt, consisting chiefly of the Pah-Utahs, Chowchillas and Washoes. I asked him how many men he had at work? He replied that it was impossible to tell, as no list of names was kept, and the men worked by the squad, and not as individuals. In explanation he added, that Indians and Chinamen were so much alike personally that no human being could tell them apart, and, therefore, for fear of paying double wages, he devised the scheme of employing, working and paying them by the wholesale. Thus, every morning a count is made of those who go to work, a second of those who eat, and, a third of those who quit at night. In this way, lengthy bookkeeping is avoided, time is saved and cheating prevented. At the present time there are about ten

As the crews began to work their way across the Nevada desert, seen above, work trains like that shown below became a familiar and much-welcomed sight.

Camps were set up at various
intervals along the desert.
At left are scenes
near Humboldt Lake.
Below, Chinese Camp,
just outside Brown's Station.

thousand Chinamen, one thousand white men and 'any number' of Indians employed on the road.

"After we got fully under way, Crocker, the superintendent of the road, came to our car, and informed us of a new regulation just made with reference to the Commissioners. He stated that in order to prevent accidents, irregular drinking had been prohibited, and if any of the party had furnished themselves with bottles or flasks they must now be surrendered. On examination, it was ascertained that the entire party, except myself, had 'pocket pistols' along. Col. Henly had a demijohn, and Mr. Marsh, of Nevada, a small hand barrel that would hold about two and a half gallons —a present he said from his wife—who cautioned him against drinking the desert water. After Crocker had taken full possession of the 'stores', he announced another regulation, that whenever the engine stopped to get water, any of the party could take a drink. He spoke feelingly of the perils of the trip, and advised us to see that our life policies were all right before we left the Colfax station.

"Everything now being in readiness, we began to ascend the upgrade. It is needless to describe what so many are familiar with. Enough to say that we crossed the Sierra Nevada Mountains on a railway, and that without accident, delay or danger of any kind. . . .

"Really, the speed is terrific, and it was some consolation after we reached Truckee to think that the worst of the journey was over. Truckee —formerly Colburn's Station—is a young and flourishing town; full of people, who all seem to be busy in the great lumber trade. Hundreds of saw-mills are at work around, and millions of feet of timber are daily flattened out into boards. It is a great place for children, for they can play at 'see-sawing' the entire twenty-four hours. In fact, I played at it myself for more than forty miles down the Truckee.

"We arrived at Reno late in the afternoon, and here beheld another new town. The noise of hammer, and plane, and saw re-echoed on all sides, and the city rises like an exhalation. It is a complete mirage on the desert, and will probably be as magnificent, and as transient. Here the road branches to Virginia City, and we found coaches awaiting our arrival, ready in a few moments to be off for the land of silver. Bent, however, upon overtaking, if possible, the end of the Pacific Railroad, we could only pause long enough to enable Baldy Johnson to call for and eat a fried mackerel for tea, and for Mr. Marsh and Col. Crocker to empty the demijohn. This done, the locomotive screamed, the bell rang, and the train was off.

"Darkness after a while set in, and our company grew silent gradually, until nothing was heard, but the snore of Frank Denver and the snort of the steam-horse. By-and-by, however, we were all aroused to witness one of the loveliest sights I ever beheld. Here, in this desolate wilderness, this

At Red Bluff, above, the lower canyon of the Truckee River crossed the line again, and then ran along the river (below) into Wadsworth.

sand desert, without a tree or a fountain within hundreds of miles of us, nature asserted her prerogative and turned showmaster for our special benefit. To the east of us, Lake Humboldt stretched for many miles, low, dark, and uninviting. All at once, the full moon started from the horizon.

"The train stopped, the engine took a drink, and so [did] the Commissioners. In truth we became hilarious. Toasts were called for and drank with vim and enthusiasm, the desert was forgotten, and all went 'merry as a marriage bell.' I only recollect one of the sentiments, it ran thus, and needs explanation, to be understood. 'General' Crocker built the road, and with Chinese labor, hence the toast: 'The Pacific Railroad—the only piece of crockery ware made out of China', elicited tremendous applause and a fresh call for the corkscrew.

"About midnight we reached our destination for the time—the Big Bend of the Humboldt. Here we were handsomely entertained at a roadside inn, and would have passed a pleasant night had not Baldy Johnson insisted on having broiled mackerel for supper; the rest of us were content with fresh trout, but nothing could appease Mr. Johnson but the salt fish. As none could be obtained, the landlord pacified him by soaking a trout for an hour in an old empty kit that Pat Harris left on his way to Unionville in 1860.

"Early the next morning, we started in fresh pursuit of the end of the road. Learning, after we passed Mill City, that the end of the road was that morning only twenty miles in advance, we made preparations to examine track in order to make our report to the Government. The *modus operandi* of examining the track was about as follows: Frank Denver took his stand on the platform of the hindmost car, and, with a small spyglass, critically scrutinized the ties, rails, and grade; while Colonel Henley laid down, on the front of the car, shut his eyes, and composed himself to sleep. The argument being this, that if the passengers could sleep the track must be level, easy, and all right; whereas, if too rough to sleep, something must be wrong with the work. I was deputized to watch Henley, and Baldy Johnson to keep an eye on Denver. Our scrutiny was entirely satisfactory. The Colonel slept profoundly, and did not wake until we overtook the end of the road just 307 miles from Sacramento.

"Here we found a very large number of men at work—principally Chinese—laying the track. The scientific part of the job is superintended by white men, but the rough mudsill work is done by the [Chinese]. A horse was furnished me by Gen. Crocker, and I rode on a gallop to the front. The grading is completed several hundred miles in advance of the track-laying, so that there is no delay in placing the rails.

"It would be impossible to describe how rapidly, orderly and perfectly this is done, without seeing the operation itself. There are just as many

210

employed as can conveniently work, and no more. Vehicles laden with ties are always in advance, and Chinese with gauge and leveling rod place them across the grade, almost as quick as thought. The car with the rails is brought up at a gallop, and six white men—three at each rail—roll the iron off the car, and drop it upon the track, with the velocity of steam. The empty car is lifted off the track, and then one fully loaded is drawn to the front, and the same operation repeated ad infinitum.

"I found that it was no joke of Gen. Crocker, that it would be no easy matter to overtake the end of the road. Taking out my watch I timed the last half mile I saw laid, and it took a little less than twenty-eight minutes. John C. Fall, who resides at Unionville, Humboldt county, recently came to San Francisco to purchase goods; and left orders at Sacramento to ship them to the end of the track. When he left home the road was completed to within a few miles of Unionville. He made all his purchases in three days and started home. His goods had preceded him; and he found, to his amazement, that, in complying with the order to ship them to the end of the track, that during his sojourn in the city the end of the track had advanced twenty-five miles beyond Unionville, and his goods were landed half way to Winnemucca! It is a fact, beyond dispute, that this company has laid over six miles of track in a single day."

Later in September the Shasta *Courier* verified the startling progress of the road: "Mr. Charles Crocker of the Central Pacific Railroad lately made the statement that if the Company were fortunate enough to receive their additional fifty locomotives now on shipboard on their way to California, in season to be employed during the coming Autumn months, the road would be completed to Salt Lake City by December. They can and do lay the track now at the rate of four miles a day. They have, we believe, some seventy-odd locomotives already, and it is to be inferred from the allusion already made, they have need of fifty more. This is railroading on a scale surpassing anything ever before conceived."

From the time the first section of the Pacific Railroad was completed back in 1864, it was understood between the government and the railroad companies that early operation of the transcontinental road was of such vital importance that many portions of the line would be hurriedly built and would require additional work after the junction was made. The government commissioners who inspected every section of twenty miles understood this, and the government bonds were not held up for minor deficiencies.

However, in order to assure a first-class road and to guarantee that the government would not advance all the subsidies to the Central Pacific and Union Pacific before the road was thoroughly operational, President Johnson, on September 25, 1868, appointed a commission of civil engineers to examine the entire road so far constructed and report upon it in accordance with instructions furnished by the Secretary of the Interior. These instructions read in part: "The rapid construction of this great national thoroughfare being deemed wholly important, it was not originally considered that in the early stages of the enterprise the standard of absolute completeness of each section should be exacted as a condition precedent to the payment of the subsidy—It becomes the duty of the executive to require that all past omissions shall now be supplied, that in lieu of temporary structures, those which are permanent and substantial shall be erected."

The Shasta *Courier* of Saturday, September 26, 1868, quoted the Salt Lake *Reporter* of September 17th: "We understand that Vice President Durant telegraphed to Governor Stanford, President of the Central Pacific Railroad Company to the following purport: 'If we lay any track on your grading we will pay you for the grading. If you lay any on ours we won't charge you a cent for it.' " On November 9, 1868, Stanford, in a letter to Hopkins, confirmed this offer. Stanford indicated it was an inducement for the C.P. to make the same offer to Union Pacific.

On October 1, 1868, the line was opened to Winnemucca, 325 miles from Sacramento. J. M. Graham later commented on the scarcity of inhabitants in northern Nevada: "What settlements were there in the desert when the line was being built? Winnemucca was a small town, there was a wayside hotel at Humboldt station, there was a little store at Mill City. There were mines south of Mill City, there was a dairy ranch 10 miles east of Winnemucca called Fairbanks Ranch, a little store at Golconda, beyond that, nothing. We used to call Fairbanks Ranch the jumping off place but there was a little saloon at Golconda. I don't remember any habitations until we touched Corinne, 20 miles east of Promontory."

"I do hope you will push the work from this on as work was never pushed before, for the interest at stake is immense," Huntington urged Crocker in a letter of October 21, 1868. "Why doesn't Stanford go to Salt Lake and stay until the roads meet? I have got the new line to Echo Summit approved. You must lay the track to the tunnel. By God, Charley, you must work as man never worked before. Our salvation is you."

Taking Huntington's suggestion, Stanford again went to Salt Lake City, where he remained for about three months. While there, he sent a number of detailed reports on his own activities and on the grading work at the eastern end. The following letters from Stanford to Hopkins are dated November 1, 8 and 9, 1868, respectively:

November 1, 1868: "Arrived here last evening. It has taken some time to make the trip, but the time has not been lost. I have now a pretty clear idea of the whole thing. I think we ought at once to create a scraper force of two hundred and fifty teams, such a force is fully equal to 1250 men.

Water tanks at the lower crossing of the Humboldt River, 254 miles.

By proper exertion it can be created so as to do much service. . . . To create this scraper force I would use horses, mules and oxen as they can be had. The scraper made by Soule and sent out here as a sample is a good one, better than the eastern scrapers. I hope this matter of scraper forces will receive immediate attention.

"I think the earthwork on the Mormon contract will be completed by the 1st. of Dec. I have agreed with another party and expect to make the contract tomorrow for the grading of so much work as they can do until they meet us from the west. Then commencing at the west end of the Mormon contract and working west. I think they will be able to do a good deal of work. It appears as though we can get all the force we may require from this end, but men are reluctant to go so far from the base of supplies as is the work west of the Mormon contract. . . .

"I am glad to find you view the accepted line of the CPRR as the true one, it is my own conclusion. In coming out and thinking the thing over I came to that conclusion and resolved to act on it. I have told Montague to organize a force here at once to have the line ready at as early a day as possible for the graders to commence at Weber and work west. At this time it appears to me that I would prefer that the Union People should commence and occupy their line before we commence work on ours. Then they certainly will not be on our line and consequently not on the Pacific RR line. But tomorrow I shall try and get posted and things may appear differently. This is Sunday and though I have been pretty busy and picked up several items I cannot see Brigham, and until he is seen but little is seen here clearly.

"But now as always the great point is to push the track. The grading though must first be done, that is not to be lost sight of. Cold weather is close at hand. I felt its breath camping out. . . ."

November 8, 1868: "Have just returned from mouth of Echo. There I met Durant [of the U.P.], but nothing came of it of sufficient importance to relate here in the short time I have for this letter if it is to go in tonight's mail. The U. Pacific track is within (80) eighty miles of mouth of Echo. They say they have the ties bedded almost the entire distance. They will put in five (5) miles temporary track if necessary to avoid delay at the tunnels on Weber.

"They are prepared to move their present forces as they come off the work about west of mouth of Weber. It certainly looks now as though they were coming west very rapidly. I hardly know what they can't do. They have an immense force to put west of Weber.

"I have made no contract for the grading between Weber and Monument Pt. except I have directed the present contractors to do the work between Monument and Promontory. I think it best to let the UP occupy

Taking on water at Winnemucca.
The rails reached this village
October 1, 1868 — 334 miles
from Sacramento.

their line and we do the same quietly with ours. But unless Huntington has matters in better shape than I am advised, I don't much fancy doing work alongside that portion of their line that they may cover with iron in six weeks. It has been storming in the Wasatch but not enough to help us. I have telegraphed to Huntington to try and meet me at Omaha. He answers he will on the 20th, but that is too far off to be altogether satisfactory."

November 9, 1868: "Your letters, also your telegram rec'd inquiring when Montague will be home. As he is due home today I do not send an answer in relation to him.

"I did not try to do anything with Durant nor he with me. We had general talk in the main. He was willing we should use his grading at Humboldt Wells and as far this way as we could use his grade before he could lay track on it. I thanked him and told him we would let him know when we reached it. He would I saw expect we should make the same offer and so I broke in on him. He resumed the subject several times, but I avoided definite talk on that subject. With our idea of grading here and laying track upon what we grade in any event I had to be cautious or else appear to be less liberal than he. We parted with the understanding expressed by me in so many words that we had done nothing to commit our respective companies to anything. To which he assented.

"Today I had to talk with Brigham Young. He will do our grading west from Ogden to the Promontory and will not make our work secondary to the U.P. That he will put plenty of men on both lines. I am satisfied he can do it. I think this is our policy. We can't stop the U.P. from grading their line, but we can through Young have our own grading and have it to ourselves to lay track on when we can reach it.

"Charley telegraphs to have the grading done to Humboldt Wells. He should expect to come this side of there with his graders.

"The Mormons will not work west of the 100 mile contract. I am doing what I can to have others work west and it looks as though we shall have a respectable force. But we must not depend on it. Do not trust that the idea of demoralizing our forces is abandoned. Durant said if we hired his men he could play the same game. I told him we never did it, that I had refused to contract with his contractors who had uncompleted contracts with him, but did not suppose he could object to contracting with those who had completed their work. To this he assented as all right."

With completion of the C.P.–U.P. transcontinental railroad close at hand, several prominent California newspapers assigned staff members to follow the progress of each road. They sent back a descriptive record of the last dash for Promontory.

The *Alta California,* in its edition of November 9, 1868, pictured the Central Pacific construction forces in action at the rail end. Their correspondent found superintendent of construction Strobridge in charge and comfortably established in a camp train, which contained hotel, telegraph office, store, kitchen, sleeping quarters, and a "home that would not discredit San Francisco." This train housed and fed the officials, the clerical force, and the Caucasian workers. The correspondent reached the camp early in the morning:

"Long lines of horses, mules and wagons are standing in the open desert near the camp train. The stock is getting its breakfast of hay and barley. Trains are shunting in from the west with supplies and materials for the day's work. Foremen are galloping here and there on horseback giving or receiving orders. Swarms of laborers, Chinese, Europeans and Americans, are hurrying to their work. On one side of the track stands the moveable blacksmith shop where a score of smiths are repairing tools and shoeing horses and mules. Close by is a fully equipped harness shop where a large force is repairing collars, traces and other leather equipment.

"To the west are the rails and a line of telegraph poles stretching back as far as the eye could reach. The telegraph wire from the last pole is strung into the car that served as a telegraph office. To the eastward stretched the grade marked by a line of newly disturbed earth. By the side of the grade smokes the camp fires of the blue clad laborers who could be seen in groups waiting for the signal to start work. These are the Chinese, and the job of this particular contingent is to clear a level roadbed for the track.

"They are the vanguard of the construction forces. Miles back is the camp of the rear guard—the Chinese who follow the track gang, ballasting and finishing the road bed.

"Systematic workers these Chinese—competent and wonderfully effective because tireless and unremitting in their industry. Order and industry then as now made for accomplishment. Divided into gangs of about thirty men each, they work under the direction of an American foreman. The Chinese board themselves. One of their number is selected in each gang to receive all wages and buy all provisions. They usually pay an American clerk—$1 a month apiece is usual—to see that each gets all he earned and is charged no more than his share of the living expenses. They are paid from $30 to $35 a month, out of which they board themselves. They are credited with having saved about $20 a month. Their workday is from sunrise to sunset, six days in the week. They spend Sunday washing and mending, gambling and smoking.

"At sunrise a signal to turn to is given from the camp train. What at first seemed confusion to the visitor soon resolved itself into orderly action. A train of about thirty cars loaded with materials and supplies had been spotted close behind the camp train. This supply train left the nearest

Powder Bluff, at the west end of Ten-Mile Canyon.

Curving irons at Ten-Mile Canyon.

supply station every morning early enough to reach the end of the track by sunrise. On it are ties, rails, spikes, bolts, telegraph poles, wire, etc.

"The rails, ties and other material are thrown off the train as near to the end of the track as feasible, and then the empty train is drawn back out of the way. At this point the rails are loaded on low flat cars, and hauled by horses to the end of the track. The ties are handled in the same way.

"Behind comes the rail gang, who take the rails from the flat cars and lay them on the ties. While they are doing this a man on each side distributes spikes, two to each tie; another distributes splice bars; and a third the bolts and nuts by which the ends of the rails are spliced together. Then comes the spikers, two on each side, to pin the rails to the ties. Two more men follow to adjust and bolt the splice bars.

"As fast as a flat car is unloaded it is turned on its side to allow the loaded cars to pass it. It is then returned to the rails and sent back for another load.

"All this time wagons are distributing telegraph poles along the grade. Cross arms are nailed onto them. Another gang working under a foreman of telegraph construction digs the holes for the poles and a third gang erects the poles. It is the aim of this third gang to keep pace with the rail gang. At times lack of wagons make it impossible to keep up the supply of poles, and the telegraph gangs, who pride themselves on never letting the track get ahead of them, utilize sage brush, barrels, ties—surreptitiously taken from the track—or anything else that would keep the wire off the ground until the supply of poles again equal the demand.

"Then comes a wagon bearing a reel of wire which unrolls as the wagon goes ahead. As the wire uncoils it is carried up on the poles and made fast to the insulators.

"Back of the track builders follows a gang with the seven or more ties necessary to complete the foundation for each rail. These are put into position and spiked by another gang, which also level up the track and leave it ready for the ballasters.

"Meanwhile on board the camp train cooks are preparing dinner, clerks are busy with accounts and records, and the telegraph wire is tapping back the needs for tomorrow in the way of materials and supplies.

"Twice a day the camp train moves to the end of the track—at noon to give all hands the hot dinner that six-hours of labor has earned and at night to give supper and sleeping accommodations.

"Immediately on reaching the end of the track at night a telegraph wire is cut in from the last pole to the telegraph car and Sacramento is notified of the number of miles of track laid."

Remaining with Strobridge, from Newcastle to the final meeting at Promontory, was his wife, the only Caucasian woman who "saw the thing through from beginning to end." The construction train on which the "Heroine of the C.P." kept house caught the eye of the news reporters. The Vallejo *Evening Chronicle* of January 11, 1869, described the mobile camp in detail:

"The pioneer train is composed of ten or eleven large cars. They look very much like houses on wheels. In the forward car is Mr. Strobridge's residence and office. It is neatly fitted up and well furnished, and an awning veranda, with a canary bird swinging at the front door, gives it [a] home-like appearance. Here Mr. Strobridge spends his time with his family and receives visitors. A battery is on the car, and an operator to work it. The train moves to the end of the track noon and night, when a wire is attached, the circuit made, and a fast telegram office is in communication.

"In the back cars of this train are eating and sleeping accommodations for five hundred men who compose the vanguard of this great modern army. Attached to the train are three or four platform cars on which carpenters, with shops fitted up in best style, are fitting telegraph poles, putting in insulators, etc., for the telegraph line.

"At every important station on the route there is a telegraph office, and through these, daily supplies are ordered up. Thus hand in hand on their sturdy march, go the twin giants, the railroad and telegraph, linked mailed purveyors of civilization which is ere long to wrest from its pristine wilderness a continent in whose broad extent Greece and Rome might be hidden away."

How were the men paid? J. M. Graham, the engineer, described the paymaster:

"East of the state line of Calif-Nevada, Mr. W. E. Brown, who was secretary of the Contract & Finance Company, would come to the end of the track and would often drive more than 100 miles in order to get in touch with the men along the line where they were working, to pay them. He carried the coin in a spring wagon and had guards along with rifles, on horseback. Sisson and Crocker Company paid all the Chinese. We always accompanied them and got paid at the same time.

"Sisson and Crocker Company had an interpreter named Sam Thayer and also a Chinese interpreter. When they came up to these gangs of Chinese, the money due them would be already counted out and they would dump the money in one of the Chinese' hats for that gang with a statement written in Chinese. There would be no time for explanations. They had to take it whether they liked it or not. This Sam Thayer claimed he could speak half a dozen Chinese dialects. If there was any claims about the pay, they would take it up with Sisson and Crocker Company later."

"If it is [within] the power of God, man, or the devil to get our rail laid to within 300 miles of Echo by, say the tenth of December, it should be done." Huntington wrote Stanford, who was still at Salt Lake City, on November 13, 1868. Six days later, the Central Pacific line was opened to Argenta, 397 miles beyond Winnemucca, the seventy-two-mile segment had been completed in one month and nineteen days. To complete the line to within three hundred miles of Echo as Huntington urged would require the laying of one hundred miles within one month, a record beyond any previous accomplishment of the C.P. Meanwhile, in Salt Lake City, Stanford continued his efforts to obtain grading crews and to hasten construction west from Ogden to connect with Crocker's forces. A series of letters he wrote in November and December told of his growing concern over the ability of the C.P. to head off the Union Pacific:

November 21, 1868: "I have let the work from Ogden west to Monument to our old contractors, Benson, Farr & West. Brigham Young has 1/4 interest in the profits. Mr. Gray and I spent part of two days on the Promontory Mts. I was so little satisfied with our line that I directed Bates to try a new one. The old line would detain us until we could make a tunnel of 800 feet through solid limestone. I was much disappointed. I had directed a party of graders to be sent out there so that we could take possession of the important points. They were within a few hours of there when we left. The UP have sent orders for their men to come off the work at Humboldt Wells and work on the Promontory. . . .

"The end of our track is not less than 300 miles from Ogden. Now how can we justify ourselves and what good can come to us in going 60 miles beyond the Pt. the Act of Congress permits and within 40 miles of the track of the UP? They having the grading substantially done from the mouth of Weber to their track and that too for most of the way as near to our line as we could build ourselves. Are they to be confined exactly to the line laid down on our maps? If so I am afraid we are liable to be complained of. . . .

"The UP are making desperate efforts to get into Echo before the winter storms and cold shall shut them out. I don't think they will get through to mouth of Weber before next spring. They have as I am informed nine bridges [ranging from 30 to 100 feet in] span to build and a trestling of about 1,000 feet, twenty to thirty feet high east of Echo Summit. . . . Even though they do have the timber all framed at Chicago, there will be some time taken up by these bridges and trestle. The timber is not yet on the ground. An ordinary winter I am confident will close them out of track west of Ogden before next spring, but the fall is unusually mild and is of great help to the UP. . . ."

December 1, 1868: "I arrived here last night from the Promontory where Col. Gray and self spent several days with Clem [Lewis M. Clement, engineer in charge of that section of the grading for the C.P.], and Bates, trying to improve the line or rather to avoid the tunnel somewhat at the expense of the alignment and save probably $75,000. We shall have one fill of about 100,000 yds. The UP have a line [surveyed] very close to ours on which they say they intend to build. After we have our line well covered I may act on the question of right of way. I am revolving the question in my mind and maybe I will by and by see clearly a course to pursue. I would be glad to talk with you all on that question. If I do not go east to meet Huntington in a few days I shall buy a release or conveyance of right of way for our road where it runs through farms. I have kept this question entirely still. Maybe something will come of it. The UP are often within a hundred feet of our line (again, surveyed, not built). I do not elaborate this but you will readily embrace it. Have a consultation on it and give me the result. . . . Of course I understand the Pacific RR has the legal right of way through all the land in Utah as none has ever been sold by the Govt. but two lines have not the right of way. . . .

"The weather here is very fine [and] would be considered such in California. The UP are making the most of it. It is greatly against us."

December 4, 1868: "Clem has sent me a profile of the line at Promontory avoiding the tunnel and it looks better than I expected. During the next week the Mormon contractors say they will have the whole work covered from Ogden to Monument Pt. Then, if I have the right of way secured, I shall be in condition to assert our line to be the only one of the Pacific RR and that others must keep off our right of way.

"The UP have crossed Bear River with their track and say they will be at the mouth of Echo by the twentieth of this month. I don't think they will be thru before the 1st January with good weather. I have taken a good deal of pains to post myself about the winters in the Wasatch and east to Cheyenne and I believe the chances are 9 out of 10 that the UP will not be at the mouth of Weber before next spring. But it does seem as if our track lagged, also, I would have strong faith in our being first to the mouth of Weber. I do think there is ground for hope. . . ."

December 8, 1868: "I started three days ago from Salt Lake for the Promontory but have concluded to stop here [at Ogden] and push the contractors into sending men to the Promontory. I think this week we will have all the important points well secured. I have determined to secure the right of way through every man's enclosure in this valley.

"The storms hold off late, but they may come yet in time to settle the question of where the roads shall meet. That is if we can come along with speed with our track. I am strongly of the opinion the UP will not get out of the Canyon with their track this winter. But we must rely upon nothing but track laying. Could not Charley, by staying out on the track, push the material forward faster? . . .

*The construction train along the Alkali Flats,
in the Nevada desert. The Superintendent's car
was made into a quite comfortable home by
Mrs. Strobridge (second from left in photo).*

*Throughout the stretch across Nevada
Indians came down to see the "iron horse,"
some of them staying to work on the line.
Here, two Paiute women pose with
their children for the photographer.*

"In thirty days, if the weather holds favorable, I think the grading will be two thirds done on each consecutive 20 miles between here and Monument Point. Promontory may make it questionable on that 20 miles, but if forces go on as I think they will, I guess it will be in condition to pass. At Humboldt Wells I think the true policy is to follow our own line disregarding entirely what the UP has done there, using their grade or not just as our line may make it necessary. . . ."

December 13, 1868: "I have held the theory steadily that the approved line is the only proper one and have acted upon it. Yet my policy seems to be the reverse of Huntington's. He writes about forcing the UP on to the accepted line or else to stop them and wonders that I do not do one or the other. Now my idea is and has been that if our theory is sound that the accepted line is the only Pacific RR line, then let the UP work off it and when they want to draw bonds on their line raise the question. It was in pursuance of this policy that I did not want our line west from Ogden so indicated that the UP would work on it, but that they should go to work on their line and give us the chance to occupy our own line without hindrance. We have by now got the line well occupied and I presume the right of way secured through all possessory claims.

"I think we are now in pretty good condition as to the line west of Ogden. But east it is another matter. Huntington in his last letter rec'd last night and of date Dec. 2nd says 'It does seem to me as tho it would be well to set men at work on the west end of the tunnel if you can get at it.'

"Now Echo Summit Tunnel is 350 miles east of our 455th mile, which may have been reached last night. Under the act of Congress, the CP was not allowed to work more than 300 miles ahead of their completed line. To go to work at Echo Summit seems to me such utter folly in every way that it can be viewed that I am satisfied that either Huntington or I completely fail to comprehend the situation. . . ."

"I think," said Huntington on December 15, 1868, in a letter to Hopkins, "it a terrible mistake that we have made in letting matters run as they have at Salt Lake. I sometimes swear terribly about it, but that doesn't do any good." On the same subject, he wrote to E. B. Crocker on December 16, 1868: "I wrote you and Stanford as soon as our line was approved, to have engineers connect our line as approved from Echo Summit to the Union Pacific line as it was being worked, and I supposed you would see the importance of it, and have attended to it at once. But up to this time I have not heard one word in reply. The Union Pacific have just filed a map that laps us by 30 miles."

During 1868, 362 miles of road were constructed—virtually the mile a day that Charles Crocker had promised. But the winter of 1868/69, one of the most severe the builders had experienced.

FOURTEEN

DASH TO PROMONTORY: *1869*

Driving of the last spike in the Pacific Railroad at Promontory, Utah, on May 10, 1869, was the final act in a dramatic rivalry that has no parallel in the history of American railroading. The fascinating details of construction activities in the Promontory Mountains are revealed through voluminous dispatches sent daily to their editors by reporters covering final stages of the contest. These, together with letters exchanged by members of the company and the personal histories recorded by many of the men who actually did the construction, give a clear and detailed account of those frenetic last four months before the rails were united.

On January 15, 1869, Stanford wrote to Hopkins:

"The weather continues remarkably good. So far for us it has been a failure in great part. Ives says two years ago last September when he was at Echo Summit snow fell four feet. Such a fall of snow this year would have saved us notwithstanding the slow progress of our track. After the report of the Special Com'rs on the UP showing clearly an unfinished road, Govt gave the UP its full amount of bonds. It is not very encouraging to us to believe that they will withhold bonds from the UP for the track through Echo and Weber because they are not exactly on our line approved by the Secty of the Interior. To me it seems what we can fairly hope for is to have our line to Ogden, on which we have worked, accorded to us, and that claiming more is to weaken our case. We are working substantially along our whole line between Ogden and Monument Pt. From Ogden to Bear River the lines are generally from 500 feet to a quarter of a mile apart. At one point they are probably within two hundred feet. From Bear River to the Promontory the UP are close to us and cross us twice, on the Promontory itself they will be very close to us, but they have so many lines,

228

some crossing us and some occasionally running within a few feet of us and no work on any, that I cannot tell you exactly how the two lines will be. They are still surveying there for a location. . . .

"Today I have been preparing affidavits to be signed by Clem [Clement], Ives and Stevenson as to variation of the UP line in Weber and Echo from approved line, and as the temporary track of about eight miles around Tunnel and heavy work west and near Echo Summit. Today Mr. Ives expects to have finished a tracing of our map filed at Washington showing variations of the UP line. I think they will be ready to go off tomorrow."

During these final months Stanford faced problems resulting from the trend of Pacific Railroad affairs in Washington, where President Andrew Johnson's administration was drawing to a close and Ulysses S. Grant was about to take office. Of some significance was General Grant's long standing friendship with General Dodge and other Union Pacific construction bosses.

Central Pacific had worked a clever stratagem that came very near succeeding. It had filed with the Interior Department maps and profiles of its proposed line from Monument Point to Echo Summit, which Secretary of the Interior Orville H. Browning had accepted. Stanford then proceeded on the theory that the Central Pacific route, regardless of the small amount of work done east of Ogden, was the true line of the Pacific Railroad, and the only one on which subsidy bonds could be issued. From his base in Salt Lake City he exerted himself to occupy and defend this line. In Washington, Collis P. Huntington filed application for an advance of $2,400,000 in subsidy bonds, two-thirds of the amount due for this portion of the line.

Union Pacific, of course, protested mightily. Its chief engineer, General Dodge, and the Ames brothers hurried to Washington and used all their influence to block the move of the Central Pacific. Browning, soon to leave office, held up the grant to the Central Pacific; and in January, 1869, he appointed a special commission headed by another army general, Major General G. K. Warren, to travel to Utah and determine the best route through the disputed territory. No subsidy bonds would be issued to the Central Pacific until the commission had reported.

On January 14, 1869, Secretary Browning sent to the commissioners a letter of instructions: "After proceeding to the western terminus of the completed track of the road of the Union Pacific Railroad Co. you will proceed to make a thorough and careful examination of the ground situated between it and the completed tracks of the road of the Central Pacific Railroad Company of California. If either of the existing routes between these termini is in all respects unobjectionable, you are at liberty to adopt

Argenta, Nevada, 1869. Three-hundred and ninety-seven miles from Sacramento.

The Argenta House.

it. If not, you will make a new location. In either case, in order that this Department may act advisedly in the premises, you will report to me specifically the facts elicited by your examinations [as well] as the reasons which governed your conclusions, and transmit an accurate map and profile of the route which you determine to be the most advantageous.

"You will also designate a point at which the two roads will probably meet in the construction of a continuous completed line."

Obviously the decision of the Secretary of the Interior to hold up the Central Pacific claim until the commissioners had issued their report was the only possible course. In spite of the friendships involved, the Union Pacific was much further advanced at that point and ready actually to occupy the disputed line, whereas the Central Pacific was still several months away. The Secretary's action, fair as it was, was a bitter dose for Leland Stanford.

On January 29, 1869, Stanford discussed the matter in a letter to Hopkins:

"I have been in hopes for some time that I should be able to answer all your letters in person, but this Commission has detained me and now I shall probably not be in Cal. before the middle of Feb. with good luck. On Monday, Feb. 1st we start to examine the lines from end of UP track in Weber Canyon through to our track. It is not expected that we will make more than twenty miles a day. The Com'rs propose to make a critical examination. From the instructions and straws [in the wind] I fear this thing is set up against us. The far off distance of our track and slow progress makes against us with great force. It is trying to one's nerves to think of it.

"The UP are detained for probably ten days more at a cut in Weber Canyon, after that they say there is nothing to stop them in track laying. They are making extensive preparations to push through this Valley, and have been surveying for light work upon 116 feet grades at the Promontory. . . .

"I fear he [Huntington] is having a hard time in trying to save what a want of foresight has jeopardized if not lost. I tell you the thought makes me feel like a dog; I have no pleasure in the thought of Railroad. It is mortification."

Meanwhile, Central Pacific again had its annual problems with the Sierra snows, which blocked the road's tracks in February, 1869. In the Virginia City *Territorial Enterprise* for Thursday, February 18, there appeared a lively account of the company's efforts to keep the line open. The newspaper's correspondent sent this dispatch from the scene:

"Wednesday morning, February 10, your humble servant left the city of Sacramento for this place. The rain was falling in torrents, and the clouds hung low over the valley, which was already flooded with the heavy

The first construction train to pass through the Palisades.

body of water that had swept down from the foothills. At Auburn, an occasional flake of snow, of huge proportions, foretold the approach of the train to the mountains; at Colfax the earth was covered, and each revolution of the engine 'drivers' was more difficult, until at Alta the train was brought to a standstill to await the arrival of the train west. The air was thick with fleecy specks; the wind swept down the heavy canyons above, the two car loads of passengers settled to a patient waiting; the youth at the telegraph office reported 'wires down in the mountains,' and right then 'trouble began.'

"The long hours of the afternoon crept slowly on. Conductor Dennison gazed on his flock of passengers pleasantly, and reported that there was no hope of progress until the coming day. And so it got dark. . . . Right here we desire to lay down as a proposition not to be gainsayed—there is no such thing as a comfortable position for sleep in a rail car seat—it is impossible.

"Morning came, and found us in the midst of a boundless waste of snow, at least two and one half feet having fallen during the night, and more coming. Patience weakened considerably, and a large amount of growling was indulged in, mixed with some merriment at the delay. Toilets were made of snow water and a finger-comb, and then a breakfast of good quality enabled us to await orders with more composure. Eight, nine, ten, eleven o'clock came, and then the order was given to take the train, with such passengers as chose, back to Sacramento.

"Five locomotives and a huge snow-plow had arrived bound to the front, and so your correspondent, with a route agent of Wells, Fargo & Co., bearing two huge sacks of letters, got aboard the locomotive *Auburn,* engineer H. Spence, and were made comfortable by that quick-eyed, strong-hearted man, who managed the huge machine with consummate skill. Hank Lancaster conducted the train, and after half an hour consumed in preparation, and to see the passenger train on its return, the signal was given for a charge at the unbroken snow bank which covered the track to the depth of nearly three feet. Two sharp whistles from the front engine, echoed by two similar shrieks from the following, and off they went. The snow was turned in huge furroughs from the track, and the bright sun came out and seemed to make partly cheerful the heavy stillness which hung around the line of road, all undisturbed except by the puffing engines. A short run and China Ranch was reached and passed, when suddenly the snow began to increase in volume, the cuts became filled, the locomotives wheezed and labored, and directly the train came to a dead stop in the middle of a huge bank of snow.

"The signal came to reverse, and haul back; half a mile down the track went the train, the advance was sounded, and with the speed of the wind

(Above, left): view from the top of the Palisades.

(Below, left): Alcove in the Palisades; water train in foreground.

*(Below): The town of Palisades, Nevada, shortly after
the line was completed, 435 miles from Sacramento.*

the immense plow swept to the snow bank. The men on the snow plow swung their arms in the air with frantic motion, the engineers each whistled a double-quick advance, each throttle-valve was pulled wide open and every pound of steam let on the cylinder, and the bank was again struck. A move of a few rods, and then another halt. So on, for hours, during which the hind engine became disabled and put back for repairs. The force was thus diminished one fifth, and the snow increasing every mile—there being at the Ranch, four miles from Alta, about five feet of snow—Conductor Lancaster shook his head, said more power must be had, and started a man to telegraph to Sacramento for assistance. So went the hours, and not until dark did the engines force the plow to the wood shed at Blue Canyon. . . .

"All day Friday was passed by Lancaster in trying to force his train along, but not a mile was accomplished, and at dusk the train backed to Alta for reinforcement. At midnight two more engines arrived, and early Saturday morning seven locomotives behind the immense plow rushed again to the fray. Passing the station with great speed, the bank was reached and gave way; curve, cut and trestle were passed, and a halt was not made until two miles had been accomplished. Bravo, Lancaster! Bully, Hawkins! Hurrah, Spence! Go it, Master Daily! Then came a lull; another back, two more runs, and at six o'clock the train made the sheds at Emigrant Gap, having accomplished four miles of track through snow that had drifted, and was from 5 to 20 feet in depth.

"The recent storm has demonstrated just this: from Truckee to Alta, the Central Pacific Railroad must be shedded—nearly every rod—to be rendered practicable in the winter. Wherever the sheds are, two engines with a plow can clear the way; in other places, ten are inadequate to the work. We predict the road will be entirely shedded before another winter. . . ."

On March 8, 1869, the Union Pacific entered Ogden, ending once and for all the dispute as to which railroad had the right to the line east of that point. "The UP track is seven or eight miles out of the Canyon, and the grade mostly finished to the base of the Promontory," the Salt Lake City *Daily Reporter* announced on March 13. "They have some heavy work there, which will, doubtless, hold them till the first of May, although they mean to have two thousand men on it by the end of the week. We can get nothing definite and reliable from the other road, but expect to when the special commission arrives."

On March 14, 1869, before returning to Sacramento from Salt Lake City, Stanford wrote one of his stronger letters to Hopkins:

"Our work is going on well and is so far advanced that there need be no delay in track laying from end of present track to Ogden in consequence of grading. The UP have changed their line so as to cross us five times with unequal grades between Bear River and the Promontory. They have done this purposely as there was no necessity for so doing.

"I think they have calculated on a report of the Special Commission favorable to this line and but for the addition of Clem [Clement] to the Commission would have got it. That the thing was set up with [Chairman] Warren and everything understood as to what the UP needed I have no doubt. His behavior has indicated that he had a part to fill. . . .

"If the UP could have got [a] report favorable to their line I conclude their intention to have been to deny that we had the right of way and claim it for themselves and that we must not get on it. Hence their crossing us and at unequal grades. They have laid track about three miles west of Ogden. I do not intend to finish up our line, but keep men scattered along it until our track is close upon them. I don't think there will be any attempt to jump our line while it is unfinished and we are working it.

"I am strongly of the opinion that if it were known that we had the bonds for unfinished work that the UP would call off their graders. They commenced to break ground last Monday on the heavy work at the Promontory. We shall serve notices for them not to interfere with our line and rest there for the present."

On March 26, 1869, the *Daily Reporter* commented on the progress of both lines:

"Corinne, March 23. The weather has cleared up beautifully and the equinoctial mud is drying fast. A raft containing 1,700 feet of piling and about 500 telegraph poles came down the river yesterday and tied up opposite the town-site, the first one and therefore worthy of note. It is the beginning of what may be a flourishing business in a few months or a year or two. Mr. Eicholtz for the U.P. Company has five pile drivers at work on the crossing of the river, and will be done driving piles by today or tomorrow. One may walk across Bear River on the finished railroad bridge within a week. The track is at Willard City, and Mr. Sharman who sets the pins for the tracklayers, pitched camp here yesterday.

"The C.P. have all their piling and bridge timber on the ground and yesterday set a steam pile driver fifty feet high. Their track is at Grouse Creek and coming on at the rate of three or four miles a day."

Five days later, the Salt Lake City *Deseret Evening News* added its comments and outlined the fierce competition between the two roads:

"Five miles west of Brigham City on this side of Bear River is situated the new town of Corinne, built of canvas and board shanties. The place is fast becoming civilized, several men having been killed there already, the last one was found in the river with four bullet holes through him and his head badly mangled.

"Work is being vigorously prosecuted on the U.P.R.R. and C.P.R.R. both lines running near each other and occasionally crossing. Both companies have their pile drivers at work where the lines cross the river. From Corinne west thirty miles, the grading camps present the appearance of a mighty army. As far as the eye can reach are to be seen almost a continuous line of tents, wagons and men.

"Junction City, twenty-one miles west of Corinne, is the largest and most lively of any of the new towns in this vicinity. Built in the valley near where the lines commence the ascent of the Promontory, it is nearly surrounded by grading camps. . . . The heaviest work on the Promontory is within a few miles of headquarters. Sharp & Young's blasters are jarring the earth every few minutes with their glycerine and powder, lifting whole ledges of limestone rock from their long resting places, hurling them hundreds of feet in the air and scattering them around for a half mile in every direction. Mr. T. E. Ticks showed me a boulder of three or four hundred pounds weight that was thrown over a half mile and completely buried itself in the ground within twenty yards of his cook room. I ate a hearty breakfast and left the spot 'sine dine'. At Carlisle's works a few days ago four men were preparing a blast by filling a large crevice in a ledge with powder. After pouring in the powder they undertook to work it down with iron bars, the bars striking the rocks caused an explosion; one of the men was blown two or three hundred feet in the air, breaking every bone in his body, the other three were terribly burnt and wounded with flying stones. Fun is fun, but standing astraddle of four or five kegs of powder and working it into the rocks with a crow-bar is a particular kind of sport that most of men wouldn't relish.

"From what I can observe and hear from others there is considerable opposition between the two railroad companies, both lines run near each other, so near that in one place the U.P. are taking a four feet cut out of the C.P. fill to finish their grade, leaving the C.P. to fill the cut thus made, in the formation of their grade.

"The two companies' blasters work very near each other, and when Sharp & Young's men first began work the C.P. would give them no warning when they fired their fuse. Jim Livingston, Sharp's able foreman, said nothing but went to work and loaded a point of rock with nitroglycerine, and without saying anything to the C.P. 'let her rip'. The explosion was terrific. The report was heard on the Dry Tortugas, and the foreman of the C.P. came down to confer with Mr. Livingston about the necessity of each party notifying the other when ready for a blast. The matter was speedily arranged to the satisfaction of both parties.

"The C.P. have about two-thirds of their heavy work done at this place, while the U.P. have just got under good headway. In other places

Machine shops and railroad yard at Carlin,
446 miles from Sacramento, January 25, 1869.

*Depot at Elko, February 8, 1869. The track switch
in the foreground was completed the next day.*

the grade of the U.P. is finished and the C.P. just beginning, so taking it 'all in all' it is hard to say which company is ahead with the work. The supposition is the two companies will meet somewhere on the Promontory, but it's my opinion that 'nobody don't know nothing about it.' One thing certain, both parties are doing their 'dirty best', and within sixty days they will meet somewhere—if they don't run off the track. . . .

"Several dance houses are now in full blast, astonishing the natives by the manner in which they are developing the resources of the Territory. I will venture the assertion that there is not less than three hundred whiskey shops between here and Brigham City, all developing the resources of the Territory, and showing the 'Mormons' what is necessary to build up a country and make it self-supporting and permanent.

"There are many heavy contractors on the Promontory, but the heaviest firm I have heard of is named 'Red Jacket' [a whiskey brand]. I notice nearly every wagon that passes have a great many boxes marked with his name."

On April 7 the first Union Pacific train steamed across the newly completed Bear River bridge and entered Corinne. At the same time the Central Pacific was still about 15 miles west of Monument Point. When the Warren Commission found that the Union Pacific was already at Ogden and had obviously won the race, the commissioners confined their investigation to the line between the two railroads. But the issue of the terminus was to be resolved in Washington, where the officials of both railroads met with representatives of the federal government.

Two backers of the Union Pacific, R. G. Hazard of Rhode Island and Samuel Hooper of Boston, together with General Dodge, met with Huntington in Washington on April 9, 1869, and reached an agreement:

"For the purpose of settling all existing controversies between the Central Pacific and the Union Pacific Railroad Companies, of fixing the place of meeting between the two roads, and of securing harmonious and united action between them in future, the following agreement has been entered into between them, to-wit:

"First: The place where the roads shall meet and connect shall be at some point within eight miles west of Ogden to be hereafter mutually agreed on by said companies. Both companies to have an equal interest and share in the town site at such junction which shall include not less than eight sections of land.

"Second: The Union Pacific company shall complete the track to the summit of Promontory Point to which place the Central shall build from the west, and the Central Pacific shall pay to the Union the cost of road without rolling stock from the terminus near Ogden as aforesaid to said Promontory Point, and shall pay to the Union one-half the cost of the

Above, the water tank at Peko.
Below and left, the stretch beneath Mount Halleck,
near Deeth, 505 miles from Sacramento.

grading by the Union between the summit of Promontory and Monument Point done at this date.

"Third: The Union shall draw U.S. bonds to the full amount per mile to the terminus near Ogden as aforesaid and the Central shall draw the balance of bonds and have the subsidy allowed by law on all that part of the track from the terminus westward."

On the following day, a joint resolution was adopted by Congress: ". . . And provided further, that the common terminus of the Union Pacific and the Central Pacific railroads shall be at or near Ogden; and the Union Pacific Railroad Company shall build, and the Central Pacific Railroad Company shall pay for and own, the railroad from the terminus aforesaid to Promontory Summit, at which the rails shall meet and connect and form one continuous line."

The Union Pacific grading crews received orders on April 11 to stop all work west of Promontory Summit, where they had grades parallel to the Central's. Three days later, Stanford ordered all work halted on the Central Pacific east of Blue Creek, the eastern base of the Promontory. The April agreement removed all cause for continued competition in grading and tracking; but competition had become a habit, and each company strained to be first at Promontory Summit, the agreed meeting place.

Ironically, the Union Pacific was in effect a contractor for the Central Pacific, its gangs working with the knowledge that the line from Ogden to Promontory Summit would be turned over to the Central Pacific.

Of unfailing interest to observers were the Central Pacific's "Big Fill" and the Union Pacific's "Big Trestle," both of which crossed a deep gorge about half way up the east slope. Farr and West began work on the Big Fill, which Stanford had predicted would require ten thousand yards of dirt, early in February, 1869, and were almost finished when a reporter from the Salt Lake City *Daily Telegraph* visited the scene on April 14: "On either side of this immense fill the blasters are at work in the hardest of black lime-rock, opening cuts of from 20 to 30 feet depth. The proximity of the earth-work and blasting to each other, at these and other points along the Promontory line, requires the utmost care and vigilance on the part of all concerned, else serious if not fatal, consequences would be of frequent occurrence. Three mules were recently killed by a single blast."

The Big Trestle was of even greater interest. The Union Pacific lacked the time to fill in the deep gorge as the Central Pacific had done. Construction superintendent Sam Reed and consulting engineer Silas Seymour therefore decided to bridge the defile with a temporary trestle, which could later, after the roads had joined, be replaced with an earth fill. On March 28, with the Big Fill still under construction, they ordered their bridge engineer, Leonard Eicholtz, to start the Big Trestle. It was about 150 feet east of, and parallel to, the Big Fill and required deep cuts at each end.

On April 23, 1869, the daily *Alta California* reported: "The space between the Central Pacific Railroad and the Union Pacific is about fifty miles. The Central Pacific is laying about four miles of track a day; the Union Pacific some days have laid the same, others only one or two, from lack of material—principally ties."

On the same day, Central Pacific engineer Clement, who was also a member of the Pacific Railroad Commission, wrote to Butler Ives in Washington: "This morning I noticed a telegram from G. M. Dodge, Chf Engr UPRR that the tracks were now only 30 miles apart. I am glad to hear it but I don't think they have made as rapid progress as should have been made— Congress, by the mutual agreement of the two companies made a compromise, which of course you have been advised through the great medicine of America, the newspapers, and will therefore not attempt to inform you of what you are already cognizant.

"We the commissioners are simply wasting our time in endeavoring to ascertain the best location from North or Ives Pass to Ogden, a fact already firmly established by the band of iron which is to hold our glorious country in one union. There is but little doubt but that there will be another *commission* appointed consisting of five (5) eminent citizens, eminent they must be, for none others could be appointed ha! ha! I don't know how this commission will end nor how it will make its report. Suffice it to say that I am heartily sick of such d——d nonsense and sincerely hope that this illegal, unjust, and humbugging progress will soon end."

Although the lines had not yet joined, emigrants were already moving west by rail, as the *Alta California* reported on April 26: "The first immigrant train for California was met at Grouse Creek, on the 11th. At 9 p.m. of the same day, the party entered Utah Territory at Rose Bud. On the morning of the 18th they reached Monument Point. Parker's Camp, as it is called, is about a quarter of a mile distant from the Lake. Here are at present three Chinese camps, the first containing 100 tents; the second, 100; and the third, 75. On the 18th a train came in from the West, consisting of 32 cars all laden with rails and ties. The road is being thoroughly ballasted as rapidly as possible, and intermediate ties put in."

Two days later, the *Alta* again noted construction progress: "END OF C.P. TRACK, Tuesday, April 27. I arrived here last evening at nine o'clock. The Central Pacific Railroad Company have laid their track to within fourteen miles of the meeting point, on the summit of Promontory Mountain, and will finish their work Thursday or Friday. They laid two miles of iron to-day, then the engine got off the rails.

"The Union Pacific Railroad Company have laid their rails to within eight miles of the Summit of Promontory Pass, and are laying a mile a day

(Left): Locomotive "Gold Run" at Terrace, Utah, with master mechanic William McKenzie; J. A. Jacobs, agent, and Charles Wright, engineer.

(Below): The locomotive "Falcon" during an inspection trip. The two men sitting on the pilot, covered with a buffalo robe, are Commissioners Clements and Blinkendoffer.

easy, but they have some difficult rock cutting to do, and some trestle work to erect, which will take twelve or fifteen days to complete. They may hurry up, or they may decide to turn on to the abandoned grade of the Central Pacific, which is within a few feet of where they are working. The united force of both companies should finish the work (by using the Central grading east of the Summit) in a week."

In April of 1869, the Central Pacific laid 10 miles and 56 feet of railroad track in a single day—a record that still challenges engineers today. Documentary evidence concerning this unparalleled feat, in the form of original time-book records, was kept by George Coley, foreman of the champion crew. A footnote on a page of the time book listing the names and "time" of eight Irishmen reads: "The above are the names of the men that laid 10 miles and 56 feet of railroad track April 28th, 1869."* Simple enough in itself, the note records one of the most colorful chapters in the building of the Central Pacific, a story in which the names of the Irish rail-handlers and their Chinese helpers will be handed down as long as there is railroad history.

Early in 1869 Crocker had predicted that his men would lay ten miles of rail in a single day, a "ridiculous boast" that was scoffed at in the rival construction camps. Rumor had it that Vice-President Durant of the Union Pacific wagered $10,000 that it could not be done, and that his money was covered by Crocker.

For several days Crocker laid his plans and marshalled his resources. Ties were hauled ahead by two-horse teams and distributed along the right of way, already graded for some distance. Rails and track materials were moved up from the rear and held in trains ready to advance. Each of the more than 4,000 men had been briefed on his particular job, and hundreds of horses and wagons were on the spot. Even the methodical Chinese, it is said, were stirred to a pitch of excitement and shared the eagerness of the few hundred Caucasians to "get at the job."

April 27, 1869, was the day selected, but an engine ran off the track early in the proceedings and compelled a postponement until the next day. This mishap brought many a laugh from the Union Pacific side, but only served to arouse the determination of Crocker's men. At seven o'clock on the morning of the twenty-eighth, sixteen cars loaded with enough iron rail and materials for two miles of track clanged to a halt at the construction front. Men scrambled to the top and threw off the fishplates** and the kegs

---

*The eight Irish rail-handlers were George Eliott, Edward Kelleen, Thomas Daley, Mike Shaw, Mike Sullivan, Mike Kenedy, Fred McNamare, and Patrick Joice.
**Metal plates for holding abutting rails in alignment.

of bolts and spikes. Others punched side stakes out of the right and left sides of alternate cars, and rails were rolled off. In eight minutes, with a noise like a bombardment, the sixteen cars were cleared. Then the train pulled back and another train of rails rolled into position.

As soon as the materials train was gone, small iron hand cars were put on the tracks. Each had a crew of six Chinese working under white bosses. Sixteen rails were loaded onto each car, together with a keg of bolts, a keg of spikes, and a bundle of fishplates. Two horses with riders were attached to each car in tandem by a long rope. When the cars were loaded and the crew on top, the horses were off on the jump. One side of the roadway was kept clear for the horses racing ahead with the material cars. On the down-grade the horses were detached, and the car went flying along with one of the crew acting as brakeman. At the same time empty cars were returning, all of them at full speed. As a loaded car came closer on the single track, the crew on the empty jumped off and lifted their car from the rails, while the full car went past with unslackened speed. Nothing was allowed to halt the continuous flow of materials to the front.

At the railhead, the gang jumped from the loaded car and another gang leaped aboard with picks, broke open the kegs and cut the fastenings on the bundles of fishplates. They threw the keg of bolts to men alongside, who filled buckets and distributed the bolts along the roadbed. Other men distributed the fishplates. The spikes were poured out over the rails; as the rails were removed for laying, the spikes dropped through the floorless car and distributed themselves.

At this point the crew of Irish rail-handlers, working under foreman Coley, moved into action. A single horse pulled the car up to the railhead, where it was blocked by a wooden-framed iron track gauge. Four men worked on each side of the track. Two seized the forward end of the rail with tongs, while two others slid the rail to the side of the car so that it rested on iron rollers. The two forward men trotted ahead the length of the rail, thirty feet, and the rear men dropped the rail into place on the ties, where it was bolted and spiked by the track gang. Then the horse pulled the car ahead, and the process was repeated. The track went forward at the rate of almost a mile an hour. The crews laid rail at a rate of approximately 240 feet in a minute and 15 seconds—about as fast as a leisurely walk.

But the rail-handlers were only eight of several hundred men at the front, every one of whom was an important cog in the smooth-working machinery. Far ahead were three "pioneers," who, with shovel and by hand, butted the ties to a rope line measured from the track-center spikes set by the surveyors. Just behind the rail-layers came the men who distributed the materials, and the spikers, and the bolters. Then came the gang that surfaced the track by raising the ends of the ties and shoveling enough ballast under-

On April 28, 1869, the Central Pacific crew laid ten miles of track in a single day, the track being moved forward at a rate of one mile per hour. Eight strong Irishmen laid a total of 3520 rails, using specially built cars hitched to two horses, in tandem, to race the materials up the newly laid track, and setting a record that challenges engineers to this day.

neath to hold them firm. Immediately following was a "reverend looking old gentleman" who sighted the line of the rails and, by motions with his hands, directed the track-straighteners. Finally the tampers came, four hundred strong, with shovels and tamping bars. From the first "pioneer" to the last tamper, about two miles away, the line of men advanced a mile in an hour.

Iron cars with their loads of rails and workers dashed up and down the newly-laid track. Foremen on horseback galloped in all directions. Keeping pace with the track-layers was the telegraph construction party. Alongside, teams hauled tool and water wagons. Chinese, with pails swinging from poles balanced over their shoulders, moved among the men with water and tea. Farther back, locomotives waited with their cars and materials. Five trains, loaded to capacity, were emptied that day. When one section was completed, the next material train rolled up as far as possible on the new track, and material for another two miles was unloaded. Moving along at the rear was the headquarters train of J. H. Strobridge and the "boarding house," a long line of wooden houses built on flat cars, looking like a small town stretching out along the line.

When a halt was called for the mid-day meal, six miles of track had been laid, and the men were confident that they would achieve their goal. Jubilant crews named their dinner stop "Victory" (now Rozel, Utah). Union Pacific officials, watching the work, were ready to concede the achievement.

After lunch the work went on, but not so rapidly. The line began ascending the west slope of Promontory Mountain, and there were many curves. Rails had to be bent, by placing the rail on two blocks and forcing it into the desired curve by blows of a heavy hammer—a time-consuming process.

When the forward march was halted at seven o'clock that evening, 10 miles and 56 feet of new track had been added to the Central Pacific. One Jim Campbell, boarding boss and later superintendent of the division, jumped into a locomotive and ran it back over the new line at a clip of forty miles an hour, just to show that the job had been well done. The task had involved bringing up and putting into position 25,800 ties, 3,520 rails, 55,000 pounds of spikes, 14,080 bolts, and other material.

Each of the rail-handlers lifted 125 tons of iron during the day, not counting their heavy rail tongs. Theirs was a wonderful exhibition of skill and strength, and they well deserved the acclaim showered on them when they proudly rode through the streets of Sacramento in a wagon during a celebration a few days later.

"Meantime," the *Alta California* reported, "the Union Pacific road creeps on but slowly; they have to build a tremendous trestle-work, over

400 feet long and 85 feet high. But their rock cutting is the most formidable work, and it seems a pity that such a big job should be necessary when the grading of the Central Pacific is available and has been offered to them. The trestle-work is like a frame gossamer; one would think that a carpenter's scaffolding were stouter.

"The loose population that has followed up the track-layers of the Union Pacific is turbulent and rascally. Several shooting scrapes have occurred among them lately. Last night a whisky-seller and a gambler had a fracas, in which the 'sport' shot the whisky dealer, and the friends of the latter shot the gambler. Nobody knows what will become of these riff-raff when the tracks meet, but they are lively enough now and carry off their share of the plunder from the working men."

On May 1, 1869, the correspondent for the *Alta* forecast completion of the road and reported on the fate of the gambler:

"Standing here, on this rising ground, a view of the whole field may be obtained. . . . Along the line of the road may be seen the white camps of the Chinese laborers, and from every one of them squads of these people are advancing. . . . The work of today leaves but four miles to be laid on the Central Pacific. These four miles are almost graded. The Union Pacific has ten miles of road to grade. The cutting in some places is very difficult, but the expectation is that the work will be completed on the 10th of May.

"In company with Mr. Strobridge, I drove yesterday to the point where the advanced posts of the two great armies of workers come close together. As we approached the Union Pacific posts, we were met by a party of white men who appeared to be in a state of unusual hilarity. The thought struck me that probably they had or were about to lay ten miles of track also; but a short distance further I found that they had only been laying out one of their own number on the side of the road. A wounded man was stretched out in a pool of blood. Some of the Central Pacific engineers, who had a little camp in the vicinity, and who were attending to the wounded man, informed us that the party whom we had met on the road had fallen upon this fellow with rifles and pistols; shots for a time rained about their little tents; one of the engineers got behind a water barrel for safety. Thirty or forty shots had been fired at the unfortunate wretch, and as he ran, one entered the left side of his face and came out at the other side, and another penetrated his leg.

"The cause of these dreadful proceedings I discovered shortly afterwards. About two miles further on is a little village of white tents; it is located in a picturesque spot in the Great Salt Lake Basin, with a portion of the lake visible in the distance; it looks smiling and calm enough in the distance. A drive through its streets recalled that every house was either a rum-mill or a grocery. If their character was no worse than this, it is pos-

sible that the scenes of riot and bloodshed which are so often enacted here would not have such tragic termination."

Bloodshed of one kind or another impeded the C.P.'s progress not at all, as the San Francisco *Evening Bulletin* reported the following day: "The Union Pacific people are pushing on the work as fast as possible. They are hauling ties and iron to the Summit, and are laying track from the Summit eastward to keep the men employed while waiting for the graders. A ride along the line from the Central Pacific station to the Union Pacific station shows that they have some heavy work to do on their side—heavier than anything the Central Pacific have had east of Humboldt Cañon. All cuts but one are nearly finished, and will be cleared up for the track-layers in three or four days, except one, and on that all the force that can be put on is working day and night, blasting. . . . The fills are not all finished, but will be in time, and, if necessary, they will put up trestle-work if they get behind. The lumber is ready at hand. The great trestle-work four miles east of the Summit is nearly finished. Mr. Casement says it is only temporary, and will be filled up during the summer. The banks of the great fill will be widened as soon as possible.

"The track-layers of the Union Pacific Company will be kept working at either end as the graders get out of the way."

But the race to Promontory was already won. The U.P. was too late. The Central Pacific reached the summit on April 30, as noted by the *Alta* of May 2: "The last blow has been struck on the Central Pacific Railroad, and the last tie and rail were placed in position today. We are now waiting for the Union Pacific to finish their rock-cutting."

Three days later, the *Alta's* reporter outlined progress on the U.P., which had finally finished the Big Trestle on May 5:

"In company with F. L. Vandenburg, General Superintendent of the telegraph, C.P.R.R., and Dan'l Casement, the veteran Union Pacific Railroad builder . . . your reporter has today ridden over the entire grade from Victory to a point east of Blue Creek and back. . . . The great Eastern line is nearly completed, and the two opposing armies . . . are melting away, and the white camps which dotted every brown hillside and every shady glen . . . are being broken up and abandoned.

"The Central Pacific force are nearly all gone already, and that of the Union is going fast. Ninety of the latter left for the East this morning, and a hundred more go tomorrow, and the rest will soon follow. Between six and seven hundred graders and one hundred track-layers are working on the Union Pacific, and now only twenty-five feet of rock-cutting remains to be finished in the Promontory Range at this moment, that is nearly all drilled and ready for blasting. Work will be carried on all night, and by tomorrow noon the grading will be entirely completed. The track-layers have just reached the long trestle-work on the east slope of Promontory Range, and will pass tonight, and can easily finish all by Friday morning, if no delay is made."

On Saturday, May 8, 1869, the San Francisco *Evening Bulletin* reported that a Chinese tong war had added to the C.P.'s problems: "Since my last dispatch a battle has occurred between two rival companies of Chinese, several hundred in number, laborers of the See Yup and Teng Wo Companies. They have been idle at Victory, eight miles from here, for a number of days past. The row occurred about fifteen dollars due from one camp to the other. After the usual braggadocio, both parties sailed in, at a given signal, armed with every conceivable weapon. Spades were handled, and crowbars, spikes, picks and infernal machines were hurled between the ranks of the contestants. Several shots were fired, and everything betokened the outbreak of a riot. At this juncture Superintendent Strobridge, with several of his men, rushed into the melee, and, with the assistance of the leading Chinamen, who were more peaceably disposed, he succeeded in separating the combatants and restoring order among the Chinese.

"The casualties include the shooting, fatally, it is supposed, of a Chinese. The ball penetrated his left side, tearing the flesh and inflicting a very ugly wound. If this man dies, another encounter will certainly follow and much bloodshed will doubtless ensue. . . ."

The date for the joining of the rails was announced in the *Alta California* for May 8: "The Union Pacific completed the rock-cutting through Promontory Point, striking the last blow this p.m. Nothing now remains to be done save a slight filling-up on the grade and the laying of about a mile and a quarter of the track. . . . This could be finished tomorrow noon, but I am told by the employees of the Union Pacific that they have been notified by telegram from the East that the ceremony of formally connecting the lines will be postponed until next Monday [May 10] to enable all the guests from the East to arrive."

On the following day, the *Alta* announced the meeting of the engines, if not yet the rails: "This afternoon the Union Pacific finished their track to a switch forty rods east of the end of the Central, on the new side track down to a point opposite the Central. At twenty minutes past four, Central [Pacific Standard] time, and fifteen minutes past five, Cheyenne time, Engine No. 66 arrived from the East with Casement, the contractors and others. No. 66 came to a halt and the engineer let off steam. . . . Engine No. 62, named the *Whirlwind,* on the Central road, standing opposite and within 100 feet, replied with a sharp whistle, and thus the first meeting of locomotives from the Atlantic and Pacific Coasts took place. The employees of both roads curiously examined each others' machines, which are radically different."

257

That day, Colonel C. R. Savage, the U.P.'s official photographer, noted in his diary: "At ½ past 12 o'clock the last rail but one was laid on the track. Arrived at Blue River. Thence to Casement's camp, where I had the honor of dining with Jack and Dan Casement in their private car. . . . Very pleasant and agreeable reception. In sight of their camp was the beautiful city of Deadfall and Last Chance. I was creditably informed that 24 men had been killed in the several camps in the last 25 days. Certainly a harder set of men were never congregated together before. The company would do the country a service in sending such men back to Omaha, for their presence would be a scourge upon any community. At Blue River the returning "democrats" so-called were being piled upon the cars in every stage of drunkenness. Every ranch or tent has whiskey for sale. Verily, men earn their money like horses and spend it like asses."

Colonel Savage's diary also records the arrival of the Central Pacific dignitaries on Saturday, May 8:

"Today a train or engine arrived with a delegation of California notables preparing for the laying of the last rail. Took three or four negatives around Casement's camp. Dined at Casement's, suppered with Mr. Sherman [Shearman], engineer. Saw Major Russell and many RR men, Mr. Hart, photographer. . . ."

The San Francisco *Evening Bulletin* of May 11, 1869, gave an account of the arrival of the Union Pacific visitors:

"General Casement today furnished trains to Governor Stanford and party, who made an excursion from this point, being also supplied with a bountiful collation and oceans of champagne. The healths of the officers of the Central Pacific Railroad were pledged and cordial greetings extended to them by General Casement. Superintendent Campbell, of the Central, proposed the health of General Casement and the officers of both roads, which was received with immense applause.

"General Hoxie, Assistant Superintendent of the Union Pacific, entertained a large party to a splendid luncheon at Taylor's Mills, a hamlet on the bank of Weber river. The most cordial harmony and good feeling marked their entertainment and all the toasts were drunk with loud applause. A special train was placed at the service of this party, and a visit was made to Ogden, which lasted about twenty-four hours.

"In consequence of the breaking of a trestle bridge, the trains of the Union Pacific are delayed in Weber Canyon. It is expected, however, that the bridge will be repaired today and the train will pass over tomorrow [Sunday]. On this train are the officers of the Union Pacific Company.

"The train from the East arrived today. The passengers are full of complaints against the Union Pacific Company. . . . They were compelled to walk around the Devil's Gate bridge, about three miles, in a drenching

Ogden, with the Wasatch Range in the background.

The Union Pacific Construction train, near Ogden.

shower with garments utterly inadequate to afford protection against the rain. They complain bitterly of the treatment which they received at the hands of the Union Pacific officials on the road this side of Cheyenne."

A great many people apparently were disenchanted with the Union Pacific, particularly a large contingent of the line's unpaid Irish workers, who took matters into their own hands and wrote a diverting addendum to history in the last few days before the celebration at Promontory. The San Francisco *Bulletin* reported the story on May 11:

"It appears that the Director's car, with the party I have named [E. P. Durant and other officials of the UP], arrived at Piedmont from Wasatch on Thursday forenoon [May 6]. Five hundred men gathered around clamoring for money. As the train was about to leave, four men armed but not showing weapons, told the conductor they did not want that car to go on. The conductor took no notice and the train moved on. The four men then loosed the pin and the car was detached. The conductor moved back to connect again, when four pistol barrels induced him to change his mind, and leave Durant and others to their fate. The men politely asked Cash and wife and others not to be concerned, and to step out; but they kept Durant and Dillon, and were disappointed to find Duff had stayed at Wasatch. They informed Durant he could not go until they were paid. Durant said, 'All right; the money is coming.' He said he was only going to look at a bridge a few miles east, and would be back tomorrow; by that time money would arrive. The men did not see it, and told Durant they thought he had better stay, and that he might not get there. They would put him on the side track; also, to prevent his car rolling off, they would chain the wheels to the rails.

"In the meantime they took possession of the telegraph office and allowed no messages but those regarding finances to go, employing their own operator. Davies, the lawyer of the Company, agreed with the men, but one of them interrupted him and thought on this occasion that the chairman of the delegates should do the talking, whereupon an Irish grader talked Tipperary law to them for two hours, complimenting Davies on his legal ability, but he must come to the Rocky Mountains to learn law.

"Durant was very cool. He had intended to stay a few days at Piedmont as he came back. There was some good fishing in the mountain streams, known as the 'muddy,' and he would go there. His grading friends consented, but thought it would help his sport if he had four or five men with muskets to accompany him. Durant thought so much company would prevent him getting a bite; so he dropped that idea.

"Next it became known that 300 troops were coming through, and there was talk of communicating with them. His custodians told him they were sorry to incommode him by taking him out of his comfortable car, but their wagons were hitched and they would have to take him to the woods for a few days. Durant, seeing the stratagem had failed, submitted to his persecutors with good grace, and on Saturday morning [May 8], after 48 hours detention, he was liberated on paying the men and contractors $253,000. Some of his fellow travelers who, though of course denouncing such outrages, had collected several thousand dollars which they hardly expected to get for months, had their jokes about Durant going fishing in 'the Muddy.' These were more frequent than pleasant to Durant's ears. Durant has had enough of the Rocky Mountain way of collecting debts. . . ."

FIFTEEN

A GOLDEN SPIKE AND
A SILVER-HEADED HAMMER: *May 10, 1869*

MUCH FOLKLORE HAS CIRCULATED about the events of May 10, 1869. Even the stories filed by the various newspaper correspondents differ greatly. For this narrative I have relied upon various eye-witness accounts, including the recollections of various company officials, and some apparently reliable newspaper reports.

In the view of David Hewes, of San Francisco, the junction of the Central Pacific and Union Pacific at Promontory could not pass without an appropriate celebration. Mr. Hewes, a member of the C.P. party, tells the story of how it all came about:

"On completion of the railroad, seeing that there was no proper sentiment being expressed by the people of the Pacific Coast, and especially by the great mining industries of the territories through which this railroad passed, it came to be my thought that the Central Pacific and Union Pacific should not be united except by a connecting link of silver rails. The two great roads, the Central Pacific and the Union Pacific, connected the two great oceans which then and for all future time must carry the commerce of the world. As the road passed over the noted gold and silver belts, and was a matter of such national and local importance to our country and state, I thought that it would naturally create some sentiment among the rich men of the Comstock, who were shipping ton upon ton of silver east in the shape of bricks. I felt hurt and mortified that there was no recognition being made of such a great event. At the last moment, I said, 'There was one last thing to be done, a last tie and a last spike to be furnished before the great work can be finished.' As an individual, I presented a gold spike and polished laurel tie,* with a silver shield on which was inscribed as follows: 'The last tie which unites in part, and helps complete the great road across the Continent.'

"Senator Stanford's brother, A. P. Stanford, was appointed to act as marshal of the occasion [the San Francisco parade of celebration]. He requested me to ask Leland, his brother, the President of the road, what signal he would send him when the road was completed. I conveyed to Leland Stanford his brother's request, and at the same time suggested to him the plan of attaching a wire to throw over the company's telegraph line and thus connecting with the Golden Spike, and have it operate in the same way like a telegraph instrument, so that signals for the firing of heavy guns by electricity could be produced. I consulted with officers of the Western Telegraph Company as to the probability of being able to fire cannon by electricity, and of firing a national salute from Fort Point at the entrance of the Golden Gate, by this means. I also consulted with General Ord [commander on the Pacific Coast] with regard to the matter. General Ord obtained permission from Washington to connect the telegraph wires with the parapet guns . . . at Fort Point. The telegraph company ran their wires about two miles to make a connection with the Fort, and a telegraphic operator was sent to take charge of the wires connecting the parapet guns."

On May 4, 1869, just two days before Leland Stanford and other invited guests were to depart from Sacramento enroute to Promontory, David Hewes picked up his gold spike from a silverware company of San Francisco, paying $25.25 for having the spike cast and engraved. The San Francisco *Alta California* of May 5, 1869, had this to say: "Mr. David Hewes left yesterday with a gold spike, manufactured for him by Messrs. Schultz, Fischer & Mahling, of this city, and which is intended to be the last spike driven on the completion of the road. This spike weighs about eighteen ounces and is valued at $350. A nugget about six inches in length is attached to the head of the spike, and will be broken off at the conclusion of the ceremonies to be made up into mementos. The following is the inscription:

" 'The last Spike. The Pacific Railroad—Ground broken January 8th, 1863; completed May—1869.

" 'May God continue the unity of our country as this railroad unites the two great oceans of the world.'

"The directors' names appear on the third face and those of the officers on the fourth.

---

*It appears that the true presentor of the laurel-wood tie was the Central Pacific's tie contractor, West Evans. It is possible that Hewes may have paid for it or suggested it to Evans.

" 'Presented by David Hewes, San Francisco.' "

The same edition of the *Alta* also mentioned the last tie: "Yesterday the attention of numerous citizens was attracted to the railroad tie which has been prepared for transmission to the junction of the two portions of the Pacific Railroad, and was on exhibition at Baldwin's jewelry store. This tie, which will be the last laid on the new road, has been already received at Sacramento, as will be seen by reference to our telegraphic dispatches."

The next day, the *Alta* described a third item: "Yesterday the Pacific Union Express Company, of this city, forwarded to Sacramento, enroute for the 'front' a silver-headed spike hammer, weighing about five pounds to be used in driving the last spike, of which so much has been written and said. This hammer, which is very neatly gotten up, is presented by the Pacific Union Express Company to the Central Pacific Railroad Company, and has upon its handle, which is of hickory, a silver plate bearing the following inscription: 'For the last spike. From the Pacific Union Express Company.' The hammer was manufactured by Messrs. Conroy & O'Connor, the silver work being done by Messrs. Vanderslice & Co."

The California delegation was first upon the ground. The Central Pacific regular passenger train, leaving Sacramento at six o'clock on the morning of May 6, bore a number of excursionists. It was closely followed by Stanford's special train—engine, tender, and superintendent's car. This car, one of the few indulgences of the road, was an official traveling home of the early Pullman style, containing a kitchen, dining conveniences, and sleeping accommodations for ten. Aboard were President Stanford, Chief Justice Sanderson, Governor A. P. K. Safford of Arizona, Clifford Gates, of Nevada, and the three government commissioners, Sherman, Haines, and Tritle, with two or three other guests. Also on board were the last spike, the last tie, and the silver-headed hammer.

On the way to Promontory, the Stanford special narrowly escaped catastrophe. Chinese, cutting timber on the mountains above the entrance to Tunnel No. 14 near the state line east of Truckee, saw the regular train pass and, unaware of the following special, skidded a log down upon the track below. The log, fifty feet long and three and one-half feet in circumference, landed in a cut, with one end against the bank and its butt upon a rail. As the train rounded the curve at this point, the engineer had barely enough time to apply brakes. The engine struck the log and was badly crippled. A guest riding on the cowcatcher was seriously injured, and the log scraped all along one side of the special car, taking the steps with it. The station at Wadsworth was ordered by telegraph to hold the passenger train until the Stanford coach might be attached. "Crocker's pets," who had made the road possible, almost dislocated the final events that were to celebrate their handiwork.

Sidney Dillon.

Monument Point, 669 miles from Sacramento.

The last emigrant wagon train heading west meets the first locomotive heading east, as they pause at the north shore of the Great Salt Lake, May 8, 1869.

The coach arrived at Promontory on Friday afternoon, May 7, in anticipation of the ceremonies set for the next day. But nothing was ready. Telegraph operators for each company were housed in tents within a few rods of each other. Stanford's group wired the Ogden office of the Union Pacific. General Casement replied that it was impossible for the U.P. delegation to arrive before Monday, as heavy rains had interrupted traffic east of Ogden. President Stanford telegraphed the disappointing news to Sacramento and San Francisco, but these two cities answered that it was too late for them to alter their own schedule of festivities. They were going to celebrate anyway, and so they did—for three days.

The official C.P. party and the other passengers were themselves in an uncomfortable situation, stranded in the rain at Promontory with a two-day wait ahead of them. Some of them hired rigs and drove to the nearest Union Pacific construction camp. General Casement ordered a special train to go out from Ogden and bring the party back. President Stanford and guests spent Friday night in his special car. On Saturday morning, May 8, the U.P. superintendent's car arrived to take them for a tour into Weber Canyon. The Stanford party gladly accepted the invitation, but returned somewhat dampened on Saturday night. The Stanford car withdrew to a more pleasant location at Monument Point siding, thirty miles west from Promontory, where there was a view of the lake. Here, they spent Sunday, May 9. The steward sallied out into the desert and shot a mess of plover. Meanwhile, San Francisco had been celebrating, and Sacramento was trying to curb the spirits of its hundreds of visitors.

It was plain to the Central Pacific excursionists that the Union Pacific indeed had encountered weather difficulties. The spring rains, unusually heavy, played havoc down through the canyons of the Wasatch, where the roadbed had been built in haste. The trains approaching from the east, bearing the first excursionists and through passengers, crept along at snail's pace upon a red flag trail. With tourist's gathered from New York, Boston, Chicago, and intermediate points, the first train had left Omaha on May 5; at darkness on May 8 it was stalled in the downpour near the exit from Weber Canyon, ten miles out of Ogden. The conductor declined to proceed until daylight; whereupon the boldest of the miserable, shivering passengers took stage for the haven of Salt Lake City, forty miles south. The Union Pacific section men were working hard to fortify the track and bridges. The Devil's Gate Bridge had to be closely watched all day Sunday and Monday, but U.P.'s operating department could give no guarantee insuring the celebration specials.

In the Promontory region, the rain continued. The plateau, Muddy Town, and the hardy construction camps were drenched, and the outlook from the Stanford car dismal. On the evening of Sunday, May 9, however,

*Tents and hastily constructed shacks
lined the track at Promontory (below).
The town was later by-passed, but
the station house and tracks at right
remained until 1942, when they
were finally torn up.*

the clouds broke, promising fair weather. The U.P.'s construction force heard that the Central Pacific was preparing early the next morning to extend its temporarily laid spur into a complete siding, thus establishing a claim to Promontory as a Central terminal. General Casement and chief engineer Dodge of the U.P. hustled their gangs and worked all night. At daybreak they had finished their own siding, and Promontory was a Union Pacific terminus. By the time the Central construction train puffed in, bearing material and Chinese workmen, the Union ballasters greeted it with a cheer.

May 10 was a fine day. The weather had cleared so cold that ice formed upon still water; but the morning dawned brightly, with a fresh breeze that ironed out the flag snapping from the telegraph pole overlooking the gap in the track, and whipped the Great Salt Lake into foam-tipped waves.

Promontory town, a single miserable street lined with canvas and rough-board shacks, was arrayed in all her festal clothes. This was her hour, the one brief moment in history when she occupied center stage. She stood upon her present, not upon her short, turbulent, and rather dubious past.

The wedding of the rails resembled a runaway marriage. The spot for the ceremony could not easily have been more remote. The plateau of Promontory Summit lay 5,000 feet above sea level. To the south, behind the camp of Promontory, the terrain rose sharply, covered with cedar; its crest and outthrust point, bordering the lake, offered a magnificent view of the vast inland sea a thousand feet below. North from the tracks the bench again rose, to form a parallel parapet. The ceremony occurred, then, in a flat valley, bare except for sagebrush and a sprinkling of scrub cedars. Its portals were concealed, and the uninvited world, except for circling buzzards, shut out.

It had been planned that the Central Pacific and the Union Pacific specials should arrive from the west and east at the same moment. But the ready construction trains were first on hand, loaded inside and out, from cabooses to the pilot cabs of the tooting engines, with cheering track and grading gangs, who poured from the cars when the trains stopped on the sidings. Others hastened to join them astride sorry grading nags, and by eight o'clock—well before the scheduled noon-time celebration—the site was crowded with spectators.

Frank Leslie's Illustrated Newspaper of June 5, 1869, described the scene: "After a pleasant ride of about six miles we attained a very high elevation, and passing through a gorge of the mountains, we entered a level, circular valley, about three miles in diameter, surrounded on every side by mountains. The track is on the eastern side of the plain, and at the point of junction extends in nearly a southwest and northeast direction. Two lengths of rail are left for today's work. We arrived on the ground

(Above): The first greeting of the iron horse at Promontory Point, May 9.

(Right): The last rail is laid, Promontory Point, May 10.

twenty minutes past eight A.M., and while we are waiting we will look about us a little. A large number of men at work ballasting and straightening the track, also building a 'Y' switch. Fourteen tent houses for the sale of 'Red Cloud', 'Red Jacket', and 'Blue Run' are about evenly distributed on each side of the track. Two engines are here."

At 8:45 A.M. the Central Pacific train arrived and was greeted by applause from the crowd. The Stanford car, drawn by the Central Pacific locomotive *Jupiter*, C.P. No. 60, fluttered red, white, and blue banners and bunting as it stood on a siding, to be pulled forward with the official party when the hour of noon came closer.

Between ten and eleven o'clock the Union Pacific's two special excursion trains arrived with the eastern officials and four companies of the Twenty-first Infantry, Major Milton Cogswell commanding. Also aboard was the Tenth Ward Headquarters Band with colorful uniforms and new instruments, which had cost $6,200 in London. They were enroute from Camp Douglas at Salt Lake, to the Presidio at San Francisco. The first train, carrying the official party, was characterized as having the most "elegant" appointments, and the largest number of passengers that had yet run over the line. Sam Bradford was at the throttle of the Rogers-built U.P. No. 119, with B. S. Mallory as conductor.

At 11:15 A.M., Central Pacific's special train, with Governor Leland Stanford's official party aboard, was pulled forward. As president, Stanford led the C.P. party over to the U.P. official train, and to the cheers of the assembled crowd, shook hands with the various members of the U.P. delegation, which had detrained to meet him. They were Vice-President Durant; courtly Sidney Dillon, chairman of the board of directors and head of the Credit Mobilier Company; the portly, white-haired John Duff from Boston; General Dodge; consulting engineer Silas Seymour; General Casement and his brother Dan; superintendents Sam Reed and James Evans; assistant superintendent Marshall Hurd; and a number of guests, including Rev. John Todd, of Pittsfield, Massachusetts, who was to bless the union of the two roads.

By now the crowd had grown to some twelve or fifteen hundred excited people. A number of ladies were present, and a few children could be seen among the spectators. Brigham Young was not present. The astute Mormon leader was in southern Utah on church and personal business, and the next Monday, was formally to officiate at the breaking of ground for his own Utah Central Railroad, which would connect the City of the Saints with Ogden. Bishop John Sharp, the "Railroad Bishop" of Utah's Mormon history, and Colonel Charles R. Savage, photographer of the day's scenes, brought Brigham Young's apologies. The capital city of Salt Lake, however, sent a deputation, and Ogden sent its mayor.

Also present were representatives from the newspapers of East and West. New York, Chicago, and Boston had their correspondents, and the Associated Press was, of course, on hand.

Under the supervision of W. B. Hibbard, superintendent of the Western Union Telegraph Company, and F. L. Vandenburg, superintendent of telegraphy for the Central Pacific, wires were run from the nearest Central Pacific and Union Pacific poles down to a special operator's kit upon a small four-legged table beside the gap between the rails. Here W. N. Shilling and W. R. Fredericks, of Western Union's Ogden office, and Howard Sigler and Louis Jacobs, Central Pacific operators, were on duty.

Amos L. Bowsher, telegraph construction boss for the Central Pacific, ran these lines and connected the wires to the last spike and hammer to be used in the ceremony. The hammer's tap would signal the world that the last spike had been driven home. A sense of awe prevailed as onlookers realized that San Francisco, Omaha, St. Louis, Chicago, Philadelphia, Washington, New York, Boston, and New Orleans were focusing their entire attention upon this small spot in the Utah desert. The sage-covered plain and blue-gray ridges shimmered in the sun and the temperature climbed to 69° by noon. Officials and guests of the occasion grouped themselves in the space to the south of the gap which was kept free of the crowd by a small detachment of infantry. Excitement mounted as construction superintendents Strobridge of the Central Pacific and Reed of the Union Pacific left the Stanford car bearing the silver-plated laurel tie. The two rails followed, Central Pacific's proudly carried by a clean, blue-frocked squad of Chinese under their boss, H. H. Minkler. The U.P. rail was carried by an Irish squad under foreman Guilford. The engine whistles shrieked, and cheers broke out. One veteran said, "We all yelled like to bust."

Another old-timer who was there later related that upon arrival of the two rails, a voice shouted to photographer Savage, "Now's the time, Charlie! Take a shot." The crew of Chinese from the C.P. "looked up, and saw the camera pointed their way." Dropping the rail, they stampeded for cover, to the joy and shouting of a delighted crowd. There was considerable argument before they would come back to lay their rail.

The crowd pressed forward. General Casement asked for space in order that all might see. The telegraph beat a tattoo of messages east and west to answer impatient inquiries from various offices:

TO EVERYBODY. KEEP QUIET. WHEN THE LAST SPIKE IS DRIVEN AT PROMONTORY POINT, WE WILL SAY 'DONE!' DON'T BREAK THE CIRCUIT, BUT WATCH FOR THE SIGNALS OF THE BLOWS OF THE HAMMER.

The instrument clicked again:

ALMOST READY. HATS OFF; PRAYER IS BEING OFFERED.

273

This message was bulletined at 2:27 P.M., eastern time, in Washington. By orders of James Gamble, head of Western Union, all wires were cleared for the news from Promontory, which had the right-of-way. Consequently, bulletins from the little telegrapher's table high in the Utah desert were read almost simultaneously by crowds collected at telegraph offices in large cities the length and breadth of the land. The Rev. Dr. Todd, of Massachusetts, offered the dedicatory prayer:

"Our Father and God, and our fathers' God, God of Creation and God of Providence, thou hast created the heavens and the earth, the valleys and the hills; Thou art also the God of mercies and blessings. We rejoice that thou hast created the human mind with its powers of invention, its capacity of expansion, and its guardian of success. We have assembled here this day, upon the height of the continent, from varied sections of our country, to do homage to thy wonderful name, in that thou hast brought this mighty enterprise, combining the commerce of the east with the gold of the west to so glorious a completion. And now we ask Thee that this great work, so auspiciously begun and so magnificently completed, may remain a monument of our faith and of our good works. We here consecrate this great highway for the good of thy people. O God, we implore thy blessings upon it and upon those who may direct its operations. O Father, God of our fathers, we desire to acknowledge thy handiwork in this great work, and ask thy blessing upon us here assembled, upon the rulers of our government and upon thy people everywhere; that peace may flow unto them as a gentle stream, and that this mighty enterprise may be unto us as the Atlantic of thy strength, and the Pacific of thy love, through Jesus, the Redeemer, Amen."

The two last rails, put into place minutes before, were then spiked with the regular iron spikes,* except at one end, where the last tie was to be inserted.

Then came the presentation of spikes.

Dr. Harkness, of Sacramento, presented Governor Stanford with the spike of pure gold, saying:

"Gentlemen of the Pacific Railroad, the last rail needed to complete the greatest railroad enterprise of the world is about to be laid; the last spike needed to unite the Atlantic and Pacific by a new line of trade and commerce is about to be driven to its place. To perform these acts the east and the west have come together. Never since history commenced her

---

*These spikes were driven by Henry Nottingham, president, Michigan, Central & Lake Shore Railroad; J. W. Haines (or Haynes), railroad commissioner and Republican candidate for governor of Nevada; F. A. Tritle, of Nevada; William Sherman, U. S. Commissioner of Inspection of San Francisco, and other friends of the railroad.

*The rival Monarchs—the Central Pacific's "Jupiter" (right),
meets the Union Pacific locomotive "No. 119" (left).
(The photograph below is by A. J. Russell, taken from the "Jupiter".)*

The celebrated meeting, and a time for photographs.
(Above): Leland Stanford, president of the Central Pacific,
is in the center of the group, holding the spike maul.
To the left (with spade) is superintendent Strobridge. The
two women are Mrs. Strobridge and a Mrs. Ryan. On the right
is T. C. Durant (with sledge on shoulder), John Duff, and Sidney Dillon.

(Left, below): Before the historic joining of the last rail,
officials of the C. P. and the U. P. gathered for a grand
group portrait. (Above): After the last tie, the last rail,
and the last spike had been taken care of, the engines of the
two companies moved forward until they touched and the respective
crews hauled out their bottles for this famous photograph.

record of human events has man been called upon to meet the completion of a work so magnificent in contemplation, and so marvelous in execution. California, within whose borders and by whose citizens the Pacific Railroad was inaugurated, desires to express her appreciation of the vast importance to her and her sister States of the great enterprise which by your action is about to be consummated; from her mines she had forged a spike, from her laurel woods she has hewn a tie, and by the hands of her citizens she offers them to become a part of the great highway which is about to unite her in closer fellowship with her sisters of the Atlantic. From her bosom was taken the first soil, let hers be the last tie and the last spike, and with them accept the hopes and wishes of her people that the success of your enterprise may not stop short of its brightest promise."

To Union Pacific Vice-President Durant, Commissioner F. A. Tritle presented a spike of silver from the Comstock Lode:* "To the iron of the East and the gold of the West, Nevada adds her link of silver to span the continent and weld the oceans."

Governor A. P. K. Safford of Arizona added a spike of alloy—gold, silver, and iron—also presented to Durant: "Ribbed in iron, clad in silver, and crowned with gold, Arizona presents her offering to the enterprise that has banded the continent and welded the oceans."

Many reports mention that Idaho and Montana also furnished spikes of silver and gold, but do not mention by whom they were presented or received.

Governor Stanford, in behalf of the Central Pacific Railroad, made the following response:

"Gentlemen, the Pacific Railroad companies accept with pride and satisfaction these golden and silver tokens of your appreciation of the importance of our enterprise to the material interests of the whole country, east and west, north and south. These gifts shall receive a fitting place in the superstructure of our road, and before laying the tie and driving the spikes in completion of the Pacific Railway allow me to express the hope that the great importance which you are pleased to attach to our undertaking may be in all respects fully realized. This line of rails, connecting the Atlantic and Pacific and affording to commerce a new transit, will prove, we trust, the speedy forerunner of increased facilities. The Pacific Railroad will, as soon as commerce shall begin fully to realize its advantages, demonstrate the necessity of rich improvements in railroading so as to render practicable the transportation of freight at much less rates than are possible under any system which has been thus far anywhere adopted. The day is not far distant when three tracks will be found neces-

---

*Some reports say it was the Hon. F. A. Fryth, of Nevada, who made this presentation.

sary to accommodate the commerce and travel which will seek a transit across the continent. Freight will then move only one way on each track, and at rates of speed that will answer the demands of cheapness and time. Cars and engines will be light or heavy, according to the speed required, and the weight to be transported. In conclusion, I will add that we hope to do, ultimately, what is now impossible on long lines—transport coarse, heavy and cheap products for all distances at living rates to the trade. Now, Gentlemen, with your assistance we will proceed to lay the last tie and last rail, and drive the last spike."

Dodge of the Union Pacific was called. As general superintendent, he spoke for his railroad in place of Vice-President Durant, who limited his appearance because of a headache. (In fact, he soon retired to his private car to rest.) Dodge said: "Gentlemen, the great Benton proposed that some day a giant statue of Columbus be erected on the highest peak of the Rocky Mountains, pointing westward, denoting that as the great route across the continent. You have made that prophecy today a fact. This is the way to India."

The crowd yelled, cheering for the United States, the Star Spangled Banner, the Pacific Railway, the officers, the men who raised the money, the men who built the grades and laid the track, and the engineers who found the way.

At this point, the silver-headed maul was presented to Leland Stanford by L. W. Coe, president of Pacific Union Express Company. The last tie upon which the rails of the two roads met was put in position by the two superintendents of construction, with J. H. Strobridge, of Central Pacific, handling the north end and S. B. Reed, of Union Pacific, the south end of the California laurel tie.

The telegraph dispatch received in the East at 2:40 P.M. announced, "We have got done praying; the spike is about to be presented."

Some wire trouble was being experienced at Omaha, and the bulletins were delayed. The Chicago office replied, "We understand. All are ready in the East."

The spikes and silver-headed maul were brought forward. "All ready now; the spike will soon be driven. The signal will be three dots for the commencement of the blows," the telegraph message flashed across the nation.

The silver spikes had been set into holes prepared to receive them, and had been partially driven by rather self-conscious guests. Doctor Durant was invited to drive his spike, and accomplished the feat gracefully.

The gold spike remained untouched. President Stanford was to have the privilege of signaling the waiting world. It was a moment of history likened afterward to the signing of the Declaration of Independence and

1863   C. P. R. R.   1869

GRAND

RAILROAD CELEBRATION

IN HONOR OF THE COMPLETION OF THE

GREAT NATIONAL RAILWAY

ACROSS THE CONTINENT.

The Completion of this Great Work will be Celebrated in
Sacramento, on the

EIGHTH DAY OF MAY, 1869,

Under the Direction of the COMMITTEE of CITIZENS

Chosen for that Purpose.

H. S. Crocker & Co's Print, Sac.

Cover of the brochure for the Grand Celebration in Sacramento.

the landing of the Pilgrim Fathers. National progress awaited only the hammer taps that signaled the end of a long campaign to level mountains and span deserts dividing a great people.

There was a hush. Inconvenienced by dangling wires, Stanford was plainly nervous. He struck an uncertain blow at the golden head—a blow to be heard "the fartherest of any by mortal man," like the first shot fired at Lexington. But he missed and he struck only the rail. That made no difference. The telegraph operator closed the circuit, and the instrument recorded "Done!"

San Francisco and Sacramento, still celebrating, received the message directly. The Omaha board grew panicky, but the operator there was fully equal to the occasion, and instantly passed the message on to Chicago.

At 2:47 P.M. in Washington, the magnetic ball on the dome of the capitol fell, and the crowd before the telegraph office began to shout. At San Francisco, the three dots had set off the heavy fire-bell in the city hall tower and triggered the discharge of 220 guns at Fort Point. At Sacramento the din of cannon, whistles, and bells drowned the uproar of thousands of excursionists brought in from valleys and mountains on free trains. At Omaha, 100 mighty guns boomed from Capitol Hill, and a cheering procession of military and civic groups took to the streets, in a noisy, rampaging excess of civic and national enthusiasm.

In New York, another hundred guns were fired. Trinity Church chanted the *"Te Deum,"* followed with "Old Hundred" on the chimes. In Philadelphia, Liberty Bell spoke in its cracked tones, and Independence Hall vibrated with the sound of joy. Buffalo echoed to the "Star Spangled Banner," sung by a mighty crowd in the streets. Chicago crowds watched four mile-long processions on land and water, which inspired Vice-President Schuyler Colfax for his evening address. In Salt Lake City, the great Tabernacle was filled to overflowing. In Ogden, where the news from the front had been received first, guns could be heard firing for fifteen minutes from courthouse, city hall, and Arsenal Hill, and all business places were closed. At two o'clock seven thousand people gathered in the new Tabernacle to hear speeches and a program by Huntington's Martial Band, which opened with "Mill May" and closed with "Hard Times Come Again No More."

At Promontory, President Stanford, after his first unremarkable blow, politely stood aside for Vice-President Durant, who with responsive courtesy proceeded to miss the spike himself!

To President Grant at Washington, the formal announcement was flashed:

PROMONTORY SUMMIT, UTAH, MAY 10, 1869

THE LAST RAIL IS LAID, THE LAST SPIKE DRIVEN. THE PACIFIC RAIL-
ROAD IS COMPLETED. THE POINT OF JUNCTION IS 1,086 MILES WEST
OF THE MISSOURI RIVER, AND 690 MILES EAST OF SACRAMENTO CITY.

LELAND STANFORD,
Central Pacific Railroad.
T. C. DURANT,
SIDNEY DILLON,
JOHN DUFF,
Union Pacific Railroad.

President Stanford and Vice-President Durant clasped hands across
the tie. The perspiring official photographers—A. J. Russell, Colonel
Savage of Salt Lake City, and Alfred Hart of Sacramento—manipulated
their slow lenses and delicate wet plates to capture the scene. The crowd
was again yelling "fit to bust"; the band tooted, the engines shrieked, and
a nine-year-old boy almost fell from his perch on a telegraph pole. Telegraph messages flooded in from east and west.

All the functionaries present were invited to tap the last spike, and it
soon bore the marks of numerous blows. The final setting of the spike was
awarded to the two engineers, Dodge and Montague. Mr. Montague struck
first and General Dodge second. Then the two shook hands. After that
there was a medley of hammering, to drive home the various spikes.

The two engines, *Jupiter* and No. 19, separated by the late gap, were
unhooked from their trains. Bearing celebrants who clung like ants, they
advanced proudly down a lane of cheering onlookers. The "stokers" (firemen) took the throttle, the "drivers" (engineers) swung out to the pilots,
each with a bottle of champagne; and as the locomotives touched noses,
the bottles were broken upon the opposite pilots, and the wine foamed
down upon the last tie, the last rails, and the last spike. Then the engineers
shook hands and the cameras clicked.*

Snorting *Jupiter* and No. 119 backed up adn hooked onto their trains.
The C.P. train retired a short space; the U.P. train crossed the junction of
the tracks, halted an instant, and majestically withdrew. The C.P. train
did the same. The transcontinental iron trail was a reality.

Scarcely had the locomotives retreated when joint crews of Central
and Union trackmen charged in with spades, crowbars, and pinchbars.
They pulled the precious spikes from the precious tie, unbedded the tie
itself, substituted a common tie, drove iron spikes home, and bolted the

---

*Everyone remained assembled for a half hour longer so the three photographers could
record the scenes from every available vantage point.

282

Parade down Montgomery Street, San Francisco, May 8, 1869.

fishplate fastenings. It was accomplished with the celerity of experts, but scarcely had the workers straightened their backs when the crowd rushed in to hack at the rails and at the tie with knives, reducing it to splinters. Six ties and two rails were demolished before the juncture was left in peace to the slower inroads of time.

At the invitation of the Union Pacific, officials and guests of both roads adjourned to the Durant Pullman—that "superb piece of cabinet work"—and read the telegrams that were pouring in. The invitation was returned, and they all adjourned to the Stanford car, where wine and speeches flowed during a "sumptuous lunch." Festivities continued in Dr. Durant's palace car where champagne flowed and oratory continued throughout the afternoon. It was nearly six o'clock that evening before the official party began to break up.

When the gold spikes were taken up, the laurel tie removed, and more businesslike substitutes emplaced, the Pacific Railroad had indeed united the nation.

But all was not as it had been planned.

After nine years of monumental engineering effort, the laying of hundreds of miles of rail through mountain fortresses and desert wastelands, untold hardship and three million dollars of personal debt, the directors of the Central Pacific encountered still more seemingly insoluble problems.

When the gold spike was rammed home, they looked forward to trade with the Orient and traffic from the Nevada mines as an immediate source of profits for the new railroad, until population, business, and agriculture could be developed in California to create trade with the eastern half of the nation. Unfortunately, that very month, the French opened the Suez Canal and virtually wiped out the C.P.'s ambitions for Far East trade; moreover, Nevada silver mining was in a depressed state that was to last for several years. Though the directors of the C.P. could do nothing about the mining situation, they quickly countered the Suez threat by starting their own shipping lines to the Orient to develop the silk and tea trade.

But their main effort was to accelerate the undertaking that was to become the second greatest achievement of its time, the building of the West. Except for a few centers, California was still a vast, unpopulated land, and they planned to open it by driving rails in all directions from the Sacramento railhead. Lines quickly proceeded into the San Joaquin Valley, to San Francisco and the bay area, and over the years north and south and west.

Seeing a future much brighter than gold, these men, despite incredible odds, had helped to link the nation. Now they would turn to the task of extending their lines over the 158,000 square miles of the Golden State. They would succeed, but nothing they could do in the future would ever match the drama and significance of that spring day in 1869, when the dream of a Pacific Railroad became a shining reality.

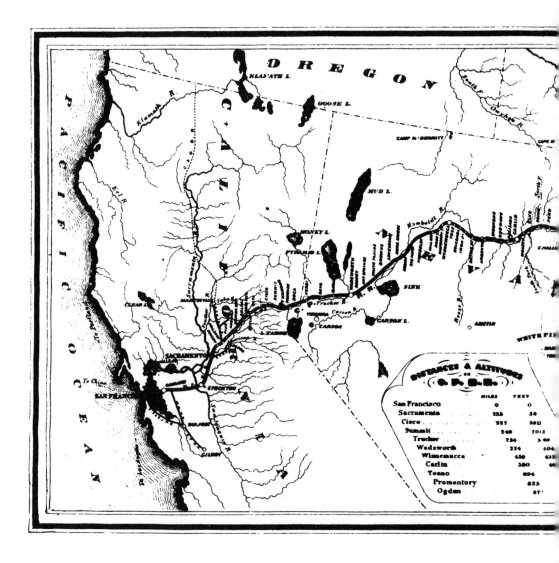

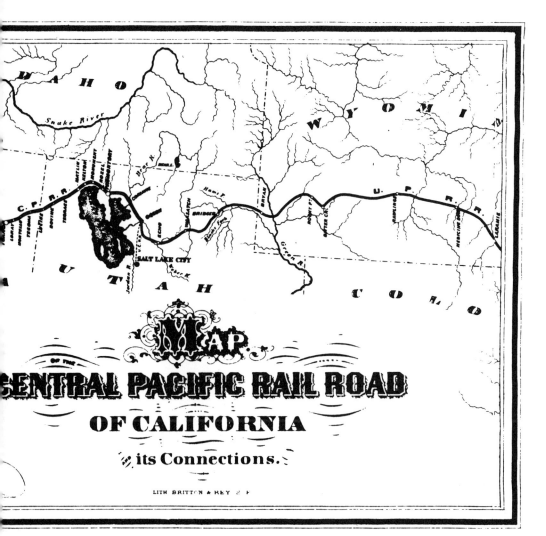

MAP

OF THE

CENTRAL PACIFIC RAIL ROAD

OF CALIFORNIA

its Connections.

LITH BRITTON & REY S.F.

The GOLDEN SPIKE at Promontory Summit signaled the end of a great pioneering era and the start of a new American epoch. It also heralded a new era of western railroad expansion. In 1869, the Big Four extended their first pioneer line into the San Francisco Bay Area and through the broad, fertile, and largely unpopulated San Joaquin Valley. They laid out towns with optimistic vigor and simultaneously launched one of America's great early public relations campaigns to attract colonists to a new West that was rapidly being opened up by advancing bands of iron.

Soon, the entire state was linked with the Overland Route. Central Pacific became Southern Pacific and grew rapidly, acquiring smaller railroads and continuing to build its own lines. Before long, the railroad again looked to the East, and in 1883—through a combination of building and acquisition in Arizona, Texas and Louisiana—another Golden Spike was driven at the Pecos River in West Texas, completing the first transcontinental railroad through the Southwest.

By 1900, when the last of the Big Four, Collis P. Huntington, had died, Southern Pacific trains were operating from Portland, Oregon, and Ogden, Utah, to New Orleans. Today, the track stretches fourteen thousand miles across twelve states, from the Pacific Ocean to the Gulf of Mexico, and through the states bordering the Mississippi River into East St. Louis, Illinois.

During more than a quarter century of growth and development, the Big Four prospered vigorously, but also called down much hatred and ill will upon themselves. As their railroad grew, so did their power—a power that was occasionally misused and greeted by an eloquent opposition from men who did not always understand or sympathize with the risks the Big Four had taken to build their fortunes. Although ruthless business antagonists, in the context of their times, the Big Four did much to promote and build a prosperity that not only swelled their own fortunes but was largely beneficial to the growing West.

In attracting settlers to the West, the railroad sought colonists not only in America but throughout the world. It moved entire families, their household furniture, pets, and livestock west on low-fare emigrant trains and settled them on their choice of lands at prices ranging from one to ten dollars an acre, payable on the installment plan. The railroad not only sold land to the farmer but often taught him how to farm it through an aggressive program designed to teach a new and prosperous agronomy. It sank wells to prove there was water, maintained experimental agricultural farms, and introduced new crops. Agricultural-display trains, such as "California on Wheels," toured the nation to create markets and attract more farmers westward. When the first effective "ice box on wheels" appeared in 1886, it became possible to transport perishables to the Midwest and East, and western agriculture exploded into a major industry.

In the interim the railroad also sought to build the West into a tourist attraction. It founded the now famous *Sunset* magazine to further encourage tourism and settlement. To attract the monied tourist, it built luxury resort hotels—the most famous of which was the Del Monte near Monterey, California—bringing new amenities to fledgling western cities. The railroad even successfully lobbied through Congress a bill that transformed Yosemite Valley, then in danger of being flooded as a reservoir, into a national park, thus saving it for future generations.

But perhaps the most notable of the railroad's achievements took place within a two-year span shortly after the turn of the century. An irrigation company engineer miscalculated, and an opening in the Colorado River broke out of control during the spring floods of 1905. Raging torrents raced through an 1,100-foot break, threatening to flood the entire Imperial Valley. Responding immediately to an urgent call from President Theodore Roosevelt, the Southern Pacific hurriedly built trestles over the break and dumped tons of rock—even entire trains loaded with rock—into the flood's path in an effort to divert it into its original channel. Time after time, seeming success came to nothing as the waters again and again tore through the break. After seven attempts, thousands of carloads of rock (which took precedence over all other traffic on the railroad's system), and an expenditure of more than three million dollars, Southern Pacific succeeded in sealing the river bank. That flood formed the Salton Sea, which remains today in the heart of the Imperial Valley. Not until 1928—twenty-two years later—did a reluctant United States Congress reimburse the railroad, returning one and a quarter million dollars in payment for a monumental job well done.

The following year, while the S.P. was still fighting the Colorado River break, a disastrous earthquake rocked San Francisco. The city was stricken by raging fires that burned for three terrible days, reducing much of it to ashes. Again rising to the emergency, Southern Pacific rushed in 1,600 carloads of food and medical supplies, and transported over 220,000 refugees to safe areas without charge. Although its own offices were destroyed, the railroad provided living quarters and supplies for the homeless, donated $200,000 for relief, and ultimately helped raise the city from the rubble in which it lay.

The railroad is still pioneering. In 1924, the S.P., sure the West was for all practical purposes settled, abandoned its efforts to attract new settlers. That campaign was replaced with another to encourage new industries and businesses, and since that time, the railroad's specialists have worked with cities and private developers to attract factories and processing plants to new sites throughout the West. Southern Pacific boasts today that for the past thirty-five years it has located an average of one new industry daily along its lines—creating new investments, larger tax bases, and thousands of new jobs.

Southern Pacific recently built a seventy-eight–mile railroad line, the Palmdale-Colton Cutoff, through rugged El Cajon Pass in Southern California. This line bypasses the congested metropolitan Los Angeles area, cutting off forty-six miles for trains moving between S.P.'s San Joaquin Valley Line and its southern transcontinental route. It is the longest railroad line built in the United States in the past quarter of a century.

Today the railroad of a hundred years ago has increased its fleet of 167 locomotives to a total of 2,300 units. Its freight-car fleet now totals 89,000 cars, many of them developed to meet specific needs and with the capacity for as much as 100 tons, compared to the mere 12 to 15 tons the tiny cars of a hundred years ago could hold.

Regardless of the many controversies that have raged—and continue to rage—about this California-based colossus, it remains a great railroad.

BIBLIOGRAPHY

As noted in both the Dedication and the Foreword to this book, most of the basic research was undertaken by the late Robert Hancocks. He left a wealth of notes and other materials he had accumulated through the years, without which this book would not have been possible. Unfortunately, many of his materials have not been cited with full bibliographic information. A man with an incredible memory, Hancocks was sometimes careless about noting where he had secured his information, although he copied the subject matter itself with meticulous care and detail. He knew what library held this letter or that, and where one could find the original to this map or that bill or document. As a result, it is difficult to prepare a fully comprehensive bibliography. The following list of sources, although only a representative sampling, should be sufficient to indicate both the scope and the authority of the research that went into making this book.

DOCUMENTS

An Act Granting Certain Persons the Right to Construct a Railroad from the Western to the Eastern Boundary of Nevada, State of Nevada, November 25, 1861.

Annual Report, Central Pacific Railroad Company of California, February, 1863.

Articles of Incorporation, Central Pacific Rail Road of California. Files of the Southern Pacific Company.

Brown, Henry: correspondence. Files of the Southern Pacific Company.

Central Pacific vouchers, 1864–1869.

Crocker, E. B.: letter to Cornelius Cole, April 12, 1865.

Gillis, John R.: *Report* to the American Society of Civil Engineers, January 5, 1870. Files of the Southern Pacific Company.

Heath, Erle, former Southern Pacific historian: interviews with J. O. Wilder, Joseph M. Graham, A. P. Partridte, and Henry Root. Files of the Southern Pacific Company.

Huntington, Collis P.: *Character of the Work; Its Progress, Resources, Earnings, and Future Prospects,* October, 1866.

Huntington, Collis P.: speech in San Francisco, May 16, 1900—Southern Pacific archives.

Investigations of the Pacific Railroad Commission, 1887-1888.

Judah, Theodore Dehone: *Initial Surveys for the Central Pacific,* 1861. Files of the Southern Pacific Company.

Judah, Theodore DeHone: *A Practical Plan for Building the Pacific Railroad,* January 1, 1857. Library of Congress.

Montague, Samuel S., Assistant Chief Engineer and later Chief Engineer of the Central Pacific: construction reports, 1863–1869.

Pacific Railroad Act, United States Congress, July 1, 1862. Also amendments of 1862, 1864, and July 3, 1866.

The Pacific Railroad Surveys, 1853–55, 12 volumes. Southern Pacific archives.

"Dutch Flat Swindle," pamphlet, published anonymously in San Francisco, August 18, 1864.

"The Pacific Railroad: A Defense Against Its Enemies," pamphlet, December, 1864.

Reports of the Board of Directors and of the Secretary, Central Pacific Railroad of California, 1861–1869.

Robinson, L. L.: letter to the Nevada Legislature, January 1864.

Sargent, A. A.: letter to Leland Stanford, February 18, 1865.

MAGAZINES AND NEWSPAPERS

Files of the San Francisco *Alta California,* 1864–1869.

Atlantic Monthly, January, 1908.

Bulletin of the Southern Pacific, 1913–1931. (These contain many interviews with surviving engineers and workers who built the Central Pacific Railroad.)

Files of the San Francisco *Chronicle,* 1868–1869.

Shasta *Courier,* January 21, 1865.

Files of the San Francisco *Daily Evening Bulletin,* 1859–1869.

Files of the Salt Lake City *Daily Reporter,* 1868–1869.

Files of the Vallejo *Evening Chronicle,* 1869.

Frank Leslie's Illustrated Newspaper, June 5, 1869.

Heath, Erle: "From Trail to Rail," published monthly from November 1926 through September 1930 in the Southern Pacific *Bulletin.*

Files of the *Territorial Enterprise,* Virginia City, Nevada, 1868–1869.

Files of the Sacramento *Union,* 1856–1869.

Wheat, Carl I.: "Life of Theodore D. Judah," California Historical Society *Quarterly,* Vol. IV, No. 3 (September, 1925).

BOOKS

Chesney, Glenn: *They Built the West* (New York, 1934).

Clark, George T.: *Leland Stanford* (Palo Alto, 1931).

Crofutt, George A.: *Crofutt's Trans-Continental Tourists' Guide* (New York, 1871).

Evans, Cerinda W.: *Collis P. Huntington* (Newport News, Va., 1954).

Greeley, Horace: *Overland Journey to California* (New York, 1859).

Lewis, Oscar: *The Big Four* (New York, 1938).

Phillips, Catherine Coffin: *Cornelius Cole: California Pioneer and United States Senator* (San Francisco, 1929).

Rae, W. F.: *Westward by Rail: The New Route to the East* (New York, 1871).

Riegel, Robert Edgar: *The Story of Western Railroads: From 1852 through the Reign of Giants* (Lincoln, 1926).

Sabin, Edwin L.: *Building the Pacific Railway* (Philadelphia, 1919).

Strassburger & Company: *Southern Pacific Company: Pioneers of Western Progress* (San Francisco, 1929).

THE FOUNDERS AND THE BUILDERS

COLLIS P. HUNTINGTON, most hated and longest lived of the Big Four, was born at Harwinton, Litchfield County, Connecticut, on October 22, 1821, the son of a farmer and small manufacturer. He was a descendant of Samuel Huntington, one of the signers of the Declaration of Independence, who later became president of the Continental Congress and governor of Connecticut and chief justice of that state's Supreme Court.

As a school boy, Collis Huntington excelled in geography and was noted for feats of memory. At the age of fourteen, already six feet tall and tremendously muscular, he left school and home to shift for himself, earning eighty-four dollars (plus board and clothing) for a year's labor. He saved every cent of it, an early indication of his extraordinary thrift, patience, and determination. "At the end of that year," Huntington later said, "I was as much a capitalist as I have ever been since."

At twenty-two, he entered business, in partnership with his eldest brother as general merchants at Oneonta, New York. There he remained until 1849 when, already married, he set out for San Francisco with other forty-niners. Enroute to California, he was detained with others for three months on the Isthmus of Panama waiting for a northbound ship. While others sat and drank, or did nothing, he bought and sold merchandise—in the process walking across the Isthmus twenty-four times. He left the East Coast with $1,200 and landed in California with $5,000.

In Sacramento, Huntington soon started a store in a small tent and shortly afterward entered a partnership with Mark Hopkins. This was so successful that by 1856 the firm was one of the wealthiest on the Pacific Coast. It was at the Huntington & Hopkins store on K Street that Theodore Judah convinced them and other California merchants to undertake the first transcontinental railroad.

Huntington later told the Pacific Railroad Commission that "in a general way, I believe that every member of the company came in at my personal solicitation. I spent many evenings until a late hour—after getting through my regular business —in going to see men, and I believe I went to see only those who were thrifty, and those I believed to be safe business men. I spent several evenings in Governor Stanford's house and he finally said he would go in. . . . I wanted him to get in because he was a good business man and a clean man in all respects. I should have said Mr. Crocker was worth more than $200,000. He was doing a thrifty business and I counted him one of the best businessmen in California."

The Big Four together had assets of less than $1,500,000 when they entered the Pacific Railroad enterprise. Although not all of them were of equal capacity, they formed an almost perfect partnership. Huntington said, "We were successful, we four, because of our teamwork. Each complemented the other in something the other lacked. There was Stanford, for instance, a man elected senator and governor, a man who loved to deal with people. He was a good lawyer. There was Mark Hopkins. He was a fine accountant and understood the value of everything. He was a thrifty man. Then, there was Crocker, the organizer, the executive, the driver of men."

Huntington himself was a very strong man. His skillful management made sure that all obligations were met promptly and that the C.P.'s bonds were counted among the best in the world. To many he was a hard, unyielding man who stopped at nothing to achieve his goal; to his family he was genial, good-humored, companionable—and a dreamer. Huntington's first wife died in 1884, and he remarried. Having no children, the "iron man" adopted a son, Archer M., and a daughter, Clara. The son later became a New York playboy, and the daughter— backed by her father's millions—married Prince Francis Hatzfeldt Wildenberg of Germany.

During his career Huntington made many enemies. Of them he said, "I am rather proud of the enemies I have made. All I ask is that they do not praise me, for then my friends would say: 'What has Huntington been doing now, that such fellows would praise him?' " Among his most bitter critics were the newspapers. At a hearing one day Huntington asked one hostile correspondent, identified only as "B," "How are you"? "B" looked nonplussed, then scowled, crowded past, and disappeared. When asked why he spoke to him, Huntington said, "I just wanted to see how big he was. I know now." ("B" may well have been the San Francisco *Examiner's* Ambrose Bierce.)

Despite his great wealth and power, innumerable interests, and the controversies that constantly revolved about him, Huntington always spoke out strongly for the working man and insisted on a day's pay for a day's work. He also had a high regard for the public. At a gathering for Southern Pacific engineers and conductors at his San Francisco home on May 6, 1897, Huntington said: "We all serve the same master—the public. I think, indeed, that of all the classes of labor in the world, from the highest to the lowest, there is no body of men who are more immediately servants of the people than we. We exist for their convenience, and we cannot live without them. At the same time, it may be justly said that without the railroad men the world today might be living in huts, and California herself would have little to recommend her except a glorious climate and the illusions of a pastoral life. Since we are, then, at once the servants and the civilizers of mankind, it would seem to be a plain duty, in the interest of ourselves as well as of the public, that we get closer to the people, acquaint ourselves with their needs, and as far as possible . . . meet their needs."

Collis Huntington died on August 13, 1900.

MARK HOPKINS, Huntington's partner, treasurer of the Central Pacific and of other activities of the Big Four, was the oldest and least colorful of the quartet. He was forty-nine when the Central Pacific was organized.

Of Puritan stock, Hopkins was born on September 1, 1813, at Henderson, New York. His family moved in 1825 to St. Clair, Michigan. At sixteen he started his business career as a clerk in a mercantile company, first in Niagara County, New York, and later at Lockport as a leading partner in Hopkins & Hughes. In 1837 he studied law as an aid to his commercial development. In 1849 he sold out and went to San Francisco, arriving on August 5 of that year. A few months later he opened a store at Placerville, hauling his own goods there by ox team from Sacramento. The next year he opened a wholesale grocery business with his friend and fellow passenger enroute to California, E. H. Miller, Jr., later secretary of the Central Pacific. In 1855 he entered partnership with Collis P. Huntington at Sacramento and continued as a member of that firm until his death.

Every project on which the Big Four embarked was submitted to Hopkins for his final approval. All had implicit faith in his judgment, honesty, and integrity. A contemporary described him as a "thoughtful, quiet man of rather slender build, who wore long, grey whiskers and a mustache, and spoke with a slight lisp." He was neither colorful nor dynamic. H. H. Bancroft reported that "Hopkins' most marked traits were less of the positive sort than those of his associates by whom he is described as 'one of the truest and best men that ever lived', and as a balance-wheel in the company. 'I never thought anything finished until Hopkins looked at it', Huntington said, 'which is praise enough.' "

He died on March 29, 1878, on an inspection tour of the new Sunset Route of the Southern Pacific—the nation's second transcontinental railroad. At a Yuma, Arizona, siding, he stretched out on a couch for a nap and quietly died, a few months short of sixty-five.

LELAND STANFORD, first president of the Central Pacific, governor of California, third president of Southern Pacific Company, and founder of Stanford University, was one of seven sons of Josiah Stanford, who farmed near Watervliet, New York, on the stage road between Albany and Schenectady. His early years were passed as a typical farm boy and a mediocre—if not dull—student, until the age of twenty, when he began the study of law at the office of Wheaton, Doolittle & Hadley of Albany. He remained with them for three years and then was admitted to practice in the Supreme Court of New York.

Also during his early years, Stanford entered his first business ventures—selling horseradish in Schenectady and chestnuts in Albany in company with his brothers. During these years, also, Stanford had his first taste of railroading—acquired when his father graded a part of the nation's first railroad, fifteen miles long, between Albany and Schenectady in 1829. He financed his law education with $2,000 made from timber cleared from land near the railroad.

During the California Gold Rush of 1849, two of Stanford's brothers headed west, but he had little desire to join the venture. He married Jane Lathrop of Albany and practiced law in Port Washington, northern Wisconsin. In 1852, however, his office and all his law books burned; almost broke, Stanford sent his wife to live with his parents and left for California, settling in the mining village of Michigan Bluff. He removed his frock coat and, with pick and shovel, started looking for gold in the American River and Placer County. Finding nothing to show for his efforts, he replaced his coat and entered the store his brothers had opened in Michigan Bluff. Within four years, he had become sufficiently wealthy to be regarded one of the leading citizens of the mining region, whereupon he left for Sacramento and entered the dry-goods-store business.

During these early years in California, Stanford earned the reputation of a fair man, and was often called upon to arbitrate disagreements among the miners. Within five years, he was taking a leading part in state politics and was the Free Soil Party's candidate for treasurer in 1857. Two years after his defeat, the party nominated him for governor—and he suffered another defeat, along with his entire ticket. He failed to carry a single county. Despite that, however, his influence spread beyond California when the party sent him as its candidate to the Chicago convention that nominated Abraham Lincoln for the presidency. It was said that he and Lincoln shared a warm friendship. After Lincoln's inauguration, Stanford remained in Washington and, some say, exerted silent but powerful influence upon national policies affecting the Pacific Coast. On his return to Sacramento, he was nominated for governor by the Republican party, in 1861, and elected by a large majority for a two-year term. His growing power and popularity undoubtedly influenced his selection as one of the backers of the Central Pacific in 1860.

After the Southern Pacific built its second transcontinental rail line across the deserts of California, Arizona, and Texas to the Bayou country and New Orleans, Stanford began following pursuits other than railroading. He ended up buying about half a million acres of California farmland. His ranch, at Vina, produced the largest vineyard in the world. Skilled vintners were brought from Europe to work in his large wineries, which were only partially successful as a business venture.

His favorite ranch, however, was at Palo Alto. Here, with a grant of twenty million dollars, he founded a university in memory of his only son, Leland Stanford, Jr., who died in Florence, Italy, in 1884. Stanford himself died at Palo Alto on June 21, 1893.

CHARLES CROCKER, under whose direction the Central Pacific was constructed seven years ahead of schedule, was an ideal head of the great working force. A cheerful man, he had a rare gift for imparting his own enthusiasm to others. William Hood, who was closely associated with Crocker during construction, said he had the gift of "sound common sense. I never heard Mr. Crocker reproving or speaking to any one except in encouragement and in a manner to increase the man's self respect and instill a desire to continue in his good opinion. He was able to convince those working under his direction that he believed they were doing their best, and they did it. Crocker, going among a large force of men, so enthused them with his spirit that, when he went away, instead of the work slackening, it went on faster than ever."

Crocker, like the others among the Big Four, was already a successful merchant when the Central Pacific was organized. A native of Troy, New York, where he was born September 16, 1822, he was only ten when he began to earn money delivering newspapers to help his father purchase a farm in Indiana, where the family moved in 1836. Here, after two years of helping to clear and cultivate the land, he went to work in a sawmill and, later, on a forge for eleven dollars a month, with board. In the winter, he attended the district school. Later he started a forge of his own, with fair success. In 1850, he crossed the Plains to California and, after two years of mining experience, established a dry-goods store in Sacramento. In 1860, he was elected to the state legislature on the Republican ticket, but after one term he gave up both politics and the dry-goods business to devote himself and his money to the Pacific Railroad enterprise. He later helped build the Southern Pacific's transcontinental line across the Southwest and founded other firms, many still surviving today, most notably the Crocker (now Crocker-Citizens) Bank. He also did much to develop California, especially in the Merced area where he constructed a reservoir to irrigate extensive tracts.

He died at Monterey, August 14, 1888. One of the men who worked for him during the Central Pacific construction had this to say in tribute: "Wherever Charley Crocker was engaged, labor and capital were just like this [*locking both hands together*] and it was some fist!"

THEODORE D. JUDAH, the driving force behind California's role in the construction of the Pacific Railroad, was born on March 4, 1826, in Bridgeport, Connecticut, the son of an Episcopal minister. The family moved to Troy, New York, and Judah studied engineering at Rensselaer Polytechnic Institute. There he got his first taste of railroad construction when he went to work on a line being laid between Troy and Schenectady. He found his career early and never abandoned it. At twenty-two he married, and at twenty-eight went to California as the chief engineer of an as yet unrealized railroad, planned to operate between Sacramento and one of the placer-mining districts east of the town (S.V.R.R.).

In *The Big Four,* Oscar Lewis has described Judah as "studious, industrious, resourceful, opinionated, humorless, and extraordinarily competent." For all that, he was also a dreamer of enormous scale and an enthusiast. One of his major enthusiasms was the concept of a Pacific railroad. Even before leaving the East, he had fallen in love with the dream of a railroad across the continent and had told his wife, "It will be built, and I'm going to have something to do with it." Once in California, he talked up the dream to anyone who would listen; his obsession, together with an already healthy residue of enthusiasm on the part of Californians, led to the convocation of the Pacific Railroad Convention in 1859 — the beginning of practical agitation for a transcontinental railroad.

Judah completed work on the Sacramento Valley Railroad in 1856—the first road in California and the only road he would ever complete. His continuing enthusiasm for the Pacific Railroad led in time to the founding of the Central Pacific Rail Road Company, and his lobbying efforts made possible the passage of the Pacific Railroad Bill of 1862—which for the first time made the dream an attainable reality. But he died in 1863, without seeing the dream fulfilled.

SAMUEL SKERRY MONTAGUE, who succeeded Theodore Judah in his duties as chief engineer for construction of the Central Pacific, was one of two sons of Richard and Content (nee Skerry) Montague, of Keene, New Hampshire. He was born on July 6, 1830.

Six years later, the family moved to Rockford, Illinois, where Samuel attended school and helped his father farm. He later attended Rockford Classical School, a private institution. He had no formal engineering education, for in those days engineering was related to digging canals or building railroads, and actual work in the field was the school in which most engineers were trained. Described by friends as diligent, persevering, and ambitious, young Montague first entered the engineering field in 1852, when he was twenty-two, working on the Rock Island and Rockford Railroad. He was later with the Peoria and Bureau Valley Railroad, and then with the Burlington and Missouri River Railroad.

In 1859, Montague and three companions joined the "Pikes Peak or Bust" gold rush to the Colorado mines. They apparently found no gold, for the party continued on to California, arriving in the fall of that same year. Montague got a job building a railroad from Folsom to Marysville, and it was then that he probably met Judah. Joining the Central Pacific on February 12, 1862 (it is believed), he worked on the location surveys Judah was making for the Pacific Railroad. On Judah's death in November, 1863, Montague was named acting engineer, and on March 31, 1868, chief engineer.

In this capacity, Montague had charge of all engineering—including location surveys through Nevada and Utah—until the railroad was completed. He continued as chief engineer for the Central Pacific, building many of the railroad's pioneer lines in California, until his death in 1883.

JAMES HARVEY STROBRIDGE, superintendent of construction for the Central Pacific, was a man of ability, command, willingness to take responsibility, and initiative under adverse circumstances.

Descended from an old New England family, Strobridge was born in Albany, Vermont, on April 23, 1827. He left home at sixteen to work as a tracklayer on the Boston and Fitchburg Railroad in Massachusetts and later contracted to build two miles of line for the Naughatuck Railroad in Connecticut. Joining the California gold rush, he left for the West on the sailing vessel *Orpheus* out of New York in January, 1849. In California, he went to work as a hay-cutter on a Sacramento Valley ranch. He managed a hay yard there until the summer of 1850, then shifted to freighting supplies to the mines for three months, and finally turned his attention to mining, locating claims at Placerville and Coon Hollow.

In 1863 he came back to the Bay Area to build the San Francisco and San Jose Railroad. The following year, he joined the Central Pacific, and was soon placed in charge of the entire construction program. W. B. Storey, who had worked under him, said that Strobridge "was particularly proud of the way in which Union Pacific was circumvented in its plan to reach the eastern base of the Sierra. U.P. did not get started building from Omaha until months after Central Pacific started at Sacramento, but hoped to cover all the relatively easy country while C.P. was getting over the mountains. A representative was sent to California to size up the situation. He inspected the work already done, saw all the difficulties, and decided that Summit Tunnel alone would take three years to complete. As soon as he was gone, Strobridge transferred forces to the east side, graded down the Truckee Canyon; hauled rail, cars, and a locomotive over the divide and laid forty miles of track; sank a shaft on the tunnel so as to work from four faces; finished the tunnel in one year instead of three; and was ready to rush the construction across Nevada enabling Central Pacific to get its share of the easy work."

After the Golden Spike ceremony Strobridge settled on a farm near Hayward, and for a number of years construction was carried on by others, by subsidiary companies, or by contract. About 1877, Crocker—dissatisfied with the pace of construction on the railroad's second transcontinental line from Los Angeles to New Orleans—sent for Strobridge, who stipulated he would not live on the site, as he had in building the Central Pacific, but would organize the work and visit it as often as necessary. He pushed the Southern Pacific through to a connection with the Galveston, Harrisburg, and San Antonio Railroad near Devils River, Texas. He later built a line from Mojave to Needles and, in 1883, began the line up the Sacramento River Canyon toward Oregon. He continued in this capacity until 1889, when he again retired to his farm and took no further active part in railroad building. He died on July 27, 1921.

JOSEPH M. GRAHAM, an assistant engineer under Strobridge and Montague in construction of the Central Pacific, was born in Crawford County, Pennsylvania, on May 22, 1842. As a small child, his parents emigrated by steamer from Erie, Pennsylvania, then to the "great West"—Illinois. At the age of five, he worked as a water boy for his father's construction gang, then building the Galena & Chicago Union Railroad, first in the state of Illinois. This work gave some basis to his claim that he began his "railroad career at an earlier date than any living man." He also did odd jobs for the construction gang on the Rock Island and Peoria Railroad, of which his older brother was chief engineer. In 1860 he attended Fulton Seminary at Lewiston, dropping out less than a year later to enlist in the Civil War. He came to California by way of Panama, in 1867, on the steamer *Ocean Queen,* at the request of Samuel Montague, whom Graham had previously known in Illinois.

Arriving in the spring of 1867, he took an engineering job and a few months later became chief assistant to Charles Cadwalader, construction engineer then completing the grading and masonry in the vicinity of Truckee. He then became construction engineer in charge of work from the California-Nevada state line east through Reno. In this capacity he set the first stakes for the towns of Reno and Wadsworth. "We did many things at that time without consuming any drawing paper," he remarked. Graham and his men handled grading, usually far ahead of the track-laying forces. He later had charge of grading near Humboldt Station, east of Golconda, in Twelve-Mile Canyon on the Humboldt River near Palisade—the heaviest construction between the Sierra Nevada and Promontory. This was finished about December 1, 1868, when he moved to the Toano Mountains until January, 1869. He did not continue on to the Promontory Mountains and therefore was not present for the last spike ceremony. Instead, he joined the celebration at Sacramento.

In later years, Graham was active in numerous railroad-engineering projects in California and Oregon until his retirement in 1917. He died in Sacramento, May, 1939.

AMOS L. BOWSHER, superintendent of telegraph construction for Central Pacific, was born in Chillicothe, Ohio, February 4, 1841. He served four years and seven months with the First U.S. Cavalry from Ohio during the Civil War and, when mustered out of the Army, went west, arriving in San Francisco, March, 1866. A letter of introduction from his commanding officer, Major A. G. Brackett, to R. P. Hammond, then superintendent of the San Francisco and San Jose Railroad, secured him a job until October, 1867, when he joined the Central Pacific in Sacramento. His first job there was boiling crossarms for telegraph poles at the original Central Pacific depot on R Street. Soon afterward he became general foreman of telegraph construction under F. L. VanDenberg and was in the front line of construction until the rails of the first transcontinental railroad reached Promontory for the Golden Spike ceremony. Later he became general foreman of telegraph construction over the entire Central Pacific and Southern Pacific systems. When the telegraph lines were leased to Western Union in 1880, Bowsher transferred to engine service. After working as a fireman for several months, he became a locomotive engineer. At the time of his retirement, March 1, 1911, after more than forty-three years of service, he was handling the Oregon Express—making his last run into Sacramento on February 28 of that year. It was Bowsher who made the wire connections to the hammer and spike which transmitted to the nation the signal that the last spike of the transcontinental railroad had been driven.

BENJAMIN WELCH, master car builder for the Central Pacific and later the Southern Pacific, built or invented many devices that helped the railroad get over the rough and rugged Sierra during the construction period. The "Bucker" snowplow was his invention, and he built nine of them at the shops. The low-cost emigrant sleeper and the luxury Silver Palace sleeper were also built by him. Welch, along with I. G. Graves, built and operated the shops of the Sacramento Valley Rail Road at Folsom. Later, he became car master on the San Francisco and San Jose Railroad, which he left for his position on the Central Pacific at Sacramento. The men who worked under him invariably liked him and called him "Uncle Ben Welch." Few other details are known of this man, although he was employed by the Central Pacific and, later, the Southern Pacific until 1899.

ARTHUR BROWN had a unique job on the railroad. Due to the special nature of railroad bridges—and to some extent other buildings as well—one man is usually in charge of such construction. He is responsible for preparation of plans and supervision of field construction. On the Central Pacific, Arthur Brown held that post during the building of the major portion of the line; when the pioneer builders encountered heavy snow problems in the highest reaches of the Sierra Nevada, it was he who designed the snowsheds and supervised their construction.

Born in 1830, at the village of Kentore near Aberdeen, Scotland, Brown was brought to Canada as a child by his widowed mother. After his schooling in Ottawa, he helped an uncle, Alexander Christie, in building railroad bridges and culverts there. Coming west with his uncle, Brown took a contract for pier construction at Victoria, British Columbia. In 1846 he journeyed south to California; the following year he accepted a job under Strobridge for a month—and stayed to take charge of bridge and building construction until the road was completed. One of his noteworthy achievements was reconstruction of a bridge over the American River, which was reopened to traffic only forty hours after it burned.

Brown remained with the railroad and its successor organizations until the early 1890's, a period in which great portions of the Southern Pacific system were built. In addition to the bridges, buildings, and snowsheds, he also was responsible for constructing the elaborate mansions of Stanford and Crocker on Nob Hill in San Francisco, and Southern Pacific's original Del Monte Hotel in Monterey. He died on March 7, 1917, at the age of eighty-seven.

REPORT

OF THE CHIEF ENGINEER ON THE PRELIMINARY SURVEY,
COST OF CONSTRUCTION AND ESTIMATED REVENUE OF
THE CENTRAL PACIFIC RAILROAD OF CALIFORNIA ACROSS
THE SIERRA NEVADA MOUNTAINS FROM SACRAMENTO TO
THE EASTERN BOUNDARY OF CALIFORNIA, OCTOBER 22,
1862.

ENGINEER'S OFFICE
CENTRAL PACIFIC R. R. OF CALIFORNIA.

SACRAMENTO, October 22, 1862.

TO THE PRESIDENT AND DIRECTORS OF THE CENTRAL PACIFIC RAILROAD COMPANY
OF CALIFORNIA:

GENTLEMEN:

In accordance with a resolution of your board, passed October 9, 1861, as
follows:

"*Resolved,* That Mr. T. D. Judah, the Chief Engineer of this Company, proceed
to Washington on the steamer of the 11th Oct. inst., as the accredited agent of the
Central Pacific Railroad Company of California, for the purpose of procuring appropriations of land and U. S. Bonds from Government, to aid in the construction of
this Road."

I beg leave to report my return to California after an absence of about ten
months, having fully accomplished the objects of my mission, a detailed and full
account of which is herewith appended, marked document "A."

A brief statement of some of the advantages accruing to your Road through its
connection with the Pacific Railroad bill, recently passed, seems necessary, in order
to realize its advantages and secure the benefits and public consideration to which it
is justly entitled.

The theory of the Pacific Railroad bill recognizes existing Companies at either
end of the road; while the central division, or portion between the states of Kansas
and California, is committed to the supervision of a company created by Act of
Congress, deriving its existing powers and authority from the bill itself.

Upon the eastern side, the right to construct the road, from the junction of the
Missouri and Kansas rivers, through Kansas, to the 100th meridian of longitude
west from Greenwich, with all the grants, donations, etc., for about 350 miles, is
given to the *Leavenworth, Pawnee, and Western Railroad Company of Kansas.*

The central division, or portion through the Territories of Nebraska, Utah, and
Nevada, to the eastern boundary of California, a distance of about 1,300 miles, is
given to the *Union Pacific Railroad Company, a Corporation created by Act of*

Congress; while the construction of the western division, reaching from the eastern boundary of California, to the navigable waters of the Sacramento River, or to the City of San Francisco, is assigned to the *Central Pacific Railroad Company of California,* to whom are made the grants of lands, bonds, etc., for that purpose.

The aid granted by the United States Government to your Road is liberal, and will materially assist in constructing and completing it.

ENUMERATION OF ADVANTAGES

The first important advantage derived by your Road, consists in the grant of the free right of way to a strip of land 400 feet in width across all Government lands.

This is a liberal width, and *precludes the possibility* of building a parallel road over your route, at many points, without occupying a portion of your lands.

Secondly. The United States Government is obliged to *extinguish the Indian title* to all lands donated to the Company, either for right of way, or to the land granted on either side of your road.

Thirdly. In order to prevent speculation by individuals, who may enter upon and take up these lands, *after* the passage of the Railroad bill, and *before the Company has time to locate its line with accuracy,* it is provided "that within two years after the passage of this act, said Company shall *designate* the general route of its road, as near *as may be,* and file a map of the same in the Department of the Interior, whereupon the Secretary of the Interior shall cause the lands within fifteen miles of said *designated* route, or routes, to be *withdrawn* from pre-emption, private entry, and sale; and when any portion of said route shall be finally located, the Secretary of the Interior shall cause the lands hereinbefore granted to be surveyed and set off, as fast as may be necessary, for the purposes herein named."

Before leaving Washington, I made a proper map, showing the general route of our road, in accordance with the provision of the bill, which map, accompanied by a written designation of the route, I filed with the Secretary of the Interior, who assured me that he would give the necessary instruction to have the same withdrawn from market. *This has been done. Such lands are now secured to us,* and cannot be pre-empted or purchased, until after our final location, and until a survey by the United States authorities of these lands.

The Department of the Interior also expressed a desire to cooperate with our Company *in preventing the cutting of timber on these lands.* It becomes, therefore, important for your board to decide if they will take any steps to prevent depredations upon these timbered lands, until a final location is made of the whole, or a part of their road.

Fourth. A grant of United States Bonds, to the amount of about $6,000,000, is made to this Company. These bonds run for 30 years, draw interest at the rate of 6 per cent, payable semi-annually, by United States Government, *who cannot redeem them until their expiration,* or for, say, 30 years, as is the case with their issue of 20-year bonds, which are redeemable, after five years, at the option of the Government.

They are, therefore, the best class of Government bonds in market, and will lead all others of her securities, now issued.

These bonds enure to your Company, as *each section of 40 miles is completed,* west of the western base of the Sierra Nevada Mountains, at the rate of $16,000 per mile — while for 150 miles from such western base easterly, the amount *is increased to $48,000 per mile,* and the same are paid over as *each section of 20 miles is completed.*

Your road exhibits a remarkably favorable peculiarity in this respect.

While most of the Railroads constructed in the United States are encumbered with issues of mortgage bonds, *on which the yearly interest must be paid, as well as the bond itself at maturity,* usually taking, for that purpose, the earnings of the road, which otherwise would be applied to the payment of dividends to stockholders.

Your road, *instead of issuing her own bonds,* for the payment of which, and the interest, she would have to provide, *receives all the benefits of nearly $50,000 per mile, or an aggregate of $6,000,000, of United States bonds,* the interest on which is regularly paid by the Government, until their maturity. It is true that Government contemplates the repayment of this loan at that time, but it is obvious that Government will furnish very nearly business enough to the road to repay them before the bonds become due. Therefore, instead of appropriating the net earnings of your road yearly, to the payment of interest on bonds, *there is no reason why such earnings* should not go to the stockholders in the shape of dividends.

This feature, peculiar to your road, is deserving of especial consideration. These bonds will, probably, command a premium in market, and whenever our present difficulties are settled, will be sought after *in preference to all other issues for foreign investment.*

Fifth. The *right to extend the road* from Sacramento to San Francisco is given to your company, with all rights, grants, donations, etc., given to that portion of the line, west of the western base of the Sierra Nevada.

Sixth. Perhaps the most important feature in the grant made to this Company exists in authorization, or *right given to it to continue on from the easterly line of the State of California eastwardly,* and construct the line of Pacific Railroad and Telegraph, until it meets and connects with the line of the Union Pacific Railroad and Telegraph, coming from the East.

This virtually concedes to your Company the right to construct at least one half of the line of the Pacific Railroad, and to receive all the grants, donations, etc., therefor, without absolutely compelling them so to do.

It becomes important, therefore, that a Railroad survey be made from the eastern boundary of the State eastwardly, to, say, Salt Lake for the purpose of determining the cost of a Railroad line, and to ascertain if sufficient inducement exists for your Company to construct said road. I am positive in the opinion that it will be found advisable *to undertake the construction of about 300 miles next easterly from the state line of California.*

VALUE OF LAND GRANTS

The United States Government donates to your Company every section of land (not sold, pre-empted, or otherwise disposed of) for a distance of ten miles upon either side of the road. Mineral lands are excepted from the operation of the act, but wherever the same contains timber, the timber thereon is granted to the Railroad Company.

The quantity of land (if it were all available to the Company) would be 6,400 acres per mile, or about 960,000 acres between Sacramento and the eastern boundary of the State. From the western base of the Sierra Nevada to State line, nearly all of these lands are covered with timber, which becomes valuable as soon as a railroad is built on which it can be transported to market.

It is always difficult to estimate the worth of timber lands, their value being dependent upon their quality, the density of the timber, the demand for and facilities for conveying it to market.

The Saratoga and Sacketts Harbor Railroad Company, of the State of New York, who have 500,000 acres of timber land in that State, in a report published by them, estimate the avails of its yield as follows:

ESTIMATED TIMBER VALUE OF LANDS BELONGING TO THE SARATOGA
AND SACKETTS HARBOR RAILROAD

Products	Quantity	Retail Price at Tidewater	Total Value at Tidewater	Corded on Line of Road	Freight on their Railroad	On Other Connecting Roads	Net Proceeds
Wood...........	30 Cords	$ 5 00	$150 00	$ 30 00	$ 75 00	$15 00	$ 30 00
Spars...........	1 128-1000	150 00	192 00	16 67	16 67	3 33	162 00
Hemlock Bark....	5 Cords	7 00	35 00	12 50	12 50	2 50	15 00
Pine Lumber.....	2,280 Feet	22 00	50 16	5 70	5 70	1 14	31 92
Spruce..........	13,680 Feet	10 00	136 80	34 20	34 20	6 84	27 36
Maple..........	6,840 Feet	15 00	102 60	17 10	17 10	3 42	47 88
Total.........			$666 56	$159 00	$161 17	$32 23	$314 16

Thus it will be seen that they estimate their spar timber at 1 128/1000 spars per acre, as yielding a net profit to them of $162 per acre or a total of $81,000,000.

The whole net proceeds of the production of their lands, they estimate at $341 per acre, or an aggregate in round numbers of $157,000,000. Their lands they assume to be worth $15 per acre, afterwards, or $7,500,000.

They estimate the freights derived from one acre of timber land and accruing to the Railroad Company, to be $161.17, which on their 500,000 acres amounts to $80,585,000. They also make the statement, based upon the production of a good farm on the Illinois Central Railroad as a guide, that there is more freight on their landed estate now ready for the cars than can be produced from the original and entire estate of the Illinois Central Railroad Company in more than one half a century.

They also state that a committee of capitalists, proposing to become interested in this work, personally traversed the route of their Road and made a report thereon, from which the following extracts were taken. They say: "The Engineer states, and your Committee confirm his statements, from personal observation, that this Road for more than seventy-five miles passes directly through a wilderness, as remarkable for its density and extent as any other in this country.

"The land for ten miles on each side of the road, and for ten miles from the margin of the lakes, is groaning under the weight of an immense amount of most valuable freight, all of which is wanted at tidewater as speedily as it will be in the power of the Road to transport it. There is more freight on the surface now ready for use than could be grown upon a cultivated country in more than half a century. The weight of lumber, etc., is about seventy tons per acre. The average weight of products of an agricultural country does not much exceed one ton per annum per acre."

Thus are the products of a timber domain estimated, *when railroad facilities are afforded* with which to carry its products to market.

It is not expected that the timber land belonging to your Company will prove as profitable as that estimated by the New York Company, *nor is this estimate here introduced to promulgate such an idea,* but for the purpose of illustrating the *difference in value* between a timber estate *without,* and one *with* facilities for conveying the same to market. While this is the case, the fact cannot be controverted that your Company possesses about 500,000 acres of timber land, which will, by the construction of your road through it, become immediately available and largely enhanced in value; and if we allow that 300,000 acres, or one-third of this land, contains *only ten trees per acre,* from which can be cut six logs twelve feet long per tree, averaging twenty-four inches square, this gives 3,400 feet, b. m., per tree, and the total quantity amounts to ten thousand millions feet of lumber, which delivered at Sacramento at, say $15 per thousand, amounts to one hundred and fifty millions of dollars; or calling this lumber worth, standing, one dollar per thousand, it would be worth $10,000,000 to the Company.

It is well known that the sugar pine of these lands often runs 125 feet high without a limb and often measures eight feet through at base—while a tree is seldom found measuring less than three and one-half feet at base. Cut but one tree per acre per year, and it gives an annual yield of 1,000 million feet of lumber—three million feet per day, equal to 5,000 tons per day, or, say, 1,750,000 tons per year.

Allowing the 500,000 acres instead, to yield fifty cords of wood per acre (a very low estimate), and it amounts to twenty-five million cords of wood, which, if delivered at Sacramento at $6 per cord, would amount to 150 millions of dollars, and pay the road about 100 millions of dollars freight.

It is well known that the supply of wood is becoming more scanty and is rising in value yearly.

What then may we estimate the value of this domain in years to come, not only to the Company as owners, but to the railroad as a source of revenue in its transportation, and to the community, who are obliged to use it.

Wood is now worth $18 per cord in Washoe, and in the winter commands $40 per cord. In fact, the cost of hauling is so great that not a few mills have been compelled to stop work, and are now idle in consequence.

How difficult it is then to realize the immense value of this estate, which belongs to your Company, *by absolute grant from the United States Government,* and to which you hold as title, which *cannot be disputed or disturbed.*

REVENUE

In estimating the revenue of your road, it is gratifying to be able to arrive so correctly at its probable business from statistics of actual business, now performed over the same route, exclusively by freight teams and stages.

It may be truly said that no road was ever constructed or contemplated in the United States, or elsewhere, that promised as large and speedy a return upon investment as the one proposed to be constructed by you between the city of Sacramento and the Washoe silver-mining district.

The extent of the existing trade now performed over this route by teams and stages can be scarcely realized, except upon careful inquiry and investigation. It is difficult to credit the statement that *over five millions of dollars per year is paid out for freight alone to Washoe,* but rigid scrutiny and investigation bears out the assertion, which seems to be entirely within bounds—and this trade is increasing and growing every day.

Your road, when *completed,* from Sacramento to Washoe, will perform—

1st. The local business of Placer, Nevada, Sierra, Plumas, and a portion of that of El Dorado County.

2nd. Over its first 25 miles, the northern business now performed by stages and steamboats.

3rd. The entire freighting and passenger business of Washoe, Esmeralda, Carson Valley, Pyramid Lake, and Humboldt, and a portion of the Salt Lake business.

It is to be observed that the freighting business to the mountains and to Washoe is now performed entirely by teams; there is no other way of forwarding goods to the interior.

The lowest price paid for freighting to Washoe is four cents per pound, or $80 per ton, and that only when the roads are in good condition.

When the roads are not in good condition, or when there is a large amount of freight offering, this price is increased to six, eight, and ten cents per pound.

A peculiarity of Washoe is that it is situated in a section of country so barren and sterile that nothing but a scanty supply of vegetables can be raised there. Every thing used there to eat or wear, all necessaries of life, as well as all manufactured goods, have to be transported by wagons or mules. The inhabitants, therefore, are absolutely compelled to draw their supplies of all kinds from the western side of the Sierra Nevada Mountains, and in paying for their supplies, to pay the additional cost of freighting by wagons at from four to ten cents per pound.

This is the business proposed to be performed by your Railroad, when constructed, and it is obvious that it will be entirely commanded by your road without competition. With a Railroad built to Washoe, this business cannot be performed by any other means, or in any other manner.

In addition to this large and increasing business may be reckoned that of supplying lumber, timber, and logs for consumption and for timbering the mines; also, fuel for consumption in the cities of Nevada Territory, and to supply the mills, a majority of which are run by steam.

As has been previously observed, wood is worth at the present time $18 per cord and in the winter will be worth $40 to $50 per cord, and many of the mills are obliged to cease running in consequence.

Your railroad will supply this fuel from the timber on its own lands, and at such a reduction in price *as will enable these mills to run through the entire year.* It is a fact worthy of observation that the construction of this road will *save to the residents of Washoe and Nevada Territory over $2,500,000 yearly.*

In order to obtain accurate information with regard to the business now performed over what is known as the Placerville Road to Washoe, I have stationed a trustworthy and reliable agent at Strawberry Valley (J. R. Atkins, Esq.), who has taken a careful and correct account of the travel passing that point for eight weeks, commencing August 16, 1862, and terminating October 10, 1862, or for a period of fifty-six days.

Every team going and returning was counted each day, and Mr. Atkins's returns present a complete statement of the weight and nature of each load, the number of horses, mules or oxen, of stages and stage passengers, buggies and occupants, riders, footmen, and loose stock.

It is to be borne in mind that these are the returns on only one road to Washoe; the different roads are enumerated as follows:

Big Tree Road.
Amador Road (new road).
Placerville Road.
Henness Pass Road.

Which comprises the Nevada Road, the Marysville, San Juan, and Downieville roads, and the Sierra Valley and Beckworth's Pass Road.

A compilation of these returns is herewith presented:

ACTUAL COUNT OF TRAVEL ON THE PLACERVILLE WAGON ROAD TO WASHOE AND NEVADA TERRITORY FOR EIGHT WEEKS, ENDING OCTOBER 10, 1862

Number of stages bound up	169
Number of stages bound down	171
Number of buggies bound up	61
Number of buggies bound down	46
Number of stage passengers up	1,287
Number of stage passengers down	785
Number of travelers, other than stage passengers, up— riders, footmen, and in buggies	1,288
Number of travelers, etc., down (including emigrants)	2,508
Loose stock, of all kinds, up	573
Loose stock, of all kinds, down	434
Number of teams bound up	4,142
Number of teams bound down	4,464
Number of animals in teams, up	22,728
Number of animals in teams, down	22,803
Number of pounds of freight, up	19,386,200
Number of pounds of freight, down	————

Teamsters are not included in the above return.

RECAPITULATION

	FOR EIGHT WEEKS			FOR ONE DAY		
	Up	Down	Total	Up	Down	Total
No. of stages	169	171	340	3	3	6
No. of buggies	61	46	107	1	1	2
No. of stage passengers	1,287	785	2,072	23	14	37
No. travelers, footmen, and in buggies	1,287	2,508	3,796	23	45	68
No. loose stock, all kinds	573	434	1,007	10	8	18
No. of teams	4,142	4,464	8,600	74	80	154
No. of animals in teams	22,788	22,003	45,591	407	407	814
No. pounds of freight.	19,286,200		20,000,000	346,185		357,000
No. tons of 2,000 lbs...	9,683		10,000	173		178

From which it appears that the daily average of loaded teams bound up is..... 74

The number of tons of freight transported daily up is..................... 178

The number of stage passengers both ways is.......................... 37

The total number of travelers, including stage passengers.................. 105

Allowing 18 days as the average time of a trip, and the number of teams and teamsters employed, amounts to 2,772, and of animals, 14,652.

At the present date, October 22, 1862, the price of freight is seven to eight cents per pound.

Estimating the yearly average of freight over the Placerville Road to be 120 *tons per day,* at an average price of *six cents per pound, and the total amount paid for freight alone amounts to $5,256,000* upon this one road.

A four-horse or -mule team, which makes the trip in about sixteen days, pays for tolls $22.75; a six-horse or -mule team pays $30 tolls. Averaging the time at eighteen days, the tolls at $25 per trip, and we find that the enormous sum of $693,000 per year is paid for tolls by freight teams.

The returns show that the stages average 37 passengers per day, which at $30 per passenger, amounts to $405,150. It is believed, however, that the total receipts of the stage line exceeds this sum.

It will be observed that 68 additional travelers per day, or nearly double the number carried by stage, pass over this road, at least one half of whom would probably take the cars were a Railroad completed.

From an entirely reliable source, I have ascertained that the total amount of silver bullion brought down by Wells Fargo's Express, for the ten months of 1862, is over 150,000 pounds, and may be safely stated at 200,000 pounds for the entire year.

Its value is not, of course, known, gold being mixed with it, but it is safe to estimate it at $30 per pound, or a total value of $6,000,000.

This is only what comes by Express, and does not indicate the amount actually taken out and retained there, or sent down by private conveyance.

It is estimated by Wells Fargo & Co. that this amount will be doubled for the year 1863, and in 1866, reach twenty-five millions of dollars.

It would, perhaps, be proper, therefore, to assume that upon the completion of your road, at a charge of one per cent, an additional revenue of at least $200,000 per year would be derived from this source. . . .

Trusting that the above report may serve to explain the prominent features of this enterprise, and soliciting your indulgence towards any imperfections or omissions it may contain, arising from want of time and unavoidable interruptions,

I am, very respectfully,

THEODORE D. JUDAH
Chief Engineer, C.P.R.R. Co. of California.

CONSTRUCTION OF THE CENTRAL PACIFIC

Sept. 1, 1865 - May 10, 1869

END OF LINE	MILES FROM SACRAMENTO	DATE OF COMPLETION
Colfax	54	*September 1, 1865*
Long Ravine Bridge	56	
Cape Horn	57	
Cape Horn Mills	59	
Secrettown	62	*May 8, 1866*
Secrettown Gap Bridge	62½	
Dixie Cut Spur	63	
Gold Run	65	*May 30, 1866*
Dutch Flat	67	*July 5, 1866*
Alta	69	*July 10, 1866*
Green Bluffs	71	
Shady Run	74	
Prospect Hill	75	
China Ranch	76	
Fort Point	76+	
Tunnel #1 (Grizzly Hill)	77	
Blue Canyon	78	
Lost Camp Spur Cut	80	
Sailor's Spur	80+	
Heath's Ravine	82	
Putnam's	82+	
Emigrant Gap	84	
Tunnel #2 (Emigrant Gap)	84	
Miller's Bluffs	88	
Crystal Lake	89	
Butte Canyon Bridge	90½	
Cisco	92	*November 29, 1866*
Tunnel #3 (Cisco)	92¼	
Tunnel #4 (Red Spur)	92½	
Tamarack	95	
Tunnel #5 (Crocker's Spur)	97	
Mountain Mill	98	
Lower Cascade Bridge	98½	
Upper Cascade Bridge	99	
Cascade	99	
Pattersons	101	
Tinkers	102	
South Yuba Bridge	102	
Soda Springs	102	
Summit	105	*November 30, 1867*
Tunnel #6 (Summit)	105½	
Tunnel #7	106	
Tunnel #8 (Black Point)	106½	
Tunnel #9 (Donner Peak)	106¾	

END OF LINE	MILES FROM SACRAMENTO	DATE OF COMPLETION
Tunnel #10 (Cement Ridge)	107	
Tunnel #11 (Tunnel Spur)	107½	
Tunnel #12 (Tunnel Spur)	107¾	
Tunnel #13 (Lake Ridge)	112	
Strongs	113	
Stanford's Mill (Cold Stream Valley)	114¾	
Miller's Mill	116	
Donner Lake	117	
Donner Creek Bridge	118	
Truckee	119	*April 3, 1868*
Proctor's	122	
Martin Creek	123	
Union Mill	125	
Prosser Creek	126	
Prosser Creek Bridge	126	
Boca	127	
Little Truckee Bridge	127½	
Clinton	130	
Cuba	132	
First Crossing of Truckee	132	
Juniper Creek Bridge	132	
Bronco	133	
Eagle Gap	133+	
Tunnel #14 (Adler Creek)	133½	
Adler Creek Bridge	133½	
Mystic	137	
Tunnel #15 (Quartz Spur)	137½	
Camp #24	137.94	
Old State Line	138	
Second Crossing Truckee	138½	
New State Line	140	
Third Crossing Truckee	141½	
Essex	142	
Verdi	143	
Fourth Crossing Truckee	145½	
Reno	154	*June 19, 1868*
Camp #37 (Truckee Meadows)	162	
Clarks	174	
Red Bluffs	178	
Wadsworth	189	*July 22, 1868*
Fifth Crossing Truckee	189	
Two-Mile Station	191	
Desert	198	
Hot Springs	208	
Mirage	216	
White Plains	223	
Humboldt (Lake)	232	
Brown's	235	*August 21, 1868*
Granite Point	242	
Lovelock's	251	
Humboldt Bridge (First crossing Humboldt)	255	

END OF LINE	MILES FROM SACRAMENTO	DATE OF COMPLETION
Oreana	262	*September 20, 1868*
Rye Patch	273	
Humboldt (Desert)	284	
Mill City (Mill Creek)	296	
Raspberry (Creek)	304	
Rose Creek	313	
Winnemucca	325	*October 1, 1868*
Tule	331	
Golconda	342	
Iron Point	353	
Stone House	366	
Battle Mountain	380	
Nebur	389	
Argenta	397	*November 19, 1868*
Shoshone	408	
Be-ow-awe	418	
Cluro	426	
Second Crossing Humboldt	428	
Sentinel Rock (Ten-Mile Canyon)	432	
Palisade	437	
Mary's Creek Bridge	444	
Maggie's Creek Bridge	445½	
Carlin	446	*January 25, 1869*
Moleen	457	
Elko	469	*February 8, 1869*
Osino	479	
North Fork Bridge	486	
Peko	489	
Halleck	497	
Deeth	505	
Third Crossing Humboldt	505½	
Bishop's Creek Bridge	515	
Tulasco	518	
Wells	526	
Cedar	532	
Moors	534	
Talbots	535	
Independence	540	
Otego	550	
Pequop	552	
Toano	562	
Loray	570	
Montello	578	
Tecoma	587	
Lucin	597	
Bovine	610	
Terrace	622	
Matlin	637	
Kelton	661	
Monument (Lake)	669	
Monument Point	674	
Rozel	682	
Promontory	690	*May 10, 1869*

C. CROCKER.

E.H. MILLER JR.

S.S. MONTAGUE.

LELAND STANFORD.

E.B. CROCKER.

MARK HOPKINS.

C.P. HUNTINGTON.

B.B. REDDING.

OFFICERS OF THE CENTRAL PACIFIC RAIL ROAD

INDEX

Text for this book is Times Roman, set by Hazeltine Typesetting, Oakland.
The book was printed and bound by Peninsula Lithograph Company, Menlo Park.
The paper is Capstan Vellum, cream white.
The cloth is Renee from Columbia Mills, Syracuse.